Marxism for Our Times

Marxism for Our Times

C. L. R. James on Revolutionary Organization

By C. L. R. James

Edited and with an introduction
by Martin Glaberman

University Press of Mississippi/Jackson

http://www.upress.state.ms.us

Copyright © 1999 by University Press of Mississippi
All rights reserved
Manufactured in the United States of America

02 01 00 99   4 3 2 1

The paper in this book meets the guidelines for permanence and durability of
the Committee on Production Guidelines for Book Longevity of the Council on
Library Resources.

Library of Congress Cataloging-in-Publication Data

James, C. L. R. (Cyril Lionel Robert), 1901–
    Marxism for our times : C.L.R. James on revolutionary organization
    / by C.L.R. James ; edited and with an introduction by Martin
    Glaberman.
        p.   cm.
    Includes index.
    ISBN 1-57806-150-4 (cloth : alk. paper). — ISBN 1-57806-151-2
(pbk. : alk. paper)
    1. Communism.   2. Socialism.   3. Revolutions and socialism.
    I. Glaberman, Martin.   II. Title.
HX44.J25   1999
335.4 — dc21   99-17326
                                                                    CIP

British Library Cataloging-in-Publication Data available

*For Peter who had to
live through all of this*

Contents

Acknowledgments

I would like to express my appreciation to Seymour Faber, Robert A. Hill, Selma James, Nettie Kravitz, Kathryne V. Lindberg, Scott McLemee, Aldon L. Nielsen, and Diane R. Voss for the help and support they provided for this book. Discussions with Alice and Staughton Lynd always helped to clarify ideas.

I am indebted to Thomas J. Moeller, Po-chung Chuang, and Carrie Marchand for helping to tame the computer. It was also useful to be so close to the Reuther Library of Labor and Urban Affairs at Wayne State University. The staff people of the Reuther Library are both knowledgeable and helpful. The Library is a significant depository of material by and about C. L. R. James with three important collections, the Raya Dunayevskaya Collection, the James and Grace Lee Boggs Collection, and the Martin and Jessie Glaberman Collection.

Seetha Srinivasan, Anne Stascavage, and the other folks at the University Press of Mississippi have been gracious, helpful, and professional in bringing this project to fruition.

Introduction

I first saw C. L. R. James when he came to the United States in 1938. He was a leader of the British Trotskyist group and a prominent figure in the international Trotskyist movement. He had already published *Minty Alley*, a novel; *The Black Jacobins*, the classic history of the Haitian revolution; *The Life of Captain Cipriani: an Account of British Government in the West Indies*; *World Revolution*, a history of the Comintern; *History of Negro Revolt*; the English translation of Boris Souvarine's biography of Stalin; and *Cricket and I*, the autobiography of the great cricketer, Learie Constantine, which James had substantially ghost-written.

In New York he lectured in the old Webster Hall to a packed auditorium on the British Empire. It was a remarkable experience, this tall dark man speaking for three hours without a note or the slightest hesitation and keeping the audience enthralled. He was an imposing orator and left a first impression on me that I never forgot.

After the New York lecture James left on a lecture tour that took him across the United States to the West Coast. After the tour he went to Mexico to spend time with Leon Trotsky who resided there in exile. It was in discussions with Trotsky on the Negro Question that he began to make his first major impact on American Marxism.

Lenin had once noted that the Negro question in the United States was a "national question." American Communists took that literally to mean that it involved controlling land and developed the demand for independence for the black belt, those areas in the South in which African Americans constituted a majority. The small and young Trotskyist movement had no significant contact with the black community, and while the Trotskyists accepted the demand for black independence, this acceptance had no serious effect on the group's activity. The discussions between Trotsky and James began to change that. James introduced the idea of the independent validity of black struggles. He found the demand for independence for the black belt acceptable if it came from the black population, although he saw no particular sign of that. But crucial to his point of view was that black struggles should not be subordinated to proletarian struggles or to the organizational discipline of a Marxist organization. Marxists, he held, should support and participate in a black mass organization without trying to control it.[1]

James already had international standing in the struggle for black liberation. He had written about Negro revolt, about the Haitian revolution, and about the development of a struggle for West Indian independence. He had been a major participant in London in a group that fought for African independence from European colonialism long before that objective was thought realistic. The group, originally International Friends of Abyssinia, protesting the 1935 invasion of Ethiopia by Italy, later became the International African Service Bureau. It included such people as Jomo Kenyatta and, later, Kwame Nkrumah. James edited its periodical, *International African Opinion*.

In 1939 James was back in New York and had taken his place as part of the leadership of American Trotskyism. In that year I left New York to take my first real job as a civil servant in Washington, D.C. I had been a member of the Trotskyist Young People's Socialist League. In Washington I became a member of the branch of the Socialist Workers Party. It was a small branch, but it included Rae Spiegel (later known as Raya Dunayevskaya), who became the major collaborator of James. In those years Washington was totally segregated and the only place a biracial group such as ours could meet was in a black funeral parlor made available by a member who worked there.

The time was one of great crisis in international Marxism. The Stalin-Hitler Pact, the outbreak of war in Europe, the Soviet invasion of Poland and Finland, all occurring at the end of a decade that featured the infamous Moscow show trials, required a major rethinking of the assumptions of the non-Stalinist Left. In 1940 the American organization, the Socialist Workers Party (SWP), split on the question of defense of the Soviet Union. A large minority, led by Max Shachtman, rejected the idea of any defense of Russia and formed the Workers Party (WP). James went with Shachtman and the Workers Party, as did the Washington branch. The official Trotskyist position—in spite of the crimes of the Stalinist dictatorship, including the murder of virtually the entire Bolshevik leadership from the time of the revolution—was that the Soviet Union was still a workers' state although degenerated.

One year later, however, the fundamental issue of the nature of the Soviet Union was up for discussion, and at the 1941 convention of the Workers Party James put forward his first major break with traditional Trotskyism and created his own organization, the Johnson-Forest Tendency, or Johnsonites. In conformity with the custom of the times to use pseudonyms, Johnson was C. L. R. James, Forest was Raya Dunayevskaya. The majority leadership of the WP presented the idea that the Soviet Union was a new type of society—

neither capitalist nor socialist — called bureaucratic collectivism. A shallow concept, bureaucratic collectivism was originally viewed as more progressive than capitalism; later it was judged as reactionary as capitalism; and ultimately, as Shachtman moved far to the right, he saw it as more reactionary than capitalism, thereby justifying his support of the Vietnam war. James introduced the theory of state capitalism, that the Soviet Union and capitalism generally represented a new stage of capitalism that was essentially statist.[2] At that convention I was one of two Johnsonite delegates who shared one and a half votes.

Raya Dunayevskaya, one of the co-authors of the theory of state capitalism, had a significant influence in convincing me of the validity of that position. She spent much of her time at the Library of Congress researching Russian sources on the nature of the Soviet economy. That was also the period in which I got to meet and know James. He was extremely persuasive in his arguments, but what distinguished him from the other party leaders who came down from New York to convince us of the correctness of their position was his fundamental humanity. He was more concerned with teaching, explaining, and learning than with battling for votes. I remember an incident a few years later, when I was the organizer in Detroit, and watched Max Shachtman, a brilliant debater, badger two young members with a battery of quotes from Marx and Lenin and Trotsky. When he realized that they still held on to their doubts, he switched to arguing that they didn't know enough to vote and should abstain. James always considered votes secondary to education, to understanding, and to listening to the doubts and the experiences of others.

Shachtman shared one element of the official Trotsky position of the Soviet Union: so long as the property was nationalized there was no national market and, while it wasn't socialist, it couldn't be capitalist. The position of James and the Johnson-Forest Tendency was based on a profound study of Marx. In *Capital* Marx had written that "in a given society the limit [of centralization] would be reached only when the entire social capital was united in the hands of either a single capitalist or a single capitalist company."[3] This excluded the possibility of a national market and was the equivalent, economically, of state capitalism. Engels took the matter further. He wrote that

> the transformation, either into joint-stock companies and trusts, or into state ownership, does not do away with the capitalistic nature of the productive forces. In the joint-stock companies and trusts this is obvious. And the modern state, again is only the organization that bourgeois society takes on in order to support the external conditions of the capitalist mode of production against the encroachments as well of the workers as of individual capitalists.

The modern state, no matter what its form, is essentially a capitalist machine, the state of the capitalists, the ideal personification of the total national capital. The more it proceeds to the taking over of productive forces, the more does it actually become the national capitalist, the more citizens does it exploit. The workers remain wage-workers — proletarians. The capitalist relation is not done away with. It is brought to a head.[4]

The identification of nationalization with workers state was done by what was essentially a verbal trick. Government ownership was called public ownership or social ownership. The public, of course, had no influence on government property, whether it was the Soviet coal trust, the British National Coal Board, the Philadelphia Navy Yard or the U.S. Post Office. By going back to the roots of Marxism James developed a theory that was in a direct line from the founders and applied their methodology to the contemporary crisis of socialism.

From that initial theoretical insight, the debate over the nature of the Soviet Union, the differences with Trotskyism began to grow. Taking a page from Lenin's response to the crisis in Marxism created by World War I and the defection of most of the socialist parties of the world to support their own governments in an imperialist war, the group, under James's guidance, returned to the roots of Marxism, studying *Capital,* the Hegelian dialectic, and the early writings of Marx. Over the next few years the Johnson-Forest Tendency developed its distinct positions on black struggles in the United States and the revolutionary potential of the working class in the U.S. and Europe.

When the Socialist Workers Party had split, the bulk of the working-class members had stayed with the SWP while the majority of the youth, mostly from the middle class in New York, had gone with the new Workers Party. In 1942, helped by the huge decline in unemployment caused by the war, the WP moved to correct what was seen as an imbalance in the membership. Young people were encouraged to move to major industrial centers and to enter industry as factory workers. I was part of this movement, and in the summer of 1942 I quit my government job and came to Detroit to help start a branch. Others came from New York, from Philadelphia, and elsewhere. The party paper, *Labor Action,* was distributed free at factory gates, especially at the massive Ford Rouge plant. The WP recognized the importance of having a significantly working-class membership and had become dissatisfied with the progress of recruiting and the growth of the party. It was in this context that James introduced a major document on organization presented for discussion in 1944. It was called "Education, Propaganda, Agitation" and is reproduced in this book. Parts of the section called "The Americanization of Bolshevism" were published by Blackwell as an appendix to James's *American Civilization.*

The language is still heavily in the Trotskyist/Leninist tradition, but the departure from orthodox Trotskyism is evident. First there is the rejection of the idea of the backwardness of American workers. James writes that *"Labor Action* is what it is because the paper is based on a certain theory. The theory is that the American working class is not class conscious to a sufficient degree. Our business in the paper, therefore, is to try to raise the masses to the next stage.... [T]he idea that the *general level of consciousness of a working class movement forbids the strong and vigorous teaching of Marxism is contrary to the whole theory and practice of the Marxist movement for a hundred years"* (10; emphasis in original).

He also begins to depart from the traditional view of the vanguard party: "The American mass party will not be built by us or by the Cannonites [the SWP]. Groups of Virginia miners, West Coast sailors, Southern sharecroppers, Pittsburgh steel workers, all sorts of 'left' formations will coalesce in time and hammer out a unified organization.... Our task is to form such a strong nucleus that the coalescence will take place around us, or even if that does not take place, our special contribution will be Marxism and the theory and practice of Bolshevism" (36). And the overwhelming emphasis is that Marxism has to be presented, to workers and to the members, rooted solidly in the American experience, much as European Marxism is rooted in the European experience.

By 1944 I became the full-time organizer of the Detroit Workers Party branch. For the leader of a minority faction this would not ordinarily have been possible. But the wartime draft kept the majority spokespersons working at their factory jobs. Through the courtesy of my draft board I had a deferment for health reasons. Among other things, this gave me the opportunity to get a closer look at the national leaders as they came through Detroit on speaking tours or as part of pre-convention discussion. One example of Max Shachtman's bureaucratic arrogance is described above. Another occurred when he had dinner at our small apartment one evening. At the end of the meal Jessie Glaberman proposed that he wash the dishes. Max, with much posturing with his arms, intoned, "I *think, you* wash dishes." On another occasion the same proposition was put to C. L. R. James. He simply got up and washed the dishes. Some time later when Raya Dunayevskaya found out about this she berated us for making James do the dishes. He, however, took it all in stride.

In 1947 negotiations began between the Workers Party and the Socialist Workers Party for reunification. When these stalled the Johnson-Forest Tendency negotiated directly with the SWP and arranged for entry into that organization. The major concern was that the Workers Party had essentially abandoned any revolutionary perspective in the United States or anywhere else and had lost all confidence in the American working class. The Socialist Workers Party, partly because of their continuing ties to the union movement and the working class, had maintained at least lip service to an American revolutionary perspective.

By agreement with the SWP leadership we arranged for three months of independence, known as the interim period, in which we could publish our own materials without being restricted as a minority caucus subject to the discipline of the majority. In those three months a massive amount of material was published that clearly indicated the distinctive character of this small Marxist tendency. This included a weekly bulletin; *The American Worker*, which combined the factory experience of a General Motors worker and a philosophical essay commenting and expounding on that; *World Revolutionary Perspectives and the Russian Question*, which left no doubt about our differences with the SWP on the nature of the Soviet Union; *The Balance Sheet of American Trotskyism*, a critical analysis of the experience of the Workers Party; and the first English translation of parts of Marx's *Economic-Philosophical Manuscripts*, which emphasized our determination to remain true to our roots in Marxism.

We were welcomed into the Socialist Workers Party, partly because the reunification with the Workers Party never materialized but significantly because of the contribution of James to party activity in relation to black struggles. The SWP, while giving verbal support to the ideas expressed by Trotsky and James about the independent validity of the struggles of African Americans, had difficulty following those ideas in practice. It was very difficult to break with the more traditional view of the American socialist left, "black and white, unite and fight," which usually meant the subordination of black struggles to the perceived limitations of the white working class. The result was a considerable amount of unrest and dissatisfaction among black workers in and around the SWP. After we entered the SWP, I moved to Flint and encountered an incident in the Flint branch which illustrated this problem. A black member of the SWP was on the executive board of the Chevrolet local. On a trip to a convention in New York he met and fell in love with a white party member. They decided to marry and settle in Flint. The party leadership never ordered them not to. But it went out of its way to make clear the importance of the fact that if the member returned to Flint with a white wife he would never get reelected to the Chevy local executive board. The pressure worked and the affair was broken up. It proved very difficult to give up the ingrained habit of subordinating the Negro Question to the working class. James's speech to the convention in 1948 got a rousing response, but the honeymoon was short-lived.

In 1948 James wrote what was eventually published as *Notes on Dialectics*. This was a study of working-class organization in the light of dialectics and marked the ultimate break with Trotskyism, the rejection of the vanguard party. The importance of this break and the theoretical validation of the James viewpoint was demonstrated eight years later in the Hungarian Revolution of 1956 (and later in the French revolt of 1968, the Czech Spring of 1968, and the Solidarity movement in Poland in 1980 and 1981). James wrote:

> Now if the party is the knowing of the proletariat, then the coming of age of the proletariat means the abolition of the party. That is our universal, stated in its baldest and most abstract form. . . .
> The party as we know it must disappear. It will disappear. It is disappearing. It will disappear as the state will disappear. The whole laboring population becomes the state. *That is the disappearance of the state.* It can have no other meaning. It withers away by *expanding* to such a degree that it is transformed into its opposite. And the party does the same. The state withers away and the party withers away. But for the proletariat the most important, the primary thing is the withering away of the party. For if the party does not wither away, the state never will.[5]

The abstract presentation of a new stage of working class activity was concretized and anticipated in these revolutionary events. The writings in this volume are a consequence of the path-breaking ideas developed by James in his study of the Marxian dialectic. Their importance cannot be overemphasized. On the one hand, no group of the left or of the right was in any way prepared to accept the possibility of proletarian revolution in the totalitarian dictatorships of Eastern Europe or in a democratic country such as France. All their assumptions proved false: that the working class needed a party to lead it in revolution; that the working class needed a press and a network of communication; that what was needed was some crisis in the society such as a depression or a war. With none of these factors in place, the workers of Hungary in forty-eight hours took over all of the means of production in that society, created a form of dual power, forced the Communist Party to reorganize under another name, and was crushed by nothing in Hungarian society but by an invasion of Soviet tanks.

On the other hand, even after the fact, the left could not deal with events that demolished their theories of the necessity of a vanguard party, and proceeded to ignore the movements in Hungary, in France, and in Poland — movements which Marx or Lenin would have pounced on to study and to hone and bring up to date their revolutionary theories.

In *Notes on Dialectics* James remarks that he has no fear of mistakes.[6] Among other things, this statement reflects the fundamental humanism of

James's concept of organization. We always understood the mutual support that organization involved to mean that members could freely expand their views to the limit because they would be protected by the organization and pulled back from ideas that might seem too outrageous. In the Trotskyist organizations you didn't dare to make mistakes because you would surely be made to pay for them in the next internal dispute. Organizational support applied to James as well as to the ordinary member. When James was forced to leave the United States in 1953, he lost a crucial aspect of that support, and that loss was reflected in the diminution of the work he was able to do.

In 1952 the decision was made to strike out on our own, and the organizational break was made with the SWP. The decision to test the waters of independence, however, came at a difficult time — the height of McCarthyism in the United States. James was arrested, confined to Ellis Island, and ultimately deported. Thereafter he lost direct contact with the organization that he had created. Furthermore, the attempt to create a new kind of workers newspaper, *Correspondence*, was handicapped by the U.S. Post Office's refusal to grant second class mailing rights and by the placing of the organization on the Attorney-General's subversive list. But this period was one of testing and problem-solving. James's writings and speeches on questions of organization are a valuable source of insights, historical information, and theory and analysis. After the organizational break the attempt to work out in practice what the rejection of the vanguard party could mean concretely became a major political priority of the organization.

The first step was to move the center of the organization from the radical and intellectual hothouse of New York to Detroit. The idea was to get away from the radical infighting of Marxist groups which detracted from their efforts with the working class and the population in general. The second was a major lecture by James on the idea that all organizations consist of three layers. The first layer was the top theoretical and political leadership; the second layer consisted of people, very often activists, who were leaders in their communities, at work, in labor organizations, youth groups, and the like; the third layer consisted of a genuine rank and file.

The problem for a Marxist organization was how to elicit the sentiments and attitudes of the rank and file and make that the fundamental basis of the organization. Formal democracy was necessary but not sufficient. Invariably, rank and file workers would vote on proposals put forward by the first or second layer. The solution, admittedly inadequate, was to insist that everyone else be quiet until the third layer had spoken. This proposition turned out to be very awkward and difficult and aroused a significant amount of resentment among those who were temporarily silenced. The ideology and practice of generations of Marxist organizations were not easily rooted out, no matter how conscious the efforts. The point was to get intellectuals discussing what workers had put forward, rather than workers discussing what intellectuals had put forward. It was a good faith attempt, but it was probably maintained essentially on the strength of James's support. I cannot say that it was successful.

One of the consequences of this emphasis on the importance of the views and experience of rank and file workers was a practice which Raya Dunayevskaya called the full fountain pen. It assumed that generally workers would not volunteer written material for our publications. It therefore devolved on middle class members interviewing workers and, in the days before the pocket tape recorder, writing down their words, typing them up, and returning to the interviewees for verification that the words represented their views and thoughts. These were often printed in our paper as small articles or letters to the editor.

In preparation for publishing *Correspondence*, a newspaper which we hoped would depart from the traditional centralization of policy and direction in an editorial board, we asked various branches to write and publish pamphlets to get the experience of producing work in areas for which they would later take responsibility. The Los Angeles branch published a pamphlet written by Selma James called *A Woman's Place*. The New York branch published *Artie Cuts Out*, the story of a high school strike in New York. The Detroit branch published Martin Glaberman's discussion of the growing bureaucratization of the unions, *Punching Out*. In addition, in this period we published *Mariners, Renegades and Castaways* by C. L. R. James, a study of Herman Melville and American civilization designed to support his struggle to stay in this country; and *Indignant Heart*, the story of a black worker who came from Alabama to work in the Detroit auto industry. It was written by Si Owen, using the pseudonym Matthew Ward (later, Charles Denby), and edited by Constance Webb.

The newspaper *Correspondence* was begun in 1953, when James was already in England. The first few issues were pretty much a mess, and they provoked a massive response from James. He sent a flood of letters criticizing the paper and telling us what we needed to do to correct the problems. Corrections were made and the paper was stabilized after the first three issues. But what happened became a foretaste of the continuing and heavy involvement of James in the day-to-day functioning of the organization, especially at points of crisis. This was made possible by the political collaboration and organizational support of Selma James who helped to maintain the James household during a very trying period. She did all of James's typing in addition to the typing she did to earn income.

In 1955 there was a split in the group and Raya Dunayevskaya took about half the organization and formed News and Letters. A split usually involves a complicated combination of factors, political, organizational, and personal. Fundamental to James's analysis of the split was his conception of the primary function of a Marxist organization: its day-to-day work needs to be sustained by continuing significant theoretical work, analyzing the problems of our society, providing key elements of Marxist theory and methodology, doing work which the organization sees and absorbs as our crucial contribution to the political world, work which no one else is doing or is capable of doing. In the period of our submergence in the Trotskyist movement we did such work — the work on state capitalism, the work on American history, the work on the sources of militancy in the American working class, the work on black struggles, etc. This apparently became lost in the struggle to maintain a paper and the grind of daily activity that did not seem to produce the kinds of response from within our membership and from outside the organization that we had earlier experienced.

Substantially reduced in size from the original seventy-five or so members, *Correspondence* was no longer a weekly or bi-weekly but became half tabloid size and published monthly or less frequently. There was a massive body of correspondence from James from 1956 on trying to guide the organization, including "American Civilization," a work James prepared for discussion by the group (very different from the document of the same name written in 1950 and published by Blackwell). With the outbreak of the Hungarian Revolution attempts to publish "American Civilization" were abandoned, and preparation began on *Facing Reality*, a book based on the events in Hungary and their application to an American revolutionary organization.

In 1962 there was another crisis. Grace Lee and James Boggs and Lyman and Freddy Paine led a split in the organization. The basis for the split was the rejection of the working class as a force for social change. They were not alone. They reflected widespread disillusionment with the working class that was evident internationally, particularly in the development of Cornelius Castoriadis and the French group Socialisme ou Barbarie. Through the technicality that Paine was the owner of *Correspondence*, James's group lost the name that had identified it and took the difficult name of Facing Reality in order to indicate our origins.

The split with the Boggses and Paines left the organization with about a half dozen members. I became the chair of the group and we tried to function without an office and without a press. "Letters on Organization" was James's attempt to guide us in this extremely difficult period. As he indicates in his letters, all of his work, particularly such work as *Mariners, Renegades and*

Castaways and *Beyond a Boundary* (his book on cricket), were designed to illustrate Marxist methodology.[7] We were gradually able to publish a newsletter, *Speak Out,* and rent an office. The '60s were much more favorable to radical organizations, and we attracted a certain amount of attention from the New Left student movements and others. The emergence of the civil rights movement, the anti-Vietnam war movement, the student movement, and so on, confirmed our basic views of the independent validity of black and other movements and reflected the way we had treated such struggles in the pages of *Correspondence.*

"Perspectives and Proposals," a collection of three talks James gave in his London flat, was designed to help the American organization to the next stage, in part by making the head of the organization a full time position, paid by the organization. As a consequence of James's proposals I made a trip to Europe in 1964 to meet representatives of organizations with Marxist politics similar to ours. I spent a week with the Jameses in London and then a couple of weeks on the continent. One of the fruits of my visit in London was a preview by James of some of the cultural wonders that I would see. In his discussion of the Medici chapel in Florence, he pointed out the political character of Michelangelo's sculptures. The Mother and Christ Child were placed to Lorenzo Medici's right. The conventional pose would have been one in which Christ looks at Lorenzo, if not adoringly, then with a certain satisfaction. However, reflecting the popular dissatisfaction with Lorenzo, Michelangelo had the Christ Child struggling to avoid looking at the figure of Lorenzo which dominates the chapel.

This analysis reminds me of a trip James and I later took to Oberlin, where he was to talk. It was spring break and much of the faculty was gone. James had been thinking for many years about the figures of the horses on an ancient Athenian frieze and how the theme had been repeated by Michelangelo and then by Picasso in Guernica. He had always had a certain respect for professionalism, and he wanted to consult with a member of the art department to exchange ideas about what he was thinking about. However, there was only one art professor on campus, and I sat to one side to observe a rather interesting discussion. On the one hand, there was James, whose look and dress were rather unprepossessing; on the other, there was this young professor. It was hard to know what the Oberlin professor expected, but he was clearly surprised by the depth of knowledge expressed by James and rather awkwardly confessed that that was not his field and he couldn't really comment on it.

We attempted to make contact with the Socialisme ou Barbarie group in Paris and learned that they had gone through the same split that we had with the Boggses. The leader of the group, Chalieu (Cornelius Castoriadis) had also abandoned the working class and had moved into a post-Marxist mode. They referred us to a small group that was based on a few Renault workers who had retained the sense of the importance of the working class. We spent an evening with a leader of this group, Jean-François Lyotard, a professor who later was seen as a guru of the French student revolt. He ultimately became a representative of post-modern thought and found a place at Emory University and the University of California at Irvine. He died in 1998.

We had better luck in Italy where radicalization of the Italian proletariat had given life to a significant movement of the non-parliamentary left. We eventually established relations with Ferruccio Gambino in Padua and Bruno Cartosio in Milan, both of whom were very much involved in American labor history. On our return to England we made contact with neo-Trotskyist groups in Great Britain. The trip essentially accomplished what James had expected, widening our horizons and establishing significant international connections. Bruno Cartosio later published an Italian translation of some of my essays with an introduction that outlined the significance of our American organization for the radical European left, a connection that began with Socialisme ou Barbarie reprinting our pamphlet on the American worker, which, in turn, influenced developments in Italy.[8]

The body of this book begins with "Education, Propaganda, Agitation" and "Marxism for Our Times," a talk given in London in November 1963 to the Solidarity Group. Originally titled, "Marxism, 1963," this piece places the rejection of the vanguard party firmly in the Marxist tradition and provides a political framework for the other documents. The final two sections, "Letters on Organization" and "Perspectives and Proposals," are both long obscure internal mimeographed documents of a tiny organization. In 1968 the Facing Reality organization held a conference that was probably the high point of the group. Contact with activists from Chicago who attended our conference led to connections with the Sojourner Truth organization. The political report given to that conference, "Theory and Practice," is presented here in an appendix, along with James's introduction, as an example of what the rejection of the vanguard party might mean in concrete organizational practice.

A word needs to be said about some of the language in these documents. From time to time James refers to Grace Lee and Raya Dunayevskaya as "those girls." The words grate on today's reader and are not acceptable and cannot be justified. However, some explanation is necessary. Apart from the times in which they were written, when such expressions were not noticed, it is important to understand that they were never intended to demean Grace or Raya. Quite the contrary. The context was always to present them as a necessary part of the leadership of the organization. In addition, under James's guidance, the organization developed feminist views far in advance of any held on the Left at the time and before the creation of the contemporary women's movement. A leader in this work was Selma James, whose pamphlet, *A Woman's Place*, was the most successful we ever published. The pages of *Correspondence* contained articles by women dealing with relations between husbands and wives, the raising of children — in short, subjects far beyond the traditional "equal pay for equal work" of the Left. The leadership of the Johnson-Forest Tendency consisted of a West Indian Negro and two women, one of them Chinese-American. This diversity was a configuration quite unique on the Left and at every other point on the political spectrum.

The 1968 conference did not bear the fruit that might have been expected. Although we had ties to the Sojourner Truth organization in Chicago and to militant African American organizations in the Detroit area, these connections did not result in increased membership, income, or support for our periodical. Instead, proposals to expand our publication and to move outward more aggressively were resisted in an organization that had reached a bare twenty-five members nationally, about half of whom were in Detroit. The kind of bickering that took place over simple organizational proposals seemed to reflect the life of a sectarian group. In my experience, a sect can survive indefinitely, but at the expense of its isolation from the real world and the destruction of its members as functioning political activists.

In 1970 I moved the dissolution of the organization. James, who was back in the United States, teaching in Washington, D.C., opposed this move. After a discussion the organization voted to dissolve, putting an end to the existence of an organization that had existed since 1941. I formed Bewick Editions to try to keep in print the work that we had done, particularly James's work. This was made possible in the 1970s by a remarkable anarchist couple, Fredy and Lorraine Perlman, who started a press in Detroit which they made available to any radical group, including groups with which they bitterly disagreed. When they lost their building and had to give up their press, Detroit radicals lost a tremendous resource.

Organizationally, the Tendency formed by C. L. R. James in 1941 has to be called a failure, but, I believe, a failure that is rich in meaning and lessons for anyone interested in a democratic, revolutionary Marxism. There were problems, internal and external, that the organization could not survive. I offer no final judgment on the reasons for our failure. It is necessary to say, however, that there were always undercurrents of resistance to some of the ideas and proposals that James put before us. And there is James's own view, expressed in these pages, that our failure stemmed from our inability to do the theoretical work required of a Marxist organization.

In 1981 I contributed an exchange of letters with James to a book edited by Paul Buhle called *C. L. R. James: His Life and Work*, published by So-journer Truth (since reprinted by Allison and Busby in England). Included in the letters was James's sharp criticism of something I had written to him and something I had written to Luke Tripp of the League of Revolutionary Black Workers.[9] When the letters appeared, Jessie Glaberman asked me if I had intended to attack James. That question took me by surprise, although I quickly understood what she meant. Did James undercut the formation of a viable American leadership by his tendency to micromanage the organization from abroad? As someone who was on the receiving end of considerable advice and criticism, which I always thought valuable and useful (although I didn't always agree), I do not have an answer. Would the organization have been more successful without James's intervention? Somehow, I doubt it.

In any case, I see considerable success alongside the failure. After the dissolution of the Facing Reality organization, the political and other work embodying James's Marxist perspectives continued and grew. George Rawick, who had come to our group in the '60s, published a multivolume work of American slave narratives, enlarging our understanding of the self-activity of the slave community.[10] I, and others, have contributed work on labor history and the American working class that continues James's revolutionary perspective. In his book, *Know-How on the Job: The Important Working Knowledge of "Unskilled Workers,"* Ken Kusterer refers to the Detroit School, a group of historians, sociologists, and activists, here and abroad, who carry on in James's tradition. A few of us tried to resume publication of a newsletter in the '80s, *Speaking Out*, but were unable to maintain it. And, of course, there is the growing interest in the life and work of James that is reflected in the increasing number of books by and about James that have been published in the last few years.

Ultimately, I suspect, a more substantial judgment on the success or failure of James as a major figure of the twentieth century will lie, not with the life or death of a particular organization, but with the body of ideas he has left as a tool to understanding our century and the next one and as a means to function in the modern world.

These ideas make Marxism relevant and useful at the end of the twentieth century. His use of Marxian methodology to develop the theory of state capitalism, his theory of race and black struggles, his critical support of third world struggles as in Ghana and Trinidad, his theories of organization, and, above all, his placing of the proletariat at the heart of Marxist doctrine (where Marx placed it) form a body of theory unmatched by any of the other groups and tendencies of the Left. His legacy is not, however, without its contradictions.

Part of the problem is the range of James's writings and activities. I once wrote, "At his funeral in Trinidad I became aware of a reality which violates my usual sectarian instincts. Everyone produces his/her own James. People have, over the years, taken from him what they found useful and imputed to him what they felt necessary."[11] James as cultural critic, James as master of the classics, James as expert on cricket, James as historian, James as major figure in the pan-African movement. That people with particular interests are attracted to a particular James is not surprising. There is, however, another side to this, the fragmentation of James.

Writing for the editors of *The CLR James Journal* in a long delayed issue, Paget Henry wrote: "As the new editor, my primary goal will be to expand the coverage to the field of ideas that James and other major Caribbean writers have shared, engaged and influenced. Hence the new subtitle of the journal."[12] The subtitle was *A Review of Caribbean Ideas*. In fact, the change was a contraction of the coverage of the journal, rather than an expansion. The concern for Caribbean ideas is important and legitimate. But it reduces James, to apply a phrase that Marx used in another connection, to a fragment of a man.

The problem is much more general. In the various symposia on the 150th anniversary of *The Communist Manifesto* held in 1998, there is hardly any reference to the working class of the industrial world, and when there is, it is only to bemoan the disappearance of working class militancy, or to announce its replacement by other categories of the population.[13] We bear the fruits of decades of Stalinist domination of Marxist theory and the tenacity of the idea of the vanguard party, which is essentially in our time the idea of the backwardness of the proletariat.

Marx thought that the proletariat was revolutionary or it was nothing. In the paragraph that is the climax to Vol. I of *Capital* Marx wrote:

> [W]ithin the capitalist system all methods for raising the social productiveness of labour are brought about at the cost of the individual labourer; all means for the development of production transform themselves into means of domination over, and exploitation of, the producers; they mutilate the labourer into a fragment of a man, degrade him to the level of an appendage of a machine, destroy every remnant of charm in his work and turn it into a hateful toil; they estrange from him the intellectual potentialities of the labour-process in the same proportion as science is incorporated in it as an independent power; they distort the conditions under which he works, subject him during the labour-process to a despotism more hateful for its meanness; they transform his life-time into working time; and drag his wife and child beneath the wheels of the Juggernaut of capital. . . . Accumulation of wealth at one pole is, therefore, at the very same time accumulation of misery, agony of toil, slavery, ignorance, brutality, mental degradation, at the opposite pole, *i.e.*, on the side of the class that produces its own product in the form of capital.[14]

"Ignorance, brutality, mental degradation"—was this the revolutionary proletariat which was to overthrow capitalism? To see it, one needs to see Marx's dialectical view of the working class. Marx and Engels said, "It is not a matter of what this or that proletarian or even the proletariat as a whole *pictures* at present as its goal. It is a matter of *what the proletariat is in actuality* and what, in accordance with this *being,* it will historically be compelled to do."[15] This is difficult for intellectuals, trained in positivist social science to comprehend, but Marx and Engels carry it further:

> Both for the production on a mass scale of this communist consciousness, and for the success of the cause itself, the alteration of men on a mass scale is necessary, an alteration which can only take place in a practical movement, a *revolution*; this revolution is necessary, therefore, not only because the *ruling* class cannot be overthrown in any other way, but also because the class *overthrowing* it can only in a revolution succeed in ridding itself of all the muck of ages and become fitted to found society anew.[16]

James could see, as Lenin and Marx could see, that to think that only with the guidance of a vanguard party could the working class be fit to make a revolution was utopian nonsense. The Russian workers who created soviets and overthrew the Tsar, the Hungarian workers of 1956, and the French workers of 1968 were workers with all the limitations imposed on them by capitalism. They were sexist; they were racist; they were nationalistic; they were influenced by the Russian Orthodox Church or by the Catholic Church. But they revolted and began to be transformed in the process.

It was James's ability to remain true to the Marxist tradition and apply it to the contemporary world which made it possible for him to understand and predict the revolutions of post–World War II Europe, the downfall of the Soviet Union and much else, while the bulk of the Left is still floundering over the question of how to transform American workers (or workers of any country) into sterling socialists, educated to following the self-proclaimed vanguard. His body of ideas will survive the demise of the small American organization that James built in the United States. The revolutionary optimism with which it is imbued will bring people to study and learn from these pages on revolutionary organization.

Notes

1. See "Revolution and the Negro," pp. 77–87, and "The Revolutionary Answer to the Negro Problem in the United States," pp. 179–87, in Scott McLemee and Paul LeBlanc, eds., *C. L. R. James and Revolutionary Marxism,* Atlantic Highlands, NJ: Humanities Press, 1994.

2. See C. L. R. James, *State Capitalism and World Revolution*, Chicago: Charles H. Kerr Publishing Co., 1986.

3. Karl Marx, *Capital*, Moscow: Progress Publishers, undated, Vol. I, p. 588.

4. Friedrich Engels, "Socialism: Utopian and Scientific," in Robert C. Tucker, ed., *The Marx-Engels Reader*, New York: Norton, 1978, p. 711.

5. James, *Notes on Dialectics*, London: Allison and Busby, 1980, pp. 175–76. Emphasis in original.

6. Ibid., p. 79.

7. In the copy of *Beyond a Boundary* that he sent me he inscribed the following: "For Marty, from Jimmy. Hoping that the time will not be very far when you will send as you receive.

I cannot prevent myself saying that within these covers, there is *everything*. I shall *in time* go into detail and will surprise even you. July 11, 1963." Emphasis in original.

8. Bruno Cartosio, "Introduzione," in Martin Glaberman, *Classe Operaia Imperialismo e Rivoluzione Negli USA*, Turin: Musolini editore, 1976.

9. What I had written to Luke Tripp was "that the policies of Negro organizations do not have to pass muster with anyone but the masses of Negroes themselves." James wrote: "That is simply not true." Paul Buhle, ed., *C. L. R. James: His Life and Work*, London: Allison & Busby, 1986, p. 159. In a speech on Black Power delivered in 1967 he said the opposite: "Who are we to stand, or rather to sit in judgment over what they decide to do or what they decide not to do?" Quoted in Paul Buhle, *C. L. R. James: The Artist as a Revolutionary*. London: Verso, 1988, p. 131. This proves, I suppose, that despite his brilliance, C. L. R. James was human and could occasionally contradict himself. In fact, there is less contradiction than meets the eye. Either view is valid, depending on the context. A Marxist group has no business lecturing a mass organization to get it to conform to some line or policy. On the other hand, a Marxist group, like any group or individual, has the right and the need to work out for itself the significance, meaning, or possible consequences of any program or activity.

10. See, George P. Rawick, *From Sundown to Sunup: The Making of the Black Community*, vol. 1 of *The American Slave: A Composite Autobiography*, Westport, CT: Greenwood Publishing Co., 1972.

11. Martin Glaberman, "C. L. R. James — A Recollection," *New Politics* vol. II, no. 4, Winter 1990, p. 80.

12. Paget Henry, "Editor's Note," *The CLR James Journal*, vol. 5, no. 1, Winter 1997, p. 2.

13. See, e.g., *New Politics*, vol. VI, no. 4, Winter 1998; *Against the Current*, no. 72, Jan.-Feb. 1998 and *Monthly Review*, vol. 50, no. 1, May 1998.

14. *Capital*, Vol. I, p. 604.

15. Robert C. Tucker, ed., *The Marx-Engels Reader*, "The Holy Family," pp. 134–35. Emphasis in original.

16. "The German Ideology," in ibid., p. 193. Emphasis in original.

Marxism for Our Times

Education, Propaganda, Agitation
Post-War America and Bolshevism

I: The General Problem of the Trotskyite Movement

We have found it necessary to make the main item on the plenum[1] agenda the organizational question. The cause is a widespread recognition of the fact that after three years of grinding work in the factories the recruiting of new members has not only been far below expectations, but from all appearances is likely to continue so. The idea that the lag in recruiting is due to the unorganized, unsystematic methods of the members has been more or less discarded. It was not a serious contribution to the question. What we are facing now and will increasingly face is the whole problem of building the mass Bolshevik party in the USA. The war in Europe is coming rapidly to an end and the whole country is aware of the tremendous social conflicts which the post-war will bring. The building of a mass party to lead the proletariat is for us the problem. This is the question I propose to discuss here, but from one aspect only, the aspect of education, propagnada, and agitation. There are others equally important. I do not propose to deal with them here.

First of all I have to make it clear what is not being done in this document.

I am not dealing with the general problem of how a party is built.

I am not touching at all upon mass trade union work except insofar as this affects or is affected by education, propaganda, and agitation.

I am not dealing with the objective situation in America except insofar as it is impossible to discuss propaganda and agitation in a vacuum.

With this limitation constantly borne in mind, we can and must remind ourselves of what we are in general attempting to do. All studies of dialectic, of historical materialism, of political economy, of the history of the working class and of the revolutionary movement are for the most part meaningless if they do not concretely contribute to and culminate in the theoretical analysis of party building. The plain fact, too often forgotten or ignored, is that in the past fifty years only one effective Bolshevik party has been built in any of the great countries of Europe and America and for that matter anywhere. The Communist Parties from their very first days were inspired and nurtured, theoretically, organizationally, and morally by Soviet Russia. From that same source they drew their early corruption. As we look back at the catastrophes they caused, their totalitarian opposition to the simplest and most elementary doctrines of Leninism, particularly in China and Germany, it is clear that whatever was responsible, these parties were Bolshevik in name only. In the last decade and a half, except in the remote and undecisive outpost of Ceylon, the Trotskyite revolutionary movement has known nothing but failure. (Britain is a special case which will be specially dealt with at another time.) Great events have come and gone. We have made no impact on them. At times, as in France between 1934 and 1936, our theory attracted widespread notice. Solid bourgeois papers devoted articles to Trotskyism as the real danger. At the Mulhouse conference of the Social Democracy in 1935 our comrades led a powerful opposition to Blum.[2] But we could do nothing effective. The great events passed us by. There is no reason at all why great events should not develop during the next few years and find us equally ineffective, left behind as before, calling other groups and parties centrist (as we justifiably called the POUM[3]), reformist, Stalinist or what not, but ourselves insignificant. There is no reason for believing that with the inevitable revolutionary upsurge of the masses, we must automatically grow until we become a large party. There was a great revolution in Spain. Every party in Spain, revolutionary and counter-revolutionary, grew except the Trotskyites. As we enter the post-war period, we, as serious Marxists, must analyze these things and try to draw some lessons.

Our Experiences, National and International

One indispensable way of doing this is by the thorough and systematic analysis of the experiences of the Trotskyite movement as a whole. This is no light task. But it is time to begin. I propose to begin as simply as possible, with the experiences of the Workers Party (WP) during its four years of existence, particularly the last two. In 1942, the party, taking conscious advantage of the national development, made a great step by incorporating itself into the broad workers movement. This was a development of fundamental importance. No party, no group, can grow and develop unless the majority of its members function and function intelligently among the workers in industry. Everything that is said here is conditioned on that. Members became immersed in union activity. The party agitation and propaganda, as was inevitable and necessary, underwent a change. *Labor Action* became a paper whose main emphasis was the activity of the workers in the union. At the same time we developed a practice of mass distribution, and half a dozen comrades would distribute thousands of copies weekly. It is not clear what was concretely expected from these distributions. We have at least the results to go by. In one area our comrades have taken an active and effective part in union work. They have distributed between a quarter and a half a million pieces of literature among the workers. Yet the results in recruiting have been practically zero. Perhaps we have now gained three members, perhaps five. This is not what the party expected. The party expected other results. It is possible that there may yet be some. It is also possible that within a year and a half the comrades in question would be unemployed, or balk at remaining in the same barren activity. If this were to take place the great effort and the great expectations will peter out. This calls, if anything ever did, for serious examination not only by the leadership but by the whole party.

Our theoretical explanation could be that the American working class, during the period of war, was not ready to join a revolutionary party even in small numbers. If this is so, then the party must recognize the fact. We attempted the impossible. The results, such as they have been, are only what could have been expected, or at least what we now see to have been inevitable. This view has not hitherto been advanced in the party.

Or it is possible to say, on the other hand, that the workers were ready to make some appreciable response to us (not, perhaps, in thousands, yet something corresponding to our efforts) but that the main failure was due to faulty party methods. If that is so, then the party as a whole bears the responsibility. No one advanced any important and concrete alternative course of action. The great value of the course we took is that it was tried out by everyone or at least nearly everyone, more or less, wholeheartedly. It is therefore impossible for anyone to say, "Had we done otherwise, the results would have been different." This writer, at any rate, is saying nothing of the kind. If, however, we agree that we did the best possible under the circumstances, that does not settle the question for the future. The party has now forecast for the coming years a period of social crisis in the United States. This can be variously interpreted.

In the *New International* and in the Internal Bulletin I have written articles which express my particular emphasis on the future development of the American working class. Soon to be freed from the restraints of the European war, and with the great experiences of 1939–1944 to help it, it now faces a political development which, when it comes, will in all reasonable probability be as violent and all-embracing as was the industrial development of the CIO a few years ago. That some millions of workers may vote for Dewey[4] would not alter the basic movement — that may even accelerate it. The whole international and national situations are conditioning substantial sections to receive extreme revolutionary agitation and propaganda. As far as it is humanly possible to see, any failure on our part over the next few years will rest squarely with the party itself. That is the way the question must be posed. If, in the next few years, there is a great social crisis, great actions by the masses (for without that there is no social crisis), and the party still remains a few hundred strong or at best continues to be so insignificant as to be unable to stamp itself upon the national consciousness, then the question of responsibility for failure becomes philosophical, if not academic. We have to recruit sufficient numbers to become an effective revolutionary party. It is in the light of this that our own recent past acquires special significance.

What then are we trying to do?

To put it briefly, we were conducting ourselves in propaganda and agitation as if we were already that mass party which we hope to become. To have 75% of our membership in the unions did not transform us into a mass party. We became a propagandist sect in the unions. That is all. And a propagandist sect, however active in the union, is not a mass party. For this reason, ten members of the CP could distribute 10,000 copies of the *Sunday Worker* in any area and confidently hope to reap results. Their paper has behind it the international power and prestige of a great modern state. The party is nationally recognized. In various spheres its actions materially affect the wages and working conditions and political life of large bodies of workers. Periodically, its nationally known speakers can visit the area and capitalize on such a mass distribution policy. It can, at a given time, throw in organizers and pull its contacts together by activity and special concentration on the area in the pages of the paper. All that was and is entirely beyond our strength. And will be for some time. Except where a union situation is hot, we are physically incapable of reaping the just reward of such mass distributions. How can ten comrades handle 5,000 readers for a paper, or even 500? We raised the political level of some thousands of workers in general. But we did not gain any substantial number of recruits that way, and cannot.

The proof of this can be seen in reverse by what took place in Missouri. There we could actually affect the lives of the workers. Since the strike in 1942, every field worker in Missouri works ten hours a day and then goes home. Nothing will make him work longer. Local 313 and the Trotskyites have the credit for this.[5] Mass distributions in the area build on a concrete foundation. At the same time, when we are ready, dozens of recruits are waiting for us. But elsewhere that is for us impossible. Any continuation of this policy in the same form can only result in wasted effort and frustration. Finally we have gained some positions in industry. But the positions gained were the result of a high level of employment. We face in time mass unemployment. The party most improbably can avoid the consequences of this. The question could not seriously be judged at the convention in January. But we may be faced with the possibilities of a return to concentration on the personal contact method of making recruits. This is the policy followed by the Cannonites,[6] it is said with good results. But the question is not by any means exhausted by mass distribution or concentration on personal contacts.

Our turn to the masses, correct, legitimate and indispensable, brought with it a particular form of agitation. We lacked the national and international drawing power of a mass party, like the Communist Party (CP). Yet in *Labor Action* which became our main weapon, we did not tell these thousands of workers what they could not learn in any other way or from any other source. What a party is, why it should exist, what has been the past of such parties, why the reader should consider that all that we did and he read must culminate soon in joining the party — that was conspicuously absent from the paper. Except for a pamphlet by Lund,[7] there is not one single piece of propagandist literature to do this recruiting job. We did not even produce a pamphlet saying what the Workers Party is about. Thus neither inside the paper nor outside of it were the mass distributions concretized. It would be a very low level of discussion which tried to prove that this was due to "lack of forces." It was a colossal mistake and nowhere so much as from the point of view of recruiting. This we must probe to its roots or we shall never correct the mistake in the way it will have to be corrected.

Labor Action As a Recruiting Agent

The present *Labor Action* must be the *foundation* of the further development of the party. There can be no return to the old *Militant* or the *Socialist Appeal* both for reasons which are well recognized by most of the members of the party and for others which will be apparent from the rest of this document. First of all, it is necessary to dispose of the broad criticism that *Labor Action* is a left-wing trade union paper. That is not only false but unless it is disposed of in the proper way, it is so easily replied to that it prevents that analysis of the paper which is necessary. *Labor Action* is *no left-wing trade union paper.* The paper is politically opposed to the capitalist *system* and the capitalist *class* as no left-wing trade union paper can be unless it is based on Marxism. To take one example. The theoretical opposition to the war is completely beyond any left-wing trade union paper that this writer has ever heard of. No left-wing trade union paper has the theoretical base of our political articles. In all these essential respects *Labor Action* is a Marxist and not a trade union paper. Furthermore, its union coverage is equally based on the concept of class. And if the party were a nationally known party the paper as it is would be a powerful recruiting weapon.

This is not a question of whether readers know that it is the paper of the Workers Party. If the paper said this in every issue on every page, it would not help matters. A reader of the paper would gather that the union question was of paramount importance. He would learn, somewhat abstractly, that labor in general should form a Labor Party. But he would read the paper for one year and get no coherent knowledge of what the Second International was and why, of the history and development of the Third International. Most important, of the historical development of the American working class, of its past, present, and future, of what the American working class stood for historically as against capitalist society, of that he would learn very little. Not only would he not learn this in general, but he would not learn the relationship of the revolutionary Marxist party to the class. He would never know what a revolutionary party was, why one should exist, what was its purpose, aims and methods, why it was an imperative necessity, what was its relation to the Labor Party and, above all, why he as an advanced worker should get into contact with it. So that even if he knew that the paper was the paper of the Workers Party, it is impossible to see how he would learn all the things that are necessary for him to know to make him into ripe material for Bolshevism. It is the lack of all this in the paper, not only explicitly but implicitly, which gives rise to the criticism that *Labor Action* is a left-wing trade union paper. To attempt to meet this criticism by saying that the critics want to go back to the old *Militant* is what has to be rooted out of all our discussion.

Let us clarify the discussion at once. One good pamphlet and six months of reading *Labor Action* should lead a substantial number of readers of *Labor Action* a long way toward joining us. It is possible that a dozen such pamphlets and a reorganized *Labor Action* would not have helped us in the past. It is possible that a reasonable section of the paper devoted specifically to educating American readers for American Bolshevism, would have left us where we are now. It is possible. But this much is certain. Unless in this field there is a drastic reorientation from top to bottom, not only of the paper but of the party, we *may* gain a few members, double our membership, even treble it in two or three years. But we shall fail completely to move organizationally with the necessities of the times. That is what we have to do, not grow in general, but grow in a certain proportion and anything else is failure.

The objective circumstances of the American working class and of the WP demand now that we get away completely from the idea of recruiting one by one or two by two. *We may have to do that for a time,* and in one sense we shall always be doing that. *But the world we live in makes it imperative for us to concentrate all our best energies into making the paper an agent for the training and recruiting of conscious Marxists.* This is a historical necessity, rooted in the development of modern civilization itself. Anyone who thinks that today, 1944, in the United States, and during the next few years, recruiting is merely a matter of personal contact "highly organized" is living in 1917. Today the whole organization of society is moving rapidly towards mass collective action on a grand scale. Workers in any numbers are repelled from small insignificant groups. The perspectives of one-by-one building up of a party to have effect in ten or twenty years have little sense to a worker in a country where organized labor is 14 million strong, and the NAACP has half a million members. Further, social and political developments are accelerated not only in space but in time. A new political organization issues at one stroke millions of pamphlets, the political leaders address the nation and the world by radio and are seen by the nation on the screen. Labor unions make special film shorts of their own. The PAC (Political Action Committees) sprang up over night. This is the age we live in. We haven't the resources to begin these things. But to us our popular press is not what *Iskra*[8] was to the early Bolsheviks. They did not have to contend against the technical facilities of the bourgeoisie that we have to contend with and the collective social consciousness corresponding to it. The odds against humble proletarian beginnings like *Iskra* and *Labor Action* lengthened enormously. *Labor Action* becomes our press, our radio, our plane, and our film short. We have to make it into something which with the necessary backing, will approach, win recruits and adherents far beyond our limited personal contact. The personal contact and the mass meeting must merely be the concluding stroke to what pamphlets and *LA* have already done.

The paper must carry such a message that as the social crisis develops, on the Eastern seaboard and the Middle West at any rate, the idea should gradually crystallize among thousands of readers, *most of them unknown to us,* that this paper should become a daily paper. The present writer believes that the American working class does not need its combativity stimulated. Any such approach on our part in particular, is not only ridiculous but presumptuous. Neither need there be any fear that the working class will not create mass political organizations. Without any assistance from *Labor Action* or the Bolsheviks, these are going to come with a violence and range which, as usual, will astonish nobody more than the radicals themselves. The whole history of labor and of labor in this country is indicative of the fact that what the American working class needs is the history and practice of Bolshevism.

That is what it needs, and that is what it can get only from us. This is what we have to translate into the paper. This is what the paper lacks and it does not lack it by accident or lack of forces.

Labor Action is what it is because the paper is based on a certain theory. The theory is that the American working class is not class conscious to a sufficient degree. Our business in the paper, therefore, is to try to raise the masses to the next stage. That stage is to make them ready for an independent labor party. When the stage is reached, the workers will then be ready for revolutionary Marxist propaganda. So that at present we are doing the best that can possibly be done. At the same time, however, on this theory and with a paper corresponding to it, we act as if we expect workers to join the revolutionary Marxist party. This is the contradiction in which the Party finds itself, in regard to *Labor Action* and recruiting.

First of all the idea that the *general level of consciousness of a working class movement forbids the strong and vigorous teaching of Marxism is contrary to the whole theory and practice of the Marxist movement for a hundred years.* Without going into that now, there is the experience of America itself during the last fifty years. Before 1914 there was the general popular agitation for socialism of Jack London[9] and later of Upton Sinclair.[10] This found a wide response among vast numbers of people. But, in addition, there was the strictly Marxist propaganda and agitation of the Socialist Labor Party and the American Socialist Party. Both of these in their various ways were socialists and Marxists speaking directly to the American workers. Such deficiencies as they had are to be explained by the fact that theoretically they were based more or less on the general standards and ideas of the European Social Democracy. The Socialist Labor Party in particular not only taught Marxism but also indulged in mass industrial work.

Secondly, they had definitive successes building from the ground up. Can anyone say that today the American working class is less class conscious than was the working class which those pioneers addressed so boldly and so consciously? The mere existence of the CIO is proof enough if proof is needed of the tremendous stage of development which the American working class has reached industrially as a class. Despite the absence of an independent labor party, the American working class is living an intense political life in the America and "One World" of today. It has had the experience of capitalist crisis in its most horrible form, of two imperialist wars, and has seen organized labor grow to be an actual and recognized social force. There has been brought home to it the political consciousness of fascism, of proletarian revolutions in Europe, of the possibilities of the productive system and the social needs of the masses of the people. All this exists today as potential material which did not exist in the days of the Socialist Labor Party and the Socialist Party. Under the circumstances what reason is there for believing that on the basis of the mass trade union work and its coverage in the paper we cannot speak boldly and directly for what we stand for, Marxian socialists seeking to build a revolutionary party in the name of scientific socialism? If we see it, we will do it.

Our INTERNATIONAL Experiences

Labor Action is not an accident. It is as it is, virtues and faults, a part of the international Trotskyite movement. It represents a stage in its development. Many of the newer comrades discuss the paper and our movement with no knowledge of what they are talking about. These questions however must be dealt with comprehensively. Lenin insisted that the problems of party building should be discussed not only among the leaders and the intellectuals, but in the press before the workers. He himself set a noble example. Let us at least begin by discussing them among ourselves with the necessary material and background.

We must see, first, the international scene in which the Trotskyite movement functioned under Trotsky and what he was trying to do from 1928 until his death in 1940.

In Europe between 1919 and 1944, with perhaps one exception, no proletarian party of any strength at all emerged independently from the proletariat. (These phenomena are to be generally explained by the capacity of capitalism to maintain illusions in the proletariat during the period. This question, though germain, it is impossible to treat here. I am merely dealing with the necessity of getting some perspective of Trotskyism and party building.) The SAP in Germany,[11] the Independent Labour Party (England), the Dutch Party led by Peter Schmitt, all were splits from the mass Social Democratic Party. Secondly, these splits were led by men who were already well-established as leaders in the Social Democratic Party. From the beginning, Trotsky, who directed the Trotskyite movement, was pretty clear as to the general situation and what it demanded. His conceptions may be divided into three periods, 1929–1934, 1934–1938, 1938–on. Each period had a separate aim and separate method. During the first period, Trotsky conceived of us as a fraction of the Communist Party. *We aimed at reintegration into an already existing mass revolutionary international organization.* Our whole propaganda and agitation aimed mainly at winning over people who understood what we were driving at. Vanguard spoke to vanguard. We were trained for that purpose and with that aim. Criticisms of the press of those days may be legitimate, but if they do not bear that in mind, they are not only useless but misleading. We did not have to make our main burden of explanation what Socialism or Bolshevism was. We operated within the framework of a false Bolshevism which we proposed to correct.

This policy was changed in 1934 with the "French Turn"[12] and we broadened our aim. *We had now as our main objective the left wing of the Social Democracy.* In Europe, in particular, this was and is a highly politicalized grouping. It more often than not had sympathetic and even intellectual affiliations with Communism and Communist Parties. It understood broadly what the problems and conflicts were about. Trotsky, aware of the urgency of the situation, aimed at splitting off substantial sections of these radicalized workers to become the nuclei of mass parties. That also was a specialized target for our activities. It was only in 1938 that that policy more or less came to an end everywhere. In 1938, the Fourth International was launched to stand on its own feet. The results are highly instructive. Except in Belgium where there was a proletarian base in the Borinage [a coal mining region] the various European parties failed to make progress. The most notorious failure was in France where the POI[13] had been established as an independent party in 1936.

Now it is important for us today to note that the American party, in a totally different environment, followed exactly the same course as the European Trotskyite parties. From 1928 to 1934 it aimed mainly at the Communist Party and was trained for so doing. From 1936 to 1938 it aimed at the American Socialist Party, a party which was and is like a Swiss group of boy scouts in comparison with the German army. However, some gains were made, more than in Europe, and in 1938 the SWP followed the international course of the Trotskyite movement and faced the American masses as an independent organization. Thus, in the ten years of its existence, in its agitation, propaganda, education, it had been a "European" party, aiming at the same specialized groups as the European parties. In the period 1928–1938 this had not been of much importance. But when the American party faced the prospect of addressing the American workers, the different stages of development of American and European [politics] at once assumed importance. The politically educated grouping in Europe, a potential soil for Trotskyism, did not and does not exist in the United States on the scale that it does in Europe. In America the split from the Socialist Workers Party came too early for any definitive conclusions to be drawn, but apart from the Russian question, there was already in the SWP in 1939, a deep conviction that the party was going nowhere "under Cannon's leadership." Burnham,[14] whose background was not in the least Trotskyite, had already begun a steady orientation towards the American scene. But Burnham was no Bolshevik and did this empirically.

By the time the WP had organized itself, the approach of war engendered the movement into factories. The WP leadership seized hold of this tendency and organized it. A radical break was made in the turn to the masses. Trotsky had seen and prepared for this turn theoretically. That was the significance of the Transitional Program. In practice, however, we had failed to make this turn. It was not until the October convention of 1941 of the WP that the turn was definitively made in the United States on the basis of the impulse given by the war. Once we recognize, however, the historical difference between the various periods we can say that the organization of this turn by the WP was one of the best things that had been done in the Trotskyite movement in the United States of America.

This time the break was made practically. Trotsky had given us the general international theory of the Transitional Program. But from a theoretical and national point of view we made the break empirically, and it has produced all the vices of empiricism. There was not worked out consciously a political ideology of a general kind, no political orientation for education, propaganda, and agitation. In the previous periods we had a theoretical basis, amply worked out. There was socialism in a single country,[15] there was the whole Russian question, there was the question of the Stalinist deviation from the Bolshevik struggle against the imperialist war, there was the Chinese Revolution, German fascism, the Popular Front in France, the Spanish question (which produced a lengthy pamphlet by Morrow), the Moscow Trials. These were our theoretical stock-in-trade from 1928 to 1938. In these we lived and thought and had our being. But with the turn to the masses those have been more or less abandoned except insofar as we make the barely necessary adaptations. But otherwise we live in what may be reasonably described as a sort of theoretical vacuum. In Europe today that is not so. Many of the old problems still remain and are for them urgent. But the theoretical accompaniment of the specific turn that we have made simply does not exist.

That is why the party talks of education but does nothing about it.

That is why *Labor Action* is as it is.

That is why the party as a whole, while very satisfied with the paper in general, yet feels that something more is needed.

That is why resolutions are passed for more socialism in the paper and nothing is done. The translation of Bolshevism, of Marxism, into terms suitable for broad masses of the American people proceeds, if at all, empirically and without any conscious plan. And this deficiency on our part we rationalize into a theory that the American masses must reach the stage of being class conscious before they are ready to accept the doctrines of scientific socialism. This is [. . .] contrary to the experience of previous Marxist organizations in the United States. We cannot say that because we have not made the attempt. It must be repeated and repeated over and over again; we were not trying to do this in the best days of the old Trotskyite movement. All such comparisons can serve only to mislead us.

Are we building an *American* party?

Look at the list of books advertised by Labor Action Book Service. It is in 1944 a curiosity. There is a book by Rochester, *Lenin on the Agrarian Question*. Simons has an old pamphlet, "Class Struggle in America." Shachtman has a 5c pamphlet on Cost-Plus, Gates one on Incentive Pay and Lund a 10c pamphlet on Plenty for All. For the rest, it is Marx to Kugelman, Lenin on the Threatening Catastrophe, Trotsky on Whither France, Plekhanov on Anarchism and Socialism, Kautsky on Ethics and Nearing on the British General Strike, and some 60 volumes of the same type. The *New International* is today a reflection and a very poor reflection of the books on this list (that I shall deal with later). But that is where we stand. To believe that we can build a mass party on such fare is a mistake, I repeat. I am not prepared to say that if there had been a change here in 1942 to 1944, we would have recruited numbers of workers. But I say without any reservations whatever that unless there is a planned, systematic, methodical but drastic attempt at reorientation, the social crisis will pass us by. *Labor Action* is, therefore, a paper of the party which has made a sharp turn to the American masses with the intention of building an American party from the ground up. But the theoretical equipment of the party is the "European" theoretical equipment which was the common heritage of the Trotskyite movement worked out over the past dozen years.

Our Problem

This is our problem. If it is not there, there is no problem and all we have to do is to go on working in the unions and hope for the best, blaming history if we do not succeed.

Let it be said at once that *the orientation which we began in 1942 must be continued.* Propagandist sect though we are (and any group which cannot effectively move masses in its own name is a propagandist sect) our place is in the union movement with the great masses. One of the great weaknesses of the European Trotskyite movement was that it would not get to the masses at the point of production but functioned among them, where it did, almost exclusively in the mass political organizations of the masses. Still more important, and this is a historical development of profound socialist significance, even before World War II, there was noticeable a powerful tendency towards drawing together of the trade unions and political organizations of the workers. In the U.S., this most capitalistic of all countries, this hitherto European tendency seems likely to attain its completest development. Inside the union movement, the American working class is living the intense political life of the times and the American political movement is likely to be tied to the union movement from the very start in an indissoluble bond. Thus, in the U.S., in particular, our place is in the union movement as the basis for our political action.

Secondly, in the next stage *there must be no change in attitude towards the CP or any other party at present on the horizon.* The CP today offers us an example of a party that is supremely well-educated for its own purposes. It can hold a meeting with 18,000 people in one month, opposing the imperialist war, and have the same people the next month supporting it. This is neither miracle nor stupidity. The party is educated with the preservation of the Soviet Union as its basis. These actions and changes are therefore perfectly intelligible to the members and sympathizers. A party like ours will waste its time trying to break through that. Furthermore we shall attract other parties by strength. Our road continues to be the American workers. Our aim continues to be to lay the foundations of a mass party from the ground up.

Here let us get the word "mass" right. A mass paper in ordinary terms is a paper that moves masses. Any organization which can publish such a paper educates and attracts, not only by concrete action, but by the means that its size and strength place at its disposal. But we have to define our terms carefully. If we distribute 25,000 copies a week, then we are meeting, for us, masses. Furthermore our whole orientation now in the paper is not towards the advanced few or even those politically educated workers who form the left wing of European Social Democracy. We, today, on an extremely narrow base, are attempting to educate and draw together a few thousand workers whom we expect to be driven toward revolutionary perspectives by the developing social crisis and our education. It is a very highly specialized situation; a country ripe for socialism, a working class in a highly charged and explosive national and international situation, but without even the education that is given by the political practice of a mass reformist party. Finally, there is another party, the Communist Party, representing Boshevism in the eyes of the masses, pushing them as hard as it can back into bourgeois-democratic illusions, perverting and distorting all the fundamentals of Marxism and skimming off the cream of the revolutionary workers as they emerge from the broad masses. These are the conditions under which we work, and everyone of them merely intensifies the importance of *Labor Action* as a paper teaching Marxism to the American workers.

It must be understood at once that changing *Labor Action* is no work of a day or of a year. No cure-all is being proposed, no list of articles and people to write them or columns in the press by qualified persons, no technical solutions to "solve" the party problem. It is a problem of a long-range policy, to be discussed inside and outside the party, a tentative plan systematically and methodically worked out by trial and error but with a clear consciousness of the aim. Some of these ideas I placed very briefly before the Political Committee nearly a year ago. Others which will follow I sketched also in outline at a city-wide meeting prepatory to the last convention which discussed the American scene.

II: The Americanization of Bolshevism

To Bolshevize America it is necessary to Americanize Bolshevism. It is time to begin. But we do not begin by writing some articles in *Labor Action* about the Bolshevik and Menshevik struggle in 1903, trying to make the readers "party-minded" by describing what our five comrades in X did or the seven in Y nearly did. No. We begin by getting a theoretical orientation and basis. Nothing can be more misleading than the idea that Americanization means seeking historical examples of revolutionary American parties and American heroes of labor with which to "inspire" the American workers and season our journalists.

Every great revolution is a truly national revolution in that it represents not only the historic but the immediate interests of the nation and is recognized as such. But every party which leads such a revolution is also a national party rooted in the economic and social life, history and traditions of the nation. Its own class ideology is cast in the national mold and is an integral part of the national social structure. In my article on Sidney Hook (signed AAB, July, October 1943, *New International*) I tried to show how truly Russian and national was Lenin, the greatest internationalist of the age. The Bolshevik Party was the same. And we shall see, it was so from its very beginning.

The Workers Party is not that. It is a long, long way from that. It has got to turn its head in that direction, a huge task if ever there was one, calling for theoretical and practical energy of a high order.

As usual, our only model is Lenin, the leader of the only effective Bolshevik party which history has known, and like the one we aim at, built from the ground up.

Lenin spent six years in preparation for his task, mastering the volumes of *Capital* that had appeared, *Anti-Dühring*, etc. He arrived in Petersburg in 1894 and from that time to 1914 his life's work was to translate Marxism into

Russian terms for the Russian people. The Russian revolutionary movement had a long tradition behind it, Herzen, Belinsky, Chernyshevsky,[16] men famous in the revolutionary movement and in Russian literature as a whole. Lenin took care to build on that tradition. His method of doing so was to do for his generation what they did for theirs, teaching Marxism to the Social Democratic Party and the Russian people in spacious terms. Here is a rough summary of his work.

(1) The most thorough exposition of theoretical Historical Materialism that exists is his long reply to Narodnik[17] falsification of Marxist theory. In Vol. XI of his *Selected Works*,[18] extracts from this study fill nearly 200 pages. It is dated 1894, is probably his first major work, is couched in Russian terms and is unsurpassed to this day.

(2) His controversy with the Narodniki on the future development of Russian capitalism fills volumes. In the course of it he made contributions to the analysis of *Capital* which remain for the most part unknown and far less understood in Western Europe and America. Yet it was Marxism applied strictly to the Russian economy.

(3) He wrote *The Development of Capitalism in Russia*,[19] a book of many hundreds of pages. It was a direct application of the most abstract Marxian economic theory to Russia.

(4) His work on party building, *What Is To Be Done*,[20] is Russian in conception and execution, Marxist classic though it is.

(5) His special work on the agrarian question in Russia stands alone.[21] It is a masterpiece of Marxism, but on Russia.

(6) His study of American agriculture, made in 1913, is a unique masterpiece.[22] He did it specially to illustrate certain aspects of the problem of Russian agriculture.

It is on this that the Russian Social Democratic movement lived. These were the theoretical and propagandist foundations of the party. This was the work that guided the agitational press of Bolshevism. The Bolshevik Party was rooted in the day-to-day work, in industrial and mass struggles, to a degree compared to which our modest efforts can claim comparison only in good intentions. Only an armor-plated ignorance could think of the Bolshevik leader as anything else but an advocate of mass activity. But as a leader he considered it *his special task* to provide those thousands of party leaders, propagandists, and agitators with material and method by which they could educate themselves and others. In this way, as Trotsky says, he also educated himself.

This was no work of an exile. It began from the day he came to Petersburg, writing leaflets about conditions in a factory, reading *Capital* to small circles of Russian workmen. In his propagandist work he was nakedly and unashamedly, and belligerently theoretical. In his study of the development of capital in Russia, he prefixed an essay on Marx's economic theory so as not to have to refer to the theory too often in the text, which nevertheless is packed with quotations from *Capital*. This was the Leninist method. It is the only method for building a Bolshevik party. It is the only way to combat bourgeois ideology. It was necessary in Russia fifty years ago, where large sections of the population were permeated by hostility to Tsarism and the existing regime and where a long line of great writers had influenced and developed the revolutionary tradition. Furthermore, in the nineties Marxism swept Russia. Marxist books were best-sellers.

Compare the modern United States, the most bourgeois country in the world where the workers are permeated with bourgeois ideology. Isn't it clear that we today need to begin this work? Isn't it clear that without it the party cannot even begin to become a mass American party? How ridiculous it would have been if Lenin had been told that the articles about unions in *Iskra* were teaching the Russian workers Marxism.

And we?

Let the reader now look at the list of pamphlets, brochures, etc., published by Pioneer Publishers in the old days, from the *Draft Program of the Comintern, Germany What Next?, The Chinese Revolution, The Spanish Revolution in Danger, Whither France*, etc., etc., and the corresponding articles in the *New International*. That was one period, one party, aiming at one group of workers and contacts. We have made a big turn to the masses. But in our theoretical conceptions and our practice, how vast is the difference? The great danger is that we shall just say, "Well, let X write a pamphlet, or Y write two. Then when we get some more forces we shall write some more." That approach is false to the core, empirical, superficial, and a positive obstacle in the progress and development of the party. We shall not get very far that way.

AMERICAN or Nothing

The more we consider this question, the more we can see the special character of the problem with which we are faced in the United States.

The classics of Marxism are European in origin and content. They require more than an ordinary knowledge of European history and particularly by an American worker. In the 1928 to 1938 days it did not matter much where we began with the Communist Party members and the radicals. Today when we have to give a class or a piece of literature to a contact, we begin perhaps with the *Communist Manifesto*. For us who aim at becoming a mass party this is in five cases out of six anomalous and will increasingly become so. Every European worker of today who reads the *Communist Manifesto* with his European experiences, his school studies and the daily life around him, social, political, literary, and artistic, at once experiences a tremendous illumination that has solid concrete associations. A French worker who reads *Class Struggles in France*,[23] *The 18th Brumaire*,[24] or *The Civil War in France*;[25] a German worker who reads *Revolution and Counter-Revolution in Germany*,[26] or the *Peasant War in Germany*,[27] finds the history of his own country made significant for him as never before.

Capital is not only a study of abstract capitalism. It is the history of English capitalist development and there is no finer introduction to the history of Great Britain. The last section on Primitive Accumulation is the historical garment of the logical capitalistic development of Western Europe. For the average American worker these books as a beginning are alien. Doubtless if he reads one he is impressed with its power and brilliance and learns something. But what they cannot give to him in sufficient measure is that sense of reality of the development of his own country, that feeling that in addition to the daily class struggle, he is part of something beyond himself that is the beginning of theoretical Bolshevism and the rejection of bourgeois ideology.

Such historical data, knowledge, general reading, social experiences as he has, the structure in which his theoretical experiences must grow, are American. We have to begin now, not to write a few pamphlets but to build up the American counterparts of the *Communist Manifesto, The 18th Brumaire*, and perhaps even more important, the American counterpart of *What Is To Be Done*. We do not wait until we become a large party to do these things. This is the way to prepare ourselves and all our supporters for the gaining of forces and the building of the revolutionary party. If in time among our efforts, we can manage at last to get one such solid pamphlet that does for United States history or the development of the labor movement or any such topic what these pamphlets do for Europe, and catch some of their spirit, we have the possibility, not only of immediate response but, in time, of reaching an ever-widening circle of concrete rewards.

This is precisely what Lenin set out to do with a grandeur, breadth, and vision that are astonishing even after years of familiarity. In every field he posed proletarian ideology against bourgeois ideology. It is impossible to build an American mass party with our propaganda consisting of Marx on France and Germany, Lenin on Russia, and Trotsky on Stalinism and Spain; supplemented by the present *Labor Action*. It is impossible for a number of average workers to become Bolsheviks unless on the basis of some systematic penetration into American development. Good Stalinists, yes. Good Trotskyites in the old days — the very old days, perhaps, but not today, for what we are going to do, NO.

That is the first point. The second is less easy to grasp but more important in the long run. For the implications of this orientation go much, much deeper. Not only do raw workers need this Americanization. *The party members from the highest to the lowest need it also.* No one has any serious grasp of Marxism, can handle the doctrine or teach it unless he is, *in accordance with his capabilities and opportunities,* an exponent of it in relation to the social life and development around him. The dialectical progression, the various stages of development, the relation between the economic basis and the superstructure, history, economics, and philosophy, all the principles and doctrines of Marxism were evolved from a profound and gigantic study by its founders of European history, of European politics, of European literature, of European philosophy. The principles have universal application. But to the extent that the conditions from which they were drawn are not familiar to the Marxists, they remain to a greater or less degree abstract, with infinite potentialities for confusion and mischief.

Either the would-be Marxist must have some serious knowledge of European history in its broadest sense, constantly renewed, amplified and developed, or the principles of the doctrine must have been incorporated, worked over, and made to live again in a study of the economic structure, social development, history, literature, and life of the country with which he has been many years familiar. Only then is he on the road to becoming a serious exponent and contributor to the doctrine. In fact and in truth only until one has dug the principles of Marxism for himself out of his own familiar surroundings and their historical past that the Marxism of Marx and Engels, Lenin or Trotsky and the famous European Marxists truly stand out in their universal application. Not only is this so. It would be a miracle if it were not so. Not only is it so for analysis, for propaganda, or for agitation. It is, abstracted from the question of personality, the basis of socialist confidence and Bolshevik morals. The Bolshevik solidity which must be the core of those who may come to us, the capacity to stand all the pressures, must be rooted in a deep, rich, wide concept of American development. The masses may not need it. But for the party cadres of this period it is imperative.

To the degree that we can teach this to masses, we develop and reinforce the hostility to American bourgeois society which is the objective result of capitalism in this stage of its development. Proletarian ideology is not merely a matter of theoretical analysis. It is the weapon and armory with which we must arm and surround the American working class and particularly those who face the enormous tasks confronting us in the present period. Unless it is rooted in the American environment and in such terms as the American worker can grasp, we cannot lift them above the instinctive class struggle, sharp as that will inevitably become. Isn't this what Lenin meant by the socialist consciousnes which the party carries to the working class?

The Proof Is in the Practice

If the above is a representation of the actual situation and the needs of the time, then a careful examination of ourselves must show not only the lack but the movement towards repairing it. The party is small and it is not difficult to get some idea of along what lines the members think. Since the birth of the Workers Party we have had two conventions. The first was in 1941 and was concerned mainly with the new orientation toward the factories. The members felt that here at last was a change from the 1928–1938 activity. The membership, the older membership in particular, was sceptical of talk and promises. It wanted results. The high point of the convention was the appearance of the comrades from Missouri.[28] It created enthusiasm and produced on the spot a substantial sum. The appearance of these workers symbolized the direct contact with the proletariat which was the aim and need of our movement. We met again in convention two years later. Once more the convention was moved to a spontaneous demonstration, this time by the document by Lund on the very question that is dealt with here. When conventions of revolutionaries behave in that way they express deep-going currents not only in the party but in the working class movement. The thing is to analyse them and see their significance.

First of all, it is obvious that in its title Lund's document has little in common with the ideas presented here. He seems to think that it is a problem of attitude, of journalistic method, of seeking "inspiration." But it is to Lund's credit that he sees the problem and has at least found time to give one exemplification of what he means in the pamphlet, "Plenty for All." For once a problem is seen at all, it is usually acted upon, whatever the difficulties.

Yet the significances of the convention demonstration was that it reflected the needs of members who were in industry, were concerned with the progress of the party in industry and were looking for ways and means to build the party deeper into industry and reap rewards in industry. In this respect the convention merely carried to its conclusion a sentiment which had been confused but clear enough at the Cleveland Conference of Active Workers.

It is now possible to summarize the party development in the minds and actions of the membership.

1. The new industrial orientation is and must remain the life-blood of the party.

2. The new *Labor Action* is a vast improvement on the old Trotskyite papers. (Not for the reasons usually given, as I have insisted all through this document, but because we are attempting what they never attempted. Losing sight of this distinction is part of the reason for our weaknesses.) The new type of paper that *Labor Action* is must form the basis and the substantial basis of any proposed orientation.

3. But at the same time the members recognize that something more is needed. This is the perpetual cry for "more socialism in the paper."

4. Clearly allied with the above is the demand for more education. The membership is deeply aware of the necessity of being educated, and it must be remembered that this membership is grappling with the problem of the American working class and that therefore its conception of education is not abstract theories but of education to make it more competent for the tasks in which it is engaged.

5. The membership feels (a) that it is time that the party began to recruit new members; (b) that it is difficult to integrate the raw workers whom we get into the existing party.

Such has been the development of the Workers Party. But as we watch this development we can see that, small as we are, we are merely reflecting in a conscious and creative manner, as befits revolutionaries, the development of the American working class itself.

After the first outburst which resulted in the formation of the CIO we had a temporary lull. But with the capitalistic preparation for the European war the American working class has been driven towards the expansion and the recognition of the social importance of organized labor. In the American press in general and in the literature issued by labor we find this rapidly growing consciousness of the importance of American labor as a force in American society. With this growth we have an increasing consciousness on the part of labor that something more is needed than the industrial struggle, a consciousness that is reflected in the PAC (Political Action Committee). Finally, all over the country and most notably among the soldiers in the army there is the growing consciousnes that more education is needed, not merely education for a better job, but specifically knowledge of American history and knowledge of the world abroad in order that they may understand the vast social developments of the time.

Thus, when the members say that we want more "socialism" in the paper and more education and must find a way of integrating raw workers into the kind of party that we are, they are demanding some theoretical orientation, material, and atmosphere which will assist them to supplement the work which they are doing among the American masses. Since 1940 the party leaders agree on this at all plenums, conventions, and conferences. Yet we remain apparently impotent. Everyone recognizes that articles about the happy life to come in the future socialist America are nonsensical. More is needed. But what, that is the question.

The reason for this is that the problem has not been seen in its full scope and depth. This, then, is the essence of the question.

Every principle and practice of Boshevism needs to be translated into American terms. Historical materialism, the Marxian economic analysis, the role of the party, the relation between democracy and socialism, the relation between the trade union and the party, reformists and revolution, the role of Social Democracy, the theory of the state, the inevitability of socialism, every single one of these can be taught, developed, demonstrated from the American economic, social, and political development. The American Revolution, the Civil War, the Knights of Labor, the Populist Movement, the Southern economy, the tremendous history of the CIO, the development of the two major parties, the political and social contributions of Paine, Jefferson, the Wilson administration, the New Deal, the NRA, the American dollar civilization, the rise and decline of the American Socialist Party, Eugene Debs, John L. Lewis, the Marxist analysis of all this is the material of our education, of our propaganda, of the creation of a Bolshevism which will break a path for us to the American masses. The ideas and principles of Marxism must be boldly and uncompromisingly presented to the American workers. The great European classics must be used, not only for their own sake, but as a means of explaining the American development.

With such a party, we shall not only be able to educate our members and give to those with whom we come in contact what they will increasingly be looking for. On the basis of our mass work, when they come to us, they will be able to feel that they belong to us. This is not only a necessary and imperative supplement to our work. It is our special contribution to the American labor movement. The two complement each other to complete what is known as scientific socialism. If one aspect is ignored, neglected, or superficially dealt with, then the other assumes an unchecked momentum of its own and does not even bring the rewards which the efforts lead us to expect.

III: The New International

I am proposing no immediate cure-all, no patent medicine to bring immediate results. Revolutionary parties are not built that way. They are built by hard thinking and hard work, and hard thinking comes first. Therefore, at the center of the proposed reorientation must be the *New International,* the theoretical journal of the party. The transformation of *Labor Action* into a direct recruiting agent, to recruit in accordance with the necessities of the time, and the reorientation of a mass propaganda must begin with the journal. We have to see, therefore, what it was, what it is, and what it must be. The journal is now ten years old, and, in accordance with the methods used herein and the ideas expressed, we must see it in the light of the historical development of the Trotskyite movement.

Between 1934 and 1938, it was a powerful and influential organ. From a strictly journalistic point of view its editing was always slipshod, but it always had the first necessity of a magazine, one strong central current and, in its later years, one minor one. The central current was Trotsky's writings on the international situation, and particularly, though not mainly, on the Russian question. Inside and outside of the [journal] he wrote with a regard for method, a comprehensiveness of knowledge and experience and a tenacity of purpose which formed the intellectual and often the editorial axes of the paper. From various parts of the world comrades who wanted to write found ideas, information, hints, and indications which could be worked up, often even phrases which could be borrowed. Not only articles, speeches, courses drew from that inexhaustible source. To write a panphlet was simplicity itself. A whole volume of 450 pages was written mainly on Trotsky's writings as basis (*World Revolution*). Isaacs' *The Chinese Revolution* directly and indirectly came from Trotsky.

It is fashionable to say that we merely repeated his views. That is true and had its weaknesses. The present writer, however, can try to sum up what he is trying to say about the period in which we live in terms of his own experience of the 1928–1938 period. When he joined the movement he found a body of ideas, a mass of pamphlets and brochures, one incomparable masterpiece, the *History of the Russian Revolution,* with its valuable appendices, soon another volume, *The Revolution Betrayed,* and a constant stream of articles, all written with a certain purpose, with the highest integrity and seriousness, with not an atom of empiricism or writing down. One went forth to do the particular battle of those days confident and fully armed. That was the source of the strength of the *New International*. If, in the next two years, for our purposes today we do one-quarter as well and our people can read and educate themselves on our material in the way we did on Trotsky's, then half our battle is won and with that, on the one hand, and our mass work on the other, *Labor Action* and the individual member will be forces to be reckoned with.

Trotsky also wrote and inspired articles on general topics such as the introduction to the *Communist Manifesto,* published in South Africa; an article on Engels; a general article on literature which appeared in *Partisan Review.* He inspired directly other articles. It is to be noted that Trotsky never wrote a single article on the United States. His introduction to *The Living Thoughts of Karl Marx* is a very broad application of the theory of Marx to familiar statistics and other phenomena of U.S. capitalism. He never wrote on the Negro question. He said that he did not have the material necessary although he had a mass of documents, memoranda, statistical material, etc., sent to him by comrades and friends. His special field was (1) the exposition of the principles of the first four congresses of the Communist International and (2) Russia.

For the period, for the audience we aimed at, it was exactly what was required, despite whatever criticisms may be made in detail. This and the work it inspired made the magazine and trained writers and propagandists.

The second trend, a minor one but nevertheless distinctive enough to be noted, was Burnham's writings on the American question. They were a new departure, consistently done and distinctive in the *New International.* Macdonald,[29] a first-class journalist, typically American, and Novack,[30] with real interest in and some knowledge of American history, showed possibilities.

Trotsky might not write about certain problems. He was keenly aware of them for he knew how parties are built. He inspired Novack to write on the Civil War, he insisted that Burnham answer Max Eastman, he continually and even impatiently asked for articles on dialectical materialism. But these were subordinate to the main general line — the exposition of the principles of the First Four Congresses.

In 1940 came the split. And since that time the magazine has steadily declined. (Nowhere in this document am I dealing with more fundamental questions such as the rightness or wrongness of the views or theories presented. That does not alter the line of argument here.) It lost Trotsky, the source of theory and ideas. It lost Burnham, Macdonald, and Novack, who, despite all their weaknesses, formed an American team who complemented each other. But worst of all, it lost a sense of direction. For a time it was difficult enough to fill its pages, but even now when there is too much material it is impossible to work out what the magazine is aiming at in theoretical education. An analysis of articles is here and at this time out of place. But to the writer, the magazine at present seems to be organized on the following basis:

1. As an organ whose main purpose is attacking the Cannonites. (And not forgetting the "Johnsonites.")

Articles, editorials, archives, before the convention and after, seem preoccupied with the proving of a case — in narrow terms. In particular, there are reprinted archives from all periods which very few readers are able to place in context. For these to be of real value, would require still more mountains of material as annotation.

2. Exposure of the aims of Stalinism in Europe, done in concrete agitational terms by warning that Russia plans to rule over labor, etc., etc.

3. Continuation in the archives of the old Trotsky-Stalin controversy.

4. An assortment of articles on varied subjects in which it is impossible to discover any orientation.

This is no question of "lack of forces." Forces fill the magazine now. What is happening to the *New International* is precisely what is happening to *Labor Action,* in the theoretical field. But *Labor Action* has the indispensable solid contact with the American working class. They give to it a central direction by their course of action. Its weakness is neglect of an empirical treatment of Bolshevism. The *New International,* however, lacking this direction, merely represents a feeble continuation from the period 1928–1938. (This is no mere "destructive" criticism. For the past year or so, the present writer has attempted to introduce into the journal at least one consistent trend along the lines of this document. I list the following articles in the *New International*:

"The Philosophy of History and Necessity," July & Oct. 1943

"Negroes in the Civil War: Their Role in the 2nd American Revolution," Dec. 1943

"In the American Tradition: The Working Class Movement in Perspective," Nov. 1943

"In the International Tradition: American Labor's Tasks," Jan. 1944

"Laski, St. Paul and Stalin," June 1944

"The American People in One World: An Essay in Dialectical Materialism," July 1944

Everyone knows what *Labor Action* is trying to do. Who can say what the *New International* is trying to do? Whatever is the aim of the magazine, it is not succeeding. At a time when we represent Marxism, when society is in such crisis that all types of theories are being eagerly discussed by all sorts of people, the magazine as an intellectual force counts for little. To deny this is to dig one's head in the sand.

Polemic the magazine must have. Bolshevism and Lenin in particular lived on polemic. The Cannonites are a legitimate target, and there are times when we have to throw all our weight into breaking them up. But we have had a long experience in these attacks and polemics, and maneuvers aimed at other parties, large and small. The concrete results have been usually in the long run pretty poor.

The most perfect example of what the *New International* is can be seen in what we produced for the ten year anniversary number. An anniversary number sums up the past, looks at the present situation, from a height so to speak, and opens up the perspectives of the future. It is a number which usually brings renewed interest and enthusiasm and a substantial number of subscribers. It is a number of which many extra copies should be printed and handed out as a card of introduction so to speak for years to come. Every reader of *Labor Action* should have felt that this was a number to get, to read, and to keep. Instead the number was a particularly bad example of what the *New International* has been for the past two years, with some 25 pages devoted to the National Question and speeches and articles by Lenin and Trotsky and Engels. Gates continues a polemic on his conception of the party. The result could have been expected. The issue has fallen flat. The wider circles it should have reached are not only untouched — even party members, if one can judge by incidental comments, have been cold where they have not approved.

This is on the positive side so far as it is positive. However, it is when we look at what the party is today and what it is trying to do, that we can see how far *Labor Action* represents one period, and the *New International* another. *Between LA and the mass approach to the American worker and the NI, there is an almost impossible gulf.*

What Should Be Done?

The first thing to recognize is that the magazine's main business is to do in theory what *Labor Action* (and the non-existent popular pamphlets) must do in practice. The central direction of the journal must be Marxism and the United States as the central directive of the old *New International* was the first four congresses of the Comintern and the international situation. With our background and with the international situation, we need never fear that the magazine will become an example of Marxist "isolationism." Our framework will always be international. At times the international aspect will predominate. Lenin was the greatest of all internationalists. But Trotsky notes that Lenin's "international period" began only in 1914. If it is true that we live in a period far more internationally united than forty years ago, yet the fact remains that once we have for the moment abandoned our preoccupation with the Communist Party and the others, genuine internationalism must be based on the national scene. To repeat ad nauseum. The theoretical journal of 1928–1938 had one aim. We have another. We must from all angles train ourselves for that. No party was ever so internationally trained as the Bolshevik Party. But this most international of all parties learned Marxism on a Russian basis, and could not have learned it in any other way. If the *New International* is not the place where we must train ourselves to do what Lenin did between 1896 and 1914, then where must it be done?

If it is urged that during the war we had a special responsibility then that responsibility is now over. France and Italy are already active. The coming period demands a reorientation of the journal.

Not only is this necessary from a national point of view but from an international. America occupies a peculiar place in international affairs today. Knowledge of this country has never formed more than a cursory part of European culture and education. In all probability the number of English universities in 1939 which gave a course in U.S. history and culture could be counted on the fingers of one hand or at most two. Today that is changed. America is the center of world attention. It is the last hope for imperialism and the old democracy. The American bourgeoisie is going to flood the world with accounts of this country, its history, its development, its politics, its ideals, etc. In the present writer's opinion substantial sections of the European bourgeoisie, and certainly the Social Democrats and liberals have no hope of salvation except in actual American overlordship or the American "ideal." As long as Roosevelt and Stalin collaborate, the whole power of Stalinism will be directed to supplementing the propagandistic efforts of the American bourgeoisie. Powerful in Europe, this trend will be overwhelming in the Far East. And even where in foreign countries there is an opposition to this trend, the opposition will of necessity concern itself with the United States. The theoretical interpretation of the United States, its past, present, and future, becomes therefore a truly international task, a part of the international struggle for socialism and the national independence of oppressed peoples. And in this, the central issue of our times, we have an exhaustive role to play.

Finally, as always in periods of crisis and never so much as in this one, the whole problem of the destiny of humanity is raised. The individual, the state, education, culture, religion, the elite, the necessity of rulers and ruled, race, all these fundamental questions are once more in the melting pot, nationally and internationally. Our contribution in this most capitalistic of all countries is to analyse these fundamental questions in our terms. This is our contribution to the international socialist debate. Marxists of each country do their own, as internationalists. Henceforth we can be certain that the European comrades will create an international journal, at least in French. Our business is internationalism with the United States as the center. We shall reprint and comment, and also contribute as we have done in the past. But henceforth the journal must know where it is going and all of us must know. I have indicated my view.

A Theoretical Journal

This obviously is no light task. Marx and Engels knew Western Europe inside out. Lenin and Trotsky were masters of all aspects of Russia. We have to do the same here. The task is not light. Neither was Lenin's task light in those days of 1894. But, a young man in his twenties, he wrote and circulated manuscripts in St. Petersburg which were written as if he were already leader of a state theoretically founded on Marxism. In every field he proclaimed the supremacy and the necessity of Marxist theory. What we have to do is not only to educate concretely. We have to train a generation which will familiarize itself with the fundamentals of Marxist theory by exercising it in this task. Its departments are four. To begin with the simplest:

1. Historical Materialism. *We haven't to do research as Lenin had to do.* In this highly organized country masses of material exist on all topics. The first American Revolution, the Second and the Third, these are *our* themes. Hitherto we have lived mentally in 1789, 1848, 1871, 1917, the Social Democracy, the Third International. We shall never be able to depart from those. They are international. But we must use them as means to an end. Our revolution is after all the American Revolution. The specific economic development of the United States, the special social relations which they produced, the political parties and the special qualities which distinguish the American from the European development. It is obvious that the leading American comrades must have accumulated knowledge and ideas about these questions. We cannot keep them in our heads any longer. Late in his career Engels planned enthusiastically to rewrite his *Peasant War in Germany in order to make it a preparation for the understanding of modern Germany.* Engels was no academic historian or lover of theory for theory's sake. He considered it his business to educate the workers from the highest possible standards.

A tremendous field is here waiting to be opened, a field which will not only bring practical results but is of the highest theoretical importance. The present writer has found that precisely because of the absence of feudal remnants in modern America, many of the most abstract analyses of Marx find their most perfect exemplification in the United States. Today this is the model capitalist country. Here increasingly in the future the utmost implications of the theory will be practically demonstrated. This is of national and international importance. The poverty of what passes for Marxist or radical thought in America is amazing. The Hackers, the Abram Harrises, the Beards[31] and the rest are all petty-bourgeois radicals spreading their poison unchecked. We have to carry on a merciless war of Marxist interpretation against their pseudo-Marxist fabrications and fantasies. The American working class, as is inevitable, is waking up to its history as a class, an inevitable stage in its socialist development. We have to treat this history as militant Marxists. A book like the Beards' *Basic History* at 69c is going to do a vast amount of mischief to workers anxious to learn. We give it credit for what is good but denounce it as Marxists. We give our own interpretation. We publish our own analysis. We publish our own studies. And peculiarly enough, that is how we make international classics. Daniel DeLeon wrote two pamphlets, *What Means This Strike* and *Two Pages From Roman History*, which, we are reliably informed, were among the treasured pamphlets of many workers in Britain.

If in the course of a year we can publish in the journal Marxist studies of the Civil War and a real Marxist analysis of the rise and social and historical significance of the CIO, we shall have accomplished a truly great beginning. From these articles *will come pamphlets, and will come a deepening of the political education in LA.* From these articles will come the historical backing necessary for the propaganda for the Labor Party. We are all aware of something missing in our propaganda for the Labor Party. It has not the fundamental theoretical basis concretely expounded. Lenin insists that from the very beginning of the socialist movement in Russia two trends appeared, opportunism and Marxism. His greatest work after 1914 was the theoretical analyses of the economic causes of this. Day after day he analyzed it economically, politically, socially. For him this education the workers needed above all. What have we done to make this a living part of the knowledge and experience of the U.S. workers and radicals? Absolutely nothing. Sure we say that the labor leaders are reactionary, pro-Roosevelt, pro-war. We say they are scoundrels. Those are just agitational statements. The general impression that our agitation gives is of reactionary labor leaders who deceive the workers. This is theoretically false. The labor leaders do not function in a vacuum. Not an issue of the *New International* should come out in which from one angle or another we did not treat from the roots up the basis of opportunism in the U.S. And in this way we perform an international service. It will not be long before its influence will appear in *Labor Action*, propagandist and agitational pamphlets and the daily work of the members.

2. Marxian economics. The sad record of the magazine here speaks for itself. It is sufficient to say that the economic question of questions in our day is the quesiton of capitalist accumulation. The debate in Lenin's day raged around the question of the realization of surplus value. The same question arose in Germany just before the last war. Rosa Luxemburg's study of accumulation also took the form of a study of realization. These were not "theoretical essays," as only a lamentable ignorance can believe. They were aspects of the class struggle expressing themselves theoretically both within and without the labor movement. The debate, as was historically inevitable, has now gone a stage further. It has moved from Vol. II of *Capital* to Vol. III. This is above all an American question. Stuart Chase, Hansen, all the government economists, all the "experts" who gave evidence before the TNEC,[32] the whole economic basis of the New Deal, all these pose this fundamental question in terms of raising the standard of living of the workers *as a means for the continued development of capitalism.*

The Stalinists have now taken this up and are preparing a highly theoretical assault upon our previous conception of Marx's *Capital. These conceptions represent the instinctive political economy of every labor leader in the country and the belief of great masses of workers.* All the labor leaders are not vulgar fakers. The workers are not fools. The basis of this belief is the obvious power of the American economy. Particularly today it seems to them obvious that by government regulation and raising of wages the American economy can function in a manner satisfactory to everybody; it is merely the wickedness and selfishness of the bad capitalists which prevents this. Yet so limited is our conception of our tasks that except for agitational shouting about the profits of capitalism and the unemployed to come, we leave these ideas to go their own unchecked way. Marx, Engels, Lenin and Trotsky, Rosa Luxemburg and Bukharin carried their opposition to these things to the point of pedantry. They were great activists all. But the classics of Marxism which we read today did a wonderful work in their day, still live and will aways live, because they tackled the false ideas of their time from the root and taught the workers by precept and example to seek bourgeois conceptions out at their source and destroy them.

The method here is important. Lenin never deviated one inch from his stand as a Marxist. He said, "This and this is Marx's view. I now propose to apply it, to Russian capitalism or agriculture or whatever it was." His work on the state was a commentary on what Marx and Engels said about it. He stood before the workers as a Marxist who based whatever he was doing on strict Marxist theory, but Marxist theory applied to Russia. This is the way a Marxist party is built: militantly, arrogantly, Marxist theoreticians, militantly and arrogantly taking it to the workers of the nation.

3. Bolshevism. This can be done in brief. It is the American counterpart of *What Is To Be Done?*

The building of the party is not advanced one inch by repeating that the party must be built. Between 1928 and 1938 we were excessively concerned about the struggles of the Left Opposition and the historical antecedents of our Trotskyite movement. This will always remain of importance to us but we have different aims now. The present writer proposes to organize some of the material in this document for publication in the *New International.* Particularly the section dealing with the international attempts at party building will be amplified. But there are also sources of experiences in American history which concern not scholars but have valuable lessons for the tasks which we are trying to do today, not only for us, but for the American workers. It is here if only in reverse, that they can learn what a genuine Bolshevik Party is. There is a wealth of experience in this country from the early German attempts to introduce Marxism to the U.S., the old Socialist Party, the various attempts at Workers Education, the beginning of the Communist Party here, successes and failures of Marxism in America. A clear sequence can be traced, of infinite value in our education and in the education of our readers.

Here then is also necessary a close study of the conditions in Russia and the methods which the Bosheviks used to build the first and only Bolshevik Party. The material exists in English and for the most part by Lenin, done both at the time and in retrospect. Written for American readers and for American workers it will have not only general educational value but concrete application to the problem of party building in the United States. Once we embrace our readers in this problem we have gone far towards making them Bolshevik in approach, that is to say, concerned about building the revolutionary party. Once we familiarize ourselves with these problems in the journal, then it will become easy for all of us to handle them naturally in *Labor Action* as it was easy in the old days to propagandize and agitate on the Socialist Party in Germany and the crimes of the Stalinist bureaucracy.

4. Dialectical Materialism. Dialectical Materialism is not something to be defended against Hook, Eastman, and Burnham. It is the philosophy and the

theory of knowledge of Marxism. To use a phrase Marx used in his early writings it is the theoretical basis of scientific humanism. Today when all thinkers are groping like drunken men, with all their points of support and reference gone, we have here a weapon whose power and value was never so great as in the prevailing confusion. In one article in particular, "St. Paul, Laski and Stalin,"[33] the present writer has tried to demonstrate how the method can be used in defence of the more general views of life and society that we stand for. But that is merely a beginning. In every field the method of logical development and historical manifestation brings results in clarification and illumination which will be felt in every sphere of our work.

Lenin was always a dialectician but it was only in 1914 that he studied seriously its origin in the Hegelian dialectic. And after that he became one of the strongest advocates of its study in Russia, demanded that extracts from Hegel and interpretations be printed in the theoretical journal. He knew and said that mistakes would be made but added that whoever was afraid of mistakes would not do anything. It cannot be said with sufficient emphasis that "defence" of the dialectic against Hook and Eastman is today the least of our problems. It is not a precious jewel in a box to be defended against them. It is a weapon to be used. In the study and practice of Historical Materialism, Marxian economics, and Bolshevism, it will be a guiding thread making points clear and helping us to make them clear to others. Contradiction, opposites, negation, negation of the negation, quantity into quality, transcendence, condition, possibility, these are not jokes or a kind of intellectual family heirloom that you "defend" fiercely against attack without ever knowing what they mean. Marx, Engels, Lenin, and Trotsky did not concern themselves with nonsense or some outworn intellectual ritual. There is today a great desire among Marxists to know more about this subject and the literature on this subject is growing. We play no part in it at all. Not only is this great interest inevitable and legitimate in general. The age we live in is one which calls for ideas and tests them ruthlessly. Dialectic will make its way with us or without. It would be to our advantage to study what is traditionally ours.

5. "Scholasticism." There is not only a way to do these things. There is a way not to do them. In the last two issues of the *New International* there has been a change in the type of articles. Douglas Ellis has written on Allied imperialism,[34] Emmett has written on "The Great Contradiction," between Vol. I and Vol. III [of *Capital*],[35] and James Barrett a long article dealing with the "Anti-Marxian Offensive."[36] With these may be classed three articles of a series on Burnham by Fahan [Irving Howe].[37] These articles typify the reverse side of what is wrong with the *New International*. An empirical approach

does not necessarily ignore theory. No Marxist admits that he ignores theory. What happens is that theory is given a special status. It becomes something divorced from the practical pursuits. A theoretician becomes a scholar, a "learned" man, and theory becomes the business of a few who have time. In other words, it becomes precisely what Lenin never let it become, a kind of cultural decoration. Articles are written which, if not written, would never be missed or asked for. For example, an article on the Great Contradiction, proving by a long list of quotations that Marx did not contradict himself, serves what purpose? The long articles on the "Anti-Marxist Offensive" dealing with Hook, Schumpeter, and others is full of knowledge and hard work but it is a typically scholastic piece. It characterizes these writers as "unfair," "illogical," subject to "technical compulsives," "falsifying Marx's theory of the state," etc., etc. In the same vein Fahan spends some invaluable twelve pages on Burnham proving that Burnham has refurbished the theory of human nature of sociology, that he has borrowed from Pareto, etc., etc. This type of writing helps nobody except those people who are interested academically in study and professorial discussions. They reek of lectures and classrooms and college journals.

First of all, the ideas of all these bourgeois writers should under no circumstances fill all that space in our journal if treated in that way. Periodically one or two or a bunch of them should be handled, preferably those who are creating an interest in labor circles. When they are dealt with, the main purpose should be twofold: (1) To show exactly what stage of bourgeois thought they repreent and how these ideas are affected by the stage of development of society and particularly of the working class. That they are illogical, traduce Marxism, etc., is nothing new. They always have and they always will. The point is in what way they do it, why, what is the relation of this type of anti-Marxism to previous ones, and what it means to the labor movement today. (2) To seize the opportunity for a positive exposition of some aspect of Marxist thought and show them up positively. Thus the renegades and anti-Marxists of the present day are all rooted in the fact that there is no powerful political labor movement in the United States. This gives their work a special American slant. And there are many similar angles. But the whole treatment should be modelled on Marx's essay on Proudhon, or Engels on Dühring, or Lenin on the Narodnik falsifiers of historical materialism, or Rosa Luxemburg on Bernstein. There is a way of doing these things. Joe Leonard's article on Williams,[38] for example, is with respect to method vastly superior to these professorial discourses.

Not only do they not do what they ought to do. In one respect they do harm for they foster exactly that attitude to theory as something on the shelf, a struggle of books against books, which the great Marxists in their practice and method constantly repudiated. This assortment of pieces will not only not raise the Marxist level of the magazine. It will not only give an illusory idea that "at least we are having some theory." It will attract only the wrong type of student who will see Hook on one side and the *New International* on the other, arguing about the same thing on different sides but in much the same sort of way. Finally, it reinforces the active party member in the sentiment that he would like to study some "theory" but he hasn't the time to spare for it. When Lenin argued on theory no one ever mistook him for a mere debater with his opponent. And both he and Marx in particular could write on the most abstruse subjects and yet make the worker who ventured into its pages feel that this has something of the utmost interest and concern to the working class. This power was not psychological. It sprang from their whole method of analysis. And that is not learned in a day. The task of the *New International* should be to teach these undoubtedly talented comrades and friends to use their talents in the Marxist manner.

Conclusion

At the meeting on the American question which preceded the 1944 convention, I listed three propagandist points as ones on which we should center our attention.

1. The Americanization of Bolshevism
2. The statification of production
3. Internationalism

Points 2 and 3 will have to wait. I have tried to abstract propaganda and agitation and education from work among the masses. But such an abstraction has all the one-sidedness of an abstraction. In actual life the mass work will guide and shape the theoretical approach at every stage. Contact with the proletariat usually results in that. But the theoretical work will guide the mass work also. The orientation outlined here will demand serious attention from all of us precisely because we are cadres for a party. The perpetual refrain of "lack of forces" is no answer. A leading comrade can go to Chicago for 14 days or go on tours lasting weeks to settle some union problem or to make speeches. The party does not collapse in their absence. But we are told that through "lack of forces" no one can find 14 days to write a pamphlet on "What is the Workers Party?" Isn't the argument ridiculous? The pamphlets are not written because the real need for them is not understood. More profoundly we have not got that body of material in the *New International*, in pamphlets and small books, which both in material and manner were such as we had in 1928–1938 and enabled us to write the kind of pamphlets or articles we needed at the drop of a hat.

Let me here conclude with the question of education, propaganda, agitation in its relation to the fundamental question of the building of the party.

The American mass party will not be built by us or by the Cannonites. Groups of Virginia miners, West Coast sailors, Southern sharecroppers, Pittsburgh steel workers, all sorts of "left" formations will coalesce in time and hammer out a unified organization. They will bring their qualities. Our task is to form such a strong nucleus that the coalescence will take place around us, or even that does not take place, our special contribution will be Marxism and the theory and practice of Bolshevism. But to do this we have to gather a nucleus of a few thousands, of whom 75% will be American workers, men and women, instinctively hostile to bourgeois society, who are workers, have been workers, and who have no other prospect in life except to be workers. They and only they can build a mass party. They are the only real mass propagandists and agitators, day after day. They exist in tens of thousands already and capitalism will create more and more thousands for us. But they need to be given, not prospects of a happy life and higher wages, but a method of thought and a conception of social development that makes their own lives and efforts intelligible to them in national and international terms. They need to know that in Marxism and the revolutionary party they have something which, even if far from being completely understood, yet is theirs. Proletarian thought, proletarian method must be for them a challenge to the bourgeoisie at all points, defeating it in theory as the workers will one day defeat it in practice. For them it must be a theory which marks off those who adhere to it from all others, giving them pride and confidence and the consciousness of a great superiority to all, however influential and famous, who do not accept Marxism. That is Bolshevism. That is what Lenin in his day and with his problems from the start strove to create.

It is with such people that we can in time grow rapidly. From now and henceforth there will be increasingly rapid breaks in the national consciousness and in the social development of the working class. This class will increasingly throw off substantial numbers of workers breaking with the traditional and petty-bourgeois ideologies. If within their own environment and of their own proletarian origin, there are trained and conscious Marxists, each of these can form at critical stages the rallying center of dozens and perhaps scores of adherents. The workers in the U.S. have no allegiance to any traditional workers parties as had the workers of Europe. Broadly speaking, the whole field is open, and by laying the necessary foundation with thoroughness and confidence we can legitimately expect the American workers, as they respond to declining capitalism, will find it impossible to pass us by.

IV: Concrete Proposals

Obviously from the whole argument above, *this will be no list of articles or proposals for columns which will solve the difficulties of the party.* I therefore merely indicate the following as immediate concrete steps for the next period in the direction outlined. Here I must revert to what is proper logical order.

The New International

A. Through straight articles or book reviews, we need as preparation for indispensable pamphlets:

1. A series of studies of the American labor movement. AFL and IWW and then AFL and CIO, along the lines dealt with in the section on the *New International* above.
2. The Civil War as the American bourgeois revolution. (Trotsky wanted to write a history of the Civil War.) This is the theoretical basis for the coming social revolution.
3. The American Revolution of 1776. From here flow all the ideology and current social thought of the country: Constitution, Bill of Rights, Founding Fathers. We have to start breaking that up, as Marxists.

From this should come in time two full length panphlets:

1. "The Communist Manifesto" of America, an analysis of American development from 1776 to today.
2. An analysis of the labor movement and its role in American history with special emphasis on the AFL and the CIO.

These should be our permanent standby. They should last forever — at least until socialism, and all our classes should begin with them and immediately after, or side by side, the *Communist Manifesto,* etc. *They must be our stamp, our label.*

B. *The whole theoretical discussion of accumulation, with a practical application to the economics of the government spending must begin. If we do two or three articles in a year, we have done well. But we must begin.*

C. The Socialist Party, the beginning of the Communist Party in this country, the Third Party, studies of these, not academic but in the Leninist manner, for our own education and the education of the workers, must begin to appear in the journal. With articles on Bolshevism and its beginnings, as a historical standard of comparison, we shall begin to create the theoretical premises for an American Bolshevism and in time do our own "What Is To Be Done?"

D. The writings of Marx, Engels, Plekhanov, and the other classics on dialectical materialism must find a place in the journal. Not every month or every three months, but steadily, so that we consciously begin to illuminate our own work with the Marxian scientific method.

We, being what we are, the above divisions are in descending order of importance. American development comes first in time and energy and space. But we have to work systematically at the others too.

Archives

Here we have two things to do:

A. The writings, letters, etc., of Marx, Engels, Lenin, Sorge, Trotsky on America have a value far beyond their scattered character. They must be collected, annotated, and published. *Lenin on Britain* is a famous and very precious volume in Britain. Lenin's two letters to the American workers, for example, should be at once reprinted in the journal.

B. We have to start reprinting and annotating some carefully chosen classics of American revolutionaries. For example, David Walker's *Appeal*, speeches of Wendell Phillips, etc.

The Negro Question

Here, as Marxist interpreters, the field is ours, Negroes and populism, Booker T. Washington, Frederick Douglass, the Garvey movement, whatever serious work we do here will not only educate ourselves but will be gobbled up by the Negro people, masses and intellectuals alike. And progressive white workers.

Party Pamphlets

We need two at once:

1. What is the Workers Party?
2. The Labor Party

They should be serious pamphlets, both cast in a *historical* mold. *Both pamphlets should be carefully coordinated,* so that the reader who reads them both should have a clear but briefly stated idea of the development of the labor movement and of the function of the two parties. Closely linked with this must be the publication of a formal Declaration of Principles and general program. This is a crying necessity.

Labor Action and the Pamphlets

A substantial section of the paper must reflect in popular form the work done on this propagandist effort. Some of the pamphlets or extracts from them must *actually appear week after week in the paper. Articles in the New International can be summarized with suitable extracts.* The party program and explanatory articles *must constantly appear in the paper.* There must be a constant tie-up, literary, *political and promotional between the New International, the solid propagandist pamphlets and the paper.*

Reviews of books should play an important part in the paper. They must not be watered down. Two reviews which have appeared or will appear in the *New International* have every place in the paper, one by Shachtman on Wilkie's *One World* and another on Wechsler's study of John L. Lewis. *Life, Time, The Saturday Evening Post, Colliers, Look,* constantly have articles of the most serious quality by highly qualified writers who do not write down. These are read by millions. A recent article in *Life* on capitalism and the free market is a case in point. These and not articles in the *New York Times* should be the target of systematic, comprehensive and fully Marxist replies by *Labor Action. Life* writes on the free market? Good. We write the Marxist view of the free market. *The Saturday Evening Post* writes about cartels and monopolies? *Next week* we write one or two articles on monopolies and cartels exposing their superficiality and preaching our own view. We say that the classic work on monopolies is Lenin's *Imperialism.* We refer to our book service. We refer to a current article in the *New International.* We denounce cartels, *but* we teach, we explain, we deliberately lift the worker above his daily struggles.

Education

The above document is not a programmatic document. Once the theoretical necessity is grasped, then the organizational arrangements, the courses of study, etc., are, to start with, a matter of collaborative effort. This, however must be said. This document repudiates entirely that conception of education which sends out documents about the speeches of Roosevelt and lists of war profits and war scandals.

Notes

1. The plenum was a meeting of the national committee of the Workers Party.
2. This refers to the Socialist Party of France. Leon Blum was the head of the party and the Prime Minister during the '30s.
3. The POUM was the Partido Obrero de Unificacion Marxista, the Workers Party of Marxist Unification of Spain, a Marxist, anti-Stalinist organizaton.
4. Thomas Dewey was the Republican presidential candidate.
5. C. L. R. James and Ernest R. McKinney (David Coolidge) of the national leadership of the Workers Party, and members of the St. Louis branch of the WP helped organize a strike of sharecroppers and tractor drivers in the cotton fields of southeast Missouri that resulted in significant gains in pay and working conditions.
6. James P. Cannon was the leader of the Socialist Workers Party. Similarly, the members of the Workers Party were often called Shachtmanites.
7. *Plenty for All* by Ernest Lund, New York: Workers Party, undated.
8. *Iskra (Spark)* was founded in 1901 as the organ of the Russian Social Democratic Labor Party and was the paper of the Communist Party of the Soviet Union.
9. Jack London (1876–1916) was a popular novelist whose most famous novel was *The Call of the Wild*. He was an avowed socialist who also wrote political novels and essays.
10. Upton Sinclair (1878–1968) was a socialist who wrote novels, plays, and essays. His novel, *The Jungle*, exposed the meat packing industry in Chicago. In the 1930s he ran for governor of California.
11. The SAP, the Socialistische Arbeiter Partei (Socialist Workers Party) was formed in October 1931 by a left grouping led by nine Reichstag members expelled from the SPD (Socialistische Partei Deutschland) in September. It was a left party which Trotsky criticized as centrist.
12. After the rise to power of Hitler with no significant resistance by the Communist Party, Trotsky drew the conclusion that the Comintern could no longer be reformed. He therefore proposed that the French Trotskyist organization enter the French Socialist Party to try to win over the more radical elements, especially the youth, in order to amass sufficient resources to emerge as an independent revolutionary force. This policy was then followed in the United States by entry into the Socialist Party.
13. The POI was the Parti Ouvrier Internationaliste (Bolshevik-Leninists) which published a paper called *La Lutte Ouvriere*.
14. James Burnham, a member of the philosophy department at New York University, was part of the leadership of the Workers Party who left soon after the dispute over the nature of the Soviet Union and developed his own theory of the "managerial society" in the United States.
15. The idea of "socialism in one country" was a major aspect of the dispute between Trotsky and Stalin. Stalin had abandoned the idea of the necessity of revolutions in other countries to support and sustain the Soviet Union while Trotsky insisted on the international character of proletarian revolution and the impossibility of creating an isolated socialist society.
16. Alexander Ivanovich Herzen (1812–1870), Vissarion Grigoryevich Belinsky (1811–1848), and Nikolai Gavrilovich Chernyshevsky (1828–1889) were Russian revolutionary democrats. Chernyshevsky was referred to by Marx in the Afterword to the

second German edition of *Capital*, although in the English edition his name was also spelled Tchernyschewsky.

17. Narodnik was a name for non-Marxists who aimed at the regeneration of Russia by "going to the people (narod)" meaning the peasantry, rather than the proletariat. The Social Revolutionary Party derived from this tendency.

18. James depended heavily on the 12 volume *Selected Works* of Lenin, long out of print. The work referred to, "What the 'Friends of the People' Are and How They Fight the Social-Democrats," can be found in Lenin, *Collected Works*, vol. 1, pp. 129–507, Moscow: Foreign Languages Publishing House, 1963.

19. Lenin, *Collected Works*, vol. 3, Moscow: Foreign Languages Publishing House, 1960.

20. Ibid., vol. 5, pp. 347–529, Moscow: Foreign Languages Publishing House, 1961.

21. See, e.g., "Capitalism in Agriculture," ibid., vol. 4, pp. 105–59. Moscow, 1960; and "The Agrarian Question and the 'Critics of Marx,'" ibid., vol. 5, pp. 103–222.

22. "New Data on the Laws Governing the Development of Capitalism in Agriculture. Part One. Capitalism and Agriculture in the United States of America," ibid., vol. 22, pp. 13–102. Moscow: Progress Publishers, 1964.

23. Marx-Engels, *Collected Works*, New York: International Publishers, 1979, vol. 10, pp. 45–145.

24. Ibid., vol. 11, pp. 99–197.

25. Ibid., vol. 22, pp. 307–55.

26. Ibid., 1979, vol. 11, pp. 3–96.

27. Ibid., 1978, vol. 10, pp. 397–482.

28. See note 5 above.

29. Dwight Macdonald (1906–1982) was a radical journalist who founded and published the magazine *Politics* from 1944 to 1949.

30. George Novack (1905–1992) was a leader of the Trotskyist movement who wrote frequently on philosophical and historical subjects.

31. Louis Hacker, Abram Harris, and the Beards were noted left-liberal authors of the period. Among their works were Hacker's *The Triumph of American Capitalism* (1940) and *The Shaping of the American Tradition*, 2 vols. (1947); Abram Harris's *The Black Worker* (with Sterling D. Spero) (1968) and *The Negro as Capitalist* (1936); Charles A. Beard wrote many works in history and political science, some with his wife, Mary R. Beard. Besides the popular, low-priced *A Basic History of the United States* (1944) there were *The Rise of American Civilization* (1933), *An Economic Interpretation of the Constitution of the United States* (1935), *Economic Origins of Jeffersonian Democracy* (1915), and critiques of the New Deal and America's entry into World War II such as *The Future Comes: A Study of the New Deal* (1933) and *President Roosevelt and the Coming of the War* (1941).

32. TNEC was the Temporary National Economic Committee formed by Congress in 1938 in order to press the New Deal's response to the counter-attacks of big business. It published a significant number of useful papers documenting the concentration of American capital and other economic problems.

33. *New International*, vol. x, no. 6, June 1944. Reprinted in C. L. R. James, *The Future in the Present*, Westport, CT: Lawrence Hill and Company, 1979, pp. 95–105.

34. Douglas Ellis, "'Peace Plans' and Historical Realities," *New International,* vol. x, no. 8, Aug. 1944.

35. W. H. Emmett, "Marx's Alleged Self-Contradiction," *New International,* vol. x, no. 9, Sept. 1944.

36. James Barrett, "The Anti-Marxian Offensive," *New International,* vol. x, no. 9, Sept. 1944.

37. A review of James Burnham, *The Machiavellians,* in *New International,* vol. ix, no. 12, Jan. 1943, vol. x, nos. 1 and 2, Jan. and Feb. 1944.

38. Joseph Leonard, "Maurice Williams and Marxism," *New International,* vol. x, no. 5, May 1944.

Marxism for Our Times

I speak as a close sympathiser of a Marxist organization whose headquarters are in the United States, and what I shall say this afternoon will try to explain an experience of it, where it is, how it has arrived there, and most essential thing, the relation of Marxism not only to politics but the way of life and thought of those who profess to live by its doctrines. I hope not only to say these things in general but what I am saying will (even if not immediately) be seen in time to be an exposition of the method and results of the doctrines of Marxism.

It will not be difficult. I don't propose to come here and put forward difficult problems before you. You are not a class; I am not a professor. But there is no doubt that a good deal of what I am saying you will find awkward, because it is so different from what, I believe, unless Britain has changed vitally from what I knew it to be last night, you are accustomed to hear — very different from what I was accustomed to learn for many years, to learn and to teach. Nevertheless we have to make the attempt. So that you will be under no misunderstanding or have no doubt or suspense, I will tell you exactly what I am going to do.

First, I shall pay great attention to the significance of Marx himself and the relation of Marx's work to the present day and the days ahead. I shall then move on to an analysis of Lenin's work and his relation to the situation in which we are. Then I propose to spend some time on an event whose positive and negative results upon Western civilization still continue to do what it has been doing since it has begun: I want to speak about the Russian Revolution, about a Marxist conception of it. After that I propose to say, not what you ought to do. I wouldn't be so rude, but what some Marxists I know have been doing and what I believe they propose to do in their perspective for the future.

[This essay is based on an address entitled "Marxism 1963" delivered in November 1963 to the Solidarity Group in London, England. It was published in the May 1965 issue of *Speak Out.* —*editor's note.*]

Unfortunately I have to begin with some few words about dialectical materialism. That is very difficult in general, yet what I shall say I hope will be very simple and obvious. But it is impossible to deal with Marxism unless upon that basis. I shall try to make it as simple as possible.

The key phrase in dialectical materialism for a Marxist is the inevitability of socialism. Now contrary to what a lot of people believe, and this they attack with great vivacity, Marx never believed in the inevitability of socialism. Neither did Lenin. Never at any time would they, as philosophers, put forward that socialism was inevitable. What Marx was very clear about, and Lenin followed him, was quite precise: Socialism *or* Barbarism. He couldn't say, it was impossible for those materialists to say, it is *bound* to be this or it is *bound* to go that way. Not at all. They said, either it goes this way or society will descend into barbarism.

Nevertheless the inevitability of socialism remains an imperative necessity for Marxists as a conception. The reason is this: we have a lot of objective facts before us, historical events, an immense variety of happenings. When you observe them you have to decide which you support, which will advance the perspectives that you have, and which are acting against these perspectives. Which, in other words, as far as you are concerned, are leading in the advance toward a socialist society and which are not, which are leading, within the basic Marxist conception, to barbarism. Therefore the inevitability of socialism becomes with a Marxist a necessity of thought, because without it he cannot think. What is happening? What do you support? What do you oppose? Literary criticism of late has made the distinction very clear. There is naturalism which describes what is taking place, and there is realism which brings to the description of what is taking place a certain critical view of what it supports and what it does not support. That is in a subject as remote as imaginative literature. In politics it is absolutely imperative. The bourgeois does not need that. He has a conception of society, the inevitability of bourgeois society. He hasn't to observe in philosphical terms. He just goes along his way. But it is necessary for a Marxist to have some criterion of judgment, and that criterion is the inevitability of socialism. This is the result of the Marxist application of the Hegelian dialectic.

I would like to spend a few more minutes on it but I shall not. I would only refer you to the introduction to the Larger Logic, where Hegel says that the positive in the negative, the unity of opposites, is the fundamental necessity for the understanding of dialectics.[1] The unity of opposites, the positive in the negative. The positive in the negative is what is in the society and is moving towards a positive resolution of its troubles and difficulties. And the negative is what is there but is constantly being negated. So that the unity of opposites is the unity of what we may call the inevitability of socialism and what stands in its way, but in reality is preparing the movement to the socialist society and the emergence of it. Marx learned that from Hegel, from the Hegelian logic. And why I emphasize that and bring that into a talk of this kind is because Marxism, the philosophy of Marxism, the method that we use, is in effect the climax of centuries of European study and of European philosophy. Marx considered himself, and we shall see the importance of that when I come to the development of the Russian Revolution, Marx considered himself the inheritor of the most important traditions of European thought and action. And dialectical materialism comes directly from Kant, and Kant you know came from Hume, at least in opposition to Hume, and all this can be related fundamentally to the *Critique of Pure Reason.* I'm not going to do that now. But I want to make it clear. Dialectical materialism is not an accident, it is not something that Marx invented. It is the result of the climax and development of the history of European philosophy, and that is the spirit in which we use it.

Now with that, I hope, clear if not accepted, I want to go on to speak of Marx and particulary the things in Marx which relate to us today. In the *Communist Manifesto,* and he quoted it in *Capital,* Marx uses a certain passage. (If I make now and then some polemical remarks you will forgive me. I confess a certain polemic feeling comes to me when I meet certain things like this, for instance: I have to deal for years with people who tell me — Marx did not foresee. I have to tell them that whatever Marx did not foresee, you do not see. You do not see what he wrote.) The key passage which he quoted from the *Communist Manifesto* in *Capital* goes like this:

> The bourgeoisie cannot exist without continually revolutionizing the instruments of production, and thereby the relations of production and all the social relations. Conservation, in an unaltered form, of the old modes of production was on the contrary the first condition of existence for all earlier industrial classes. Constant revolutions in production, uninterrupted disturbance of all social conditions, everlasting uncertainty and agitation distinguish the bourgeois epoch from all earlier ones. All fixed, fast-frozen relations, with their train of ancient and venerable prejudices and opinions, are swept away, all new formed ones become antiquated before they can ossify. All that is solid melts into air, all that is holy is profaned, and man is at last compelled to face with sober senses his real conditions of life, and his relations with his kind.[2]

In other words, that is where the process is moving, the process of human relations. Marxism is *not* fundamentally a process of what is happening to the economy, and how much production you have and how much accumulation, etc. That is not what Marx is mainly concerned with at all. For Marx economic relations are relations between people. The relations between people and things, means of accumulation, are property relations. Marxism, especially at this advanced stage, is concerned with human relations. Over and over again we will see it. I have to refer to only a few. "Man is at last compelled to face with sober senses his real conditions of life, and his relations with his kind."[3] I want to state, and we shall come to that a little later, I believe mankind is very near to that realization. Very near to an understanding of the relations, of the conditions in which we live and our relations with other people. And not only we, this is not a question of the advanced countries; all over the world, the great masses of the people are extremely near to this understanding, and that is what Marx said would be the result of the constant disorders and changes in capitalist production. So somebody turns up parading automation and tells me: Marx didn't foresee. I confess to a certain impatience. A man who speaks about constant changes in relations of production, constant disorders, everything being changed, that is the bourgeois nature of production, that is what it will do, to tell him he didn't foresee is enough to get him very angry. They used to ask him: but what must the workers do to make the socialist society? The question was and is absurd. How could he say what the workers will do when he spoke about constant disorders, constant changes in relations of production and so forth? He used to reply: the workers will do what it is necessary to do, and he used the phrase which I use very often, which I love very much. He said, "I am not going to write any recipes for the cook shops of the future."

So that is the basic position which we have to remember today. Automation should not put us in any dither. I'm going to talk about it in a few minutes but it shouldn't put us out. It is one of the constant revolutions in production and the haphazard destruction of previous modes of production, etc. Marx says not the socialist society but capitalist relations have to work in that way. And then, within a page or two of that passage, he makes a fundamental statement as to the nature of capitalist society. There he slips for a moment, I'm not going to go into that, into some rather strained writing. He always was in great command of himself but here you could see control had escaped him, what he was trying to say had got out of discipline. Within about six or seven lines he says twice, capitalist society will perish, it will not continue to exist, unless it solves (not the realization of profit and the limitations of the market, that is not what he is saying at all), he says society will perish unless it solves the condition of the worker in relation to the process of production. I find few Marxist writers have understood that. There was one who understood it from the start, till the day he died, and that was Lenin. Marx says, what is necessary is that the working class, the working man, now reduced to a mere fragment of a man, has got to be made into a fully developed individual, fit for any variety of labors, ready to face any change in production and a man for whom all the social functions (I wish you would take note of that — it is not only the work that he does in the factory), *all the social functions* he performs are to be expressions of his natural and his acquired characteristics.

> But if, on the one hand, variation of work at present imposes itself after the manner of an overpowering natural law, and with the blindly destructive action of a natural law that meets with resistance, at all points, Modern Industry, on the other hand, through its catastrophes imposes the necessity of recognizing, as a fundamental law of production, variation of work, consequently fitness of the laborer for varied work, consequently the greatest possible development of his varied aptitudes. It becomes a question of life and death for society to adapt the mode of production to the normal functioning of this law. Modern Industry, indeed, compels society, under penalty of death, to replace the detail-worker of today, crippled by life-long repetition of one and the same trivial operation, and thus reduced to the mere fragment of a man, by the fully developed individual, fit for a variety of labors, ready to face any change of production, and to whom the different social functions he performs, are but so many modes of giving free scope to his own natural and acquired powers.[4]

That is the socialist society. It has nothing to do with any plan; the plan is totally subordinate. We are all bewildered by the Russian Revolution and its plan and its statistics and the transformation of the peasantry (into what? God knows. The Russians themselves don't know), but all this drowns out mankind as the primary concern. That is the socialist society. The transformation of the worker into the main object and concern of production and society. Everything else flows from that. And then Marx goes on to speak about education; what is a socialist education going to be? He says the man, his wife, and the children will probably be educated in one and the same process, all built around the factory, which means that the factory will be a very different thing from what it is today. Then he says, upon that basis you will have a new conception of the family, and he gives a historical view of the family. All this business of not only vanguard party, but of planning, and the raising of the statistics of the economy is utterly foreign to Marxism as I understand it. And also to Lenin. That has grown up with Trotsky and Stalin, both of them arguing about it.

Now Marx was a dialectician and when we look at his method we have to understand his use of the dialectic. In the Introduction to Vol. III of *Capital,* Engels says that his method was to analyze very closely and to leave the last chapter of whatever he was doing for an analysis of things as he saw them *and the perspectives which he saw flowing from that.* That is the structure of

Vol. I, that is the structure of Vol. III. That was the basis that Lenin worked on and that is the basis that we have to work on. That also will need some very careful explanation.

Marx, at the end of *Capital,* Vol. I, had already written, so we are told in the Introduction to Vol. III, had already written what we know now today as Vols. II and III or most of it. But at the end of Vol. I he wrote one of the most remarkable pieces of writing in the whole of human history, The Historical Tendency of Capitalist Accumulation. I am going to refer to that when I speak, as I do at the end, of the effect of the death of Mr. Kennedy in the modern world. We will begin to understand the effect this has had by basing ourselves on the Historical Tendency of Capitalist Accumulation: let that wait until we come to it.

When Marx wrote that chapter in 1867 nobody believed that what he described was going to take place, except the Marxists. The whole world to a large degree was non-capitalist. And even in the advanced countries, the kind of society Marx describes, far less the kind of forecast that Marx made in 1867 in that chapter, did not exist in the large majority of countries. But that is the kind of thing that the Marxist does. The Historical Tendency of Capitalist Accumulation in 1867 said what was going to take place in capitalist society with the utmost confidence and boldness and in a language that remains today one of the miracles of human achievement.

Now I have to go on to Vol. III which Marx did not live to finish. In the last chapter of Vol. III, the last section, Part 7, "The Revenue and Their Sources," he was preparing obviously to do for the whole of capital and for capitalist society as a whole something along the lines that he had done in The Historical Tendency of Capitalist Accumulation in Vol. I. I have to refer to three points that he makes.

Point number one: Marx says he is concerned only with the ideal average of what takes place in capitalist production. He says in a particular country the working class and its wages, which are the basis of the whole structure, are the result of climatic conditions, of historical conditions which may have assumed the character of second nature to the particular people. He says he is not going into those in any particular country or in general. He says, I'm not interested in that. All these variations are historical matters but in general what I'm doing here is not that, I am concerned with the ideal average. That's all. At the end of some 3000 pages he deals with what is before him but he constantly moves from that into a general analysis of what has happened, what is happening, and what he sees for the future. And after this warning that you do not mistake what he is trying to do, so that you can't accuse him of not foreseeing, he says, foresee? I've not been trying to foresee;

that does not interest me; I am dealing with fundamental processes, the ideal average.

He then proceeds to write one of the most neglected passages in Marxism. Marx in these last chapters, in particular in a chapter called "The Analysis of Distribution," says that capitalist production is distinguished by two dominant features. Two. Number one is that the production of commodities is the predominant feature of the capitalist mode of production. And then he goes on to say that primary to that is the fact that in the capitalist process of production labor power is a commodity. I am sure you have heard that many times. You know it by heart. I doubt if you have heard many times the conclusions that Marx draws and which in reality he has been drawing all through. He says that the moment you have labor power as a commodity in the process of production there follows automatically the process of circulation, the gaining of what is called profit, the transference of profit into means of power of the ruling class and the transference of that profit into further means of production, etc., etc. He says the whole process flows from the fact that the workers' labor power is a commodity.

Now I would like to hear your response to that when the time comes. It took me years to understand the first passage I quoted to you and other passages in which he talks about the kind of worker that is needed in a socialist society and the only way in which capitalist society can be prevented from falling to pieces. This fact, *the* fact that matters, is the workers' labor power being treated as a commodity. That has to be destroyed or basically altered. *You have to think it out.* That is the issue. Because as long as it continues you can plan, you can appoint as many new ministers as Mr. Wilson[5] will appoint, you can do whatever you like. Labor power as a commodity results in an ideal average, an essential movement of capitalist production as Marx described it.

And what is the second feature, distinguishing feature, of capitalist production? I don't as a rule believe in miracles but I believe in dialectical miracles. I don't know what was in Marx's head. The last chapter of Vol. III consists of a page and a half in which he said he would take up the classes.[6] He never reached it. But this second feature of capitalist production is something that in 1963 is very strange to read. He says, unlike production with slaves, serfs, etc., the essential feature of capitalist production is that it creates a hierarchy of managers and officials who are placed in opposition to the workers in the process of production itself. In other words, he has stripped away the question of property, he has stripped away the question of ownership, he has stripped away all regional and what might seem fundamental relations, and he pointed his finger to the essential nature of the capitalist society. It needs a number of officials, a hierarchy of managers, whose function is placed in direct opposition to the masses of the workers in the process of production.

I don't know what you think about that. I find it very strange in view of what has happened in the Communist states and what is happening in the underdeveloped countries.

So those are the two. Labor power as a commodity from which the whole thing flows and then, inevitably, as a result of that, a hierarchy of managers in the process of production who are placed in a position compelling them to act in opposition to the great masses of the workers. (May I here add that in these countries, the more economically advanced the capitalist development, the more the hierarchy of managers and the greater the opposition.) And Marx's conception of socialism was that the main concern and concentration of production, of society, had to be the creation from the working class, of a certain type of person taking a certain role in production which was absolutely opposed to his labor power being treated as a commodity. This is the significance of the phrase, be his payment high or low. I assure you that you do not know what that means.

Now with that clear (or unclear), I can move on. You see, of course, the relation of those apparently abstract conceptions to what is taking place today. Of every one-hundred socialists you will find ninety-nine of them think in terms of the plan and of raising of the salary of the worker and of giving him some more fringe benefits; instead of three weeks vacation, well, socialism will give him four, and so on. But the breakup of the old system concentrating the complete attention of the society to make it understand that the first thing to do is to make the development of that worker, his material and spiritual development, the first condition of progress, otherwise society is going to fall apart, as it is falling apart; *that* the average socialist does not know, does not accept, as the basis of the Marxist position.

I have now to move to Lenin.

In 1917, about February of 1917, Lenin gave a lecture to the Swiss workers which I hope a lot of you know, in Lucerne or Geneva or some such place in Switzerland, and he said: we who are now living may not be living to see the world revolution.[7]

Let me warn you, my friends. The spirit, the attitude, that is pervasive, particularly among revolutionaries who live with it every day: the revolution does not happen or is defeated, and finally they begin to look upon the revolution as a necessity but somewhat abstract. They either commit the folly of preaching to workers that they *ought* to make a revolution, the quicker the better; or they convince themselves that the idea of revolution is utopian. Watch Lenin's conception of his work. In February 1917 he said: we who are members of the Marxist movement may not live to see the world revolution. That was a month or six weeks, I believe, before the Russian Revolution; we who are Marxists and revolutionaries may not live to see the world revolution. Despite this grim realism Lenin was of course actively organizing his party. *But at the same time he was preparing one of the greatest revolutionary documents* since *Capital* or the *Communist Manifesto.* This was *State and Revolution,* and *State and Revolution* corresponds to The Historical Tendency of Capitalist Accumulation, which Marx wrote in 1867 and which nobody at the time could see was anywhere in sight. *State and Revolution* is a revolutionary document. It is a revolutionary document for the twentieth century based on the possibilities and premises of a socialist society. Lenin actually wrote it in about July because the Russian Revolution broke out. He had long prepared the documents and when he had to fly [into temporary exile] from Petrograd he put the documents together and wrote the book.

But the combination to me is very striking, the combination of his personal uncertainty as to when the revolution would take place and the work that he pertinaceously did. This is how we as Marxists must think. He was concerned with the objective circumstances of bourgeois society at that stage, and he drew as bold and as complete and precise as possible rejection of bourgeois society and an outline of the state in a period of socialist revolution. Some of you may note today, may have already arrived at or have found statements which go further than *State and Revolution.* Apart from Lenin himself, I don't know any, except those that come from Hungarian workers in the Hungarian Revolution. About economy and the functioning of the economy and the functioning of the workers in the economy, and the development of society and what kind of society it was likely to be, Lenin was as bold and as confident as Marx was bold in his chapter on the Historical Tendency of Capitalist Accumulation, although he didn't know when the revolution would take place. That is the work a Marxist does. That is the function which Marxists have to carry out.

Now all through the Russian Revolution, 1917–1923, Lenin, while keeping his eye on the reality, never failed to indicate how socialists should think. That duality of Lenin from 1917 to 1923 is in my experience the greatest triumph of the human mind. (Students at universities study Aristotle and Wittgenstein.) I want to spend five minutes on the last articles Lenin wrote. He was on his deathbed; I believe he had already lost his power of speech. You will find them in the *Selected Works,* vol. 9.[8] The important one, or the decisive one, is an article "On Cooperation." It is about nine pages long, you may have read it before. I read it for more than nine years before I began to understand it, i.e., accept it. (All writers on Lenin—I know them well, I have myself written on the subject and I have had to pay attention to it — E. H. Carr, Souvarine whose book I translated, Isaac Deutscher, Trotsky himself, the whole lot of them, you will read their books on Leninism and its development right through from the beginning to the end — they have nothing to say of *any* value about the two things I'm going to mention now — Lenin's last articles in which, after years of illnesses, he summed up the Russian Revolution.)

He stated that there are two things we need. He says, number one is the education of the peasantry to take a proper function in cooperative movements, and then, as was his habit, he added, for the economic development of Russia we have to educate the peasantry, he put that in again. And the second thing, he said, is that this government we have, it is no good at all. The apparatus of government has to be improved. And he wrote another article in which he said: we have thirteen departments of government; one of them, the Department of Foreign Affairs, is reasonably good. All the others are no good whatever. *Absolutely no good.* He said, we talk of soviets and socialism. He said, we would be fortunate if we had arrived at the stage of bourgeois culture. These systems of government we have here, these organizations of government, are absolutely hopeless. Then he did something he very rarely did. He said, if we are not going to settle down to tackle them seriously, we'd better leave them as they are. Like Abraham Lincoln on Emancipation, he knew the immensity of the problem. And to this day you can confound most of the learned students of Leninism and of the Russian Revolution with this: what exactly did he propose as the way the revolutionaries should work? Those are the two things he said: to educate the peasants to take part in cooperative societies, and, secondly, to improve, fundamentally change, the apparatus of government. Collectivization? Mechanization? Improvement of this or that? Lenin naturally wrote often about these things but they were not his main concern.

These two points were his last will and testament to the party and that was, I am sure, because he understood that it was the conception of social relations, the institutions and the functioning of people in them that determined the condition and the movement of society. And that great student of Marxism and anti-capitalist was never going to write that it was the question of the proper use of the plan or the mechanical development of the productive labor in Russia that was decisive. He could not write that; he could not write it. He would write about economic development and that one and the other, say this is what we have to do, etc., etc. But in any total view of what was to happen, his social perspectives, it was absolutely clear to him, a Marxist to the last degree, it was the condition of the mass of the population in society that decided whether it was a socialist society or a society approaching socialism, or not. One of his phrases which he repeated in essence about fifty times: God grant that our children or our children's children in Russia will see socialism. He knew what was going on. He knew the limitations. So in those last three articles he went on to say that these two things are needed.

What was his perspective then? In a famous article, "Better Less, But Better,"[9] he says plainly what his perspective is. He says, *we have to hold on until the world revolution.* In so many words. He was a plain speaker. He was not like Trotsky, brilliant in exposition, marvelous in ideas, and so forth. He was, on the contrary, very simple. Nobody's language was so closely related to the facts he was dealing with. In bourgeois society Abraham Lincoln reached that stage. And in the revolutionary movement, Lenin alone. He says, what we have to do is to hold on, and he continues: India, China, Russia, the majority of working people are being swept into the revolutionary movement. That is our salvation. Now he might have been right or he may have been wrong; he might have been this or he might have been that. But that is what he thought. And there is not Marxism today unless it is very clear that we continue that tradition and not what has grown up instead, as the Marxist tradition, a lot of wearisome scholasticism about the plan and socialism in a single country. That is the view we have of Lenin and that is the way in which his work has guided us.

Now we have reached a good way. I want now to take up as an exposition of Marxism, as the method of Marxism, and also as an analysis of a fundamental feature of the world in which we live with both positive and negative features, I want to take up the Russian Revolution.

Some of you may have studied the history of Russia. In any case what I say here may appear strange, but it will not in any way to the ordinary educated person be something difficult to grasp. You can grasp and reject; you can grasp and keep. What I'm saying is a little unusual, but it is easy enough to follow.

It begins with Pushkin in 1800. Pushkin was born, I think, in 1801. After the French Revolution Europe made some tremendous advances, intellectually in philosophy. And I hope I have made it clear, though brief, and I want to make it clear again, that Marxism was the result of the work done by Hegel, Fichte, and Schelling after the French Revolutiion, in which they took the great traditions of European philosophy a great distance further. But the country which led Europe in every section of intellectual and creative effort, middle class and proletarian, the country which went to the head of European civilization and remained there, was Czarist Russia followed by the first years of the Russian Revolution. I want to give you some names. I can't prove it but I want you to understand it. After the French Revolution, and the bourgeoisie began to take power in other places, in the particular country which was the most backward country in Europe but which had this advantage, that the intellectual element among the bourgeoise and the left wing of the aristocracy were excluded from government by the Czarist autocracy and the church and the military, and therefore were compelled to exercise powers that they would normally have exercised in government, the law, etc., in Western civilization; they exercised them in the creative achievements of the intellect. Pushkin. There is nothing like him in Western literature. Except perhaps Goethe, but Pushkin is a more modern man. After Pushkin, Gogol, Dostoevsky, Tolstoy, Turgenev. What is there in Western literature to touch them?

The greatest master of the short story for the last one hundred fifty years is not a Frenchman, de Maupassant, it is Chekhov. And then you come to drama. Who in Western Europe from 1800 to 1963 writes anything as Chekhov wrote, made such discoveries? And it was not only literature as such. Chekhov found that great master of stage presentation, Stanislavsky, and the two of them worked together. Western Europe has nothing to show like that. In the thirteenth edition of the Encyclopedia Brittanica you will read an essay on stage production by Stanislavsky. (I hope they have kept it in in the new edition.) I know of no finer piece of writing or any exposition of any doctrine anywhere. That was the level of the Russian intellectuals. In music it is the same. I don't know any European country who could compare for variety and power to the Romantic musicians, Tchaikowsky, the really native Moussorgsky, and finally, he had to run away from there, but he came from there, Stravinsky.

In ballet it is the same. The foremost names in the history of ballet from the nineteenth century to the present day is, what? You know them, I'm sure: Diaghilev and Fokine. They came from Russia. Some of them had to come to Western Europe in order to develop themselves.

Even in painting (in really modern painting, I don't know what is happening — I read that Kandinsky, one of the originators of modern painting, came from Russia.) This business can be continued indefinitely. Marx himself paid tribute to the greatest political and creative writer of the nineteenth century. I hope you know his name: Tchernychewsky.[10] Marx used such terms about him. *Capital* was understood, I believe, it was translated in Russia before it was done in any other European country. And [a writer in a St. Peterburg paper] made an analysis of the dialectic and Marxism which Marx quoted, and he said: This is what the fellow says I'm saying. I couldn't say it better myself. You'll find it in the introduction to *Capital*.[11]

Belinsky originated modern literary criticism, after the great Romantics gave it a social basis.

In other words, they were ahead in every department, these Russian intellectuals, and I attribute it — the fact itself cannot be challenged — I attribute it to the situation in which they were. That we can argue about. But the fact is, in every respect they were and they remain first in Europe to this present day — at least in comparison to bourgeois society. Since 1924 Stalin managed to ruin it, nevertheless that is what happened.

Now the peculiar thing is this, that the Russian proletariat and the Russian party achieved the same distinction in the development of Europe that the intellectuals achieved. These intellectuals did what they did because they were able to incorporate the discoveries of Western Europe and apply them to a particular situation in which they were compelled to be revolutionary, or, generally speaking, opposed to the existing regime. The same thing happened to the proletariat. What happened to the Russian proletariat is this: In addition to an extremely backward environment, Western capital exported capital to Russia, and it was accepted by Russian capitalists. In the same way that Western intellectual creativeness exported its discoveries to and was taken over by the Russian intellectuals, the Russian capitalists took over Western capital. So that about 1890 there began to develop on the backwardness of Russia (with very little commodity production, vast numbers of peasants, not even a high standard of manufacture, but still elementary handicraft production), there was placed upon this backwardness, large-scale, modern factory production of the most advanced kind.

And that is where Lenin and the Bolshevik Party came from.

Lenin was born in 1870. This kind of factory production in Russia began to make itself felt in about 1890. He was then twenty years old. And Lenin and the Bolsheviks grew side by side with the development of this capitalism and the Russian proletariat it created. He wrote the first book, *The Development of Capitalism in Russia*,[12] in about 1898, in which he has the figures for modern, large-scale factory production, about 820 thousand people, that was all, in a population of 100 million people. Lenin's mental conceptions and his view of the party and his view of the proletariat and his understanding of Marxism grew side by side with the growth of the Russian proletariat from 1870 to 1917, and it was the product of this special development. In other words, it was a part of the same type of special development as that which created the Russian intellectuals. In the tremendous activities and energies which they were displaying, in trying to find out what was the road for Russia, the way in which they showed such brilliance in every direction, Lenin was one of them. God had not made a wonderful man, or he was not *merely* a man of great ability; he found this section of Russian society, this modern factory production, and while everybody did this and that, sought here and there, he fastened on to this section and held on to it from start to finish. That was the origin of the Vanguard Party. It was not a theory. It was not merely the result of police persecution and Czarist brutality. Lenin hoped that in time to come he would be in opposition in the Russian parliament which they hoped to create, as in Britain and in Germany, the Labor Party was in opposition — that was all he was thinking of — that is what he thought at the time. But in all the conflicts he kep his eye always fastened on this section of the Russian proletariat which became the most advanced section of the Russian proletariat which became the most advanced section of the European proletariat.

At first Lenin himself didn't understand them very well. He began somewhere in 1899 very bitter and angry against the people who opposed him. He said, the proletariat has to be instructed by the intellectuals.[13] He was quite wrong and he knew it. A little later he said so and wrote an article on Tchernichevsky about 1909 which is one long apology for saying what he had said; but he was dealing with a proletariat that was born yesterday, that had no traditions whatever.

As the Russian proletariat developed, Lenin developed the Bolshevik Party. It was a specific organization which was the result of that specific section of the Russian proletariat as a part of Russian history. It has no significance or validity elsewhere. It was as much Russian as Tolstoy's non-resistance, or the Slavophils, or Dostoevsky. That is what the Russian Revolution was. That is what the Russian Vanguard Party was. And the Russian proletariat led Lenin, Lenin did not lead that section of the Russian proletariat, that is a gross mistake. Trotsky is chiefly responsible for this transformation of history. Because in 1905, December 1905, this section of Russian society created the general strike. Nobody had done that before. Rosa Luxemburg was very clear on that. They made the general strike. And then later on when the revolutionary movement developed, they did more than that. They rejected parliamentary democracy altogether and they created the Soviets. Lenin had nothing to do with that. It is in relation to that proletariat which is to be seen in relation to the whole of Russian development in relation to Europe, that the Vanguard Party emerged.

And Lenin knew that very well. He knew what the party was. His great emphasis was not fighting against other parties who were interfering and who would mislead the proletariat. But unfortunately when the revolution began in Western Europe, there was the Second International with a party. And the Bolsheviks formed an International in opposition to the Second. They had to. But before he died, in 1924, after he had been ill for some months, Lenin came into the Fourth Congress of the Communist International and he told them: "Look, these resolutions, I wrote some of them myself, and they are pretty good, they are quite correct, but I don't think you all understand them. They are too Russian. Take them away for one year and study them. And then come back and then we will be able to see what we shall be able to do."[14] And I can trace right through his clear conception that this thing which had developed in Russia was specific to Russia and had to be seen outside of Russia with extreme care and caution, and by 1922 he was saying, well, I don't think it will work out there.

Now that is one section of the Russian Revolution which has poisoned all political relations because the masses of the people don't read Lenin, and they say, well, there was a great revolution and the Bolshevik Party led it, so they saw revolution in terms of the party. And their party has achieved nothing. Now this is very serious. In not one place has it led any successful revolution, at any time, anywhere. All it has to its credit is a record of continuous failure. Now that is a problem we have to deal with. Why? The reason is because the original Vanguard Party was the result of a specific situation in Russia, as specific as that which produced Dostoevsky, Tolstoy, the Slavophils, Belinsky; and the Russian proletariat which made the Vanguard Party was a specific creation of Russia, and when transferred to Western Europe the Vanguard Party hasn't done very well — to put it mildly.

Now that is one side of it. The other side is what has happened to the revolutionary movement under the guidance of Trotsky. That has been nothing else but an absoute disaster. I am not speaking about Healy.[15] Healy doesn't interest me; I don't care whether he has five thousand or ten thousand people; that means, or will mean, nothing at all. I am speaking about the influence which Trotsky has exercised and still exercises on the corruption of Marxism and the corruption of the things that Lenin brought into the movement in continuation of Marx.

I am going to present two quotations this evening. One at the end from Lenin and one from Trotsky. The first one is from the chapter on the art of insurrection in Trotsky's *History of the Russian Revolution.* This is the greatest history of an event that I know. I personally prefer to read Michelet's *History of the French Revolution*; but that is purely personal. This book is more advanced and understands a great deal more than Michelet understood, although Michelet understands much more than Trotsky in certain respects not unrelated to what we are examining. But I want to refer you to the center of the confusion which permeates this history from start to finish, and which continues in all Trotsky's writings. This is not only in the history of the Russian Revolution, because if I took a single point one could always argue, that's not exactly what he meant, you are taking it too literally and that type of evasion. That cannot work here. The passage I refer to is Trotsky's own summation of what has happened, a summation made for the benefit of leaders of revolutions in the future. It was written about 1932. He had had about fifteen years to think it over. He writes as usual brilliantly, so that his mistake is unmistakable and glaring. He says:

"To overthrow the old power is one thing. To take power is another. The bourgeoisie may win power in a revolution not because it is revolutionary but because it is bourgeois." (Lenin never made a statement like that, never.) Now he goes on to explain why. "It has in its possession property, education, the press, and a network of strategic positions, and a hierarchy of institutions." That, he says, is what the bourgeoisie has. And then he proceeds to say, "Quite otherwise with the proletariat."[16] That is absolutely false and I'm going to deal with it at once.

The proletariat in England has some property, though not much. It has education, in some respects, social respects, the most advanced experience in the country. It has a press. It has a network of strategic positions — ask the bourgeoisie. It has a hierarchy of institutions. And what it hasn't got it could take over in twenty-four hours. *The Times? The Guardian?* The proletariat could take over that material and run it within two hours. In fact they run them now. As a matter of fact, in Arab countries and in the rest of the underdeveloped countries, they know enough politics to know that when they make a revolution the first thing to do is to rush for the radio station. When they get hold of it they know what to say.

Let us continue with Trotsky. He says, "Quite otherwise with the proletariat." Quite otherwise. The proletariat, as he sees it, has nothing, is nothing. This is a Russian intellectual, full of talent, but one who has never grasped the essentials of Marxism because he grew up in an awkward country, a difficult country, in which there were these special conditions. He never saw who and what was the vanguard of society. In that, his famous theory of Permanent Revolution wandered about in the air. He could never join anybody to do anything about it. And when the Russian Revolution was over, in India and China his theory of Permanent Revolution fell apart. That, however, is by the way. He goes on to commit the permanent blunder.

"Quite otherwise with the proletariat. Deprived in the nature of things of all social advantages . . ." Entirely false. He could not stand up in the British Empire today and tell the British proletariat that it was "deprived in the nature of things of all social advantages. . . ." The proletariat is the most advanced section of British society. I've spoken about that and I am prepared to speak of it again at any time. The things that matter in Britain, the proletariat is reponsible for. To mention two, the end of Empire and the end of unemployment as a necessary part of society. Sometimes through the Labour Party, sometimes they have to force the Labour Party, but Trotsky thinks otherwise. "Deprived in the nature of things of all social advantages, an insurrectionary proletariat can count only on its numbers, its solidarity, its cadres (that is the party), and its official staff (that is the party leadership)."

That is his conception, that is what he is writing in 1932. And that is what he wrote until he died. You remember the famous passage in *Germany, the Key to the International Situation?* He says, "Retreat you say, you who were yesterday leaders of the Third Period."[17] You see whom he is talking to? He isn't talking to the German people. He is talking, as he always did, to the Communist Party. "Retreat you say, you who were the leaders of the Third Period. Leaders and institutions can retreat. Individuals can hide. But the working class will have no place to hide in the face of Fascism." Very brilliant and very true. And he goes on to say, "If the party were to give way and not lead the proletariat. . . ." In all his writings you can trace it. He is concerned not with the proletariat; he still thinks of it always in terms of the backward Russian proletariat, not the advanced section either. That is how he always thinks. That's why he writes *The Spanish Revolution in Danger*; another pamphlet on the danger to the revolution in France. Stalin is ruining the revolution in China. That is what Trotsky spent all his life doing. Because the proletariat as such, and its tremendous social advantages and what it meant to modern society, that he never saw. Lenin was very clear as to what was happening to that section of the proletariat in Russia and the backwardness of the rest of Russia *and* the relation of that to the rest of the world. And he saw that because that had helped to make him what he was. He had helped to make it what it was, but it had helped to make him what he was. In 1890 it began and he went along with it to 1917–1923.

And that is where we are today. I am not speaking about people who read Trotsky. Many of the Stalinists who wanted to break away from Stalinism were faced with Trotsky's theories, and particularly his theory that Stalin would restore capitalism in Russia. Trotskyism did not grow because it was riddled with falsities. And the great mass of the population which judges events by tremendous happenings saw that the Russian Revolution was led to power by means of a revolutionary party which formed an international, and believed for many years — and to some extent still believes — that that is the way in which a revolution must succeed. Utterly false. From 1934 to 1957 the history of the revolutionary uprisings and movements prove the exact opposite. The Vanguard Party is a dangerous anachronism.

I come now to the last section of what I have to say. You have been very patient and I assure you I won't keep you very long. What have Marxists to *do*?

We have to deal with certain problems of Marxism. I hope you understand that. I hope that for us, we cannot possibly, being what we are and having the views we hold, do otherwise than what Lenin did in the early months of 1917. Although he didn't know when the revolution would come, he sat down and drafted that tremendous document, *State and Revolution,* giving an idea and perspective of what the socialist society would be, what under a revolution, a state would do. That is what we consider our task to be. And please note: this is the way Lenin did it: he took quotations from Marx; he took quotations from Kautsky; he took quotations from Engels; he took quotations from Pannekoek, and various people; and he said, this is what *they* said, but the present world is not like that, they have misinterpreted Marx, etc. In other words, he continued a tradition. He couldn't start as if he were born way up a coconut tree. He said, this is where we have reached up to here — which is what Marx had done with philosophy, Kant and Hegel — and he says, from here we go on; and he made his analysis. That is what we have to do.

I believe we have a tremendous tradition to continue. That is our tradition. And there is something we can learn from the history of Marx and Lenin also. There are an immense number of organizations, small, everywhere. None of them are very likely to grow to any particular size, that is to say, to any great weight. They may or may not. (One did in Ceylon. But I don't think that Ceylon is a model for us.) But the proletariat itself must move; this is what Lenin insisted on. Particularly after 1917, he insisted, everything created in a socialist movement, and in the basic movement of modern society, is created by the revolutionary proletariat. Everything new in Russia, he continually said, was created and maintained by the revolutionary proletariat and could not have been created otherwise. (Somebody should make a list of those statements.) There must be no misunderstanding about that. Some of us are working here, some there and everywhere, and have a great deal of work to do. But some time or other the proletariat is going to decide to intervene and to act. And then all these tendencies will acquire solidity, solidarity, and a certain weight in the community or some will disappear.

Now we continue the tradition of Marxism, and we are very hostile and are going to take some pains to deal with elements in that tradition which in our opinion are mischievous and harmful. But there is something else we have to do. We have to do what Marx did in the Historical Tendency of Capitalist Accumulation, and what Lenin did in *State and Revolution,* and what Trotsky never did — what Trotsky said was that the proletariat has nothing but solidarity and leaders. We have to look around, because Marx's method and Lenin's was to examine what was taking place and then, in the light of the general Marxist analysis of society, add its expectations, to draw some conclusions.

We have to continue that tradition. We have to say that they were *here* yesterday and we start from the same place today, but tomorrow we expect such and such. We are living in a society in which certain conclusions of Marx and Lenin are very obvious. You haven't to preach Marxism to the population as Lenin had to do. Today, life teaches Marxism to everybody. But if you wish to exercise an assured continuation of a tremendous tradition, you have to be serious students of Marxism. At least that's what we think. And we take the case, I want to take as an example, the case of the late President Kennedy. His is a very striking example.

Kennedy was shot the other day. In regard to the situation in the U.S., Cockburn this morning in the *Sunday Telegraph* says what nobody has said and what has been obvious for a long time, that this shooting could be the introduction, the preliminary, to a situation in the United States in which mortal forces cross swords. I feel very regretful that a Marxist has not said that. My U.S. friends will say that, no doubt; one of them *has* said it, but we haven't got the thing out in time.

In regard to this assassination, I want you to note the kind of analysis which is required of a Marxist and which only a close study and continuation of Marxism will give you. Otherwise you are guessing and you might succeed and you might not. About the murdered president, a lot of people are saying, "Oh, this was a wonderful man. He had beautiful features, and he used to write books, and he was so active and energetic, and he brought intellect back into American government, and his wife was very beautiful, and he loved his children, and he was a millionaire." Now true or not true, all of that is of little importance. Why Kennedy's death has had such importance in the world today, everywhere, is due fundamentally, this is where you have to begin, to points made by Marx in the Historical Tendency of Capitalist Accumulation. If you don't begin there you are lost entirely. Centralization of the means of production and socialization of labor at last reach a point. . . . The point they have reached, that was the significance of Kennedy.

Let us move on to the concrete. What is the problem they have on both sides of the Iron Curtain? DeGaulle says that he must have his deterrent. And Home says, well we mustn't spread the deterrent, but we must have one. And Kennedy says, well, you all must have the deterrent, but let us join and let me be in complete control of it. That means nothing but the centralization of the means of production. That is what it is. That gives him his world-wide significance. Whether he was tall or short, handsome or ugly, or what, the rulers of Russia, the ruler of the United States today, occupies that position in regard to the process of production on a world scale. Centralization of the means of production means: the man who will press the button is the man in charge of the whole process of production on which they depend for their very existence. That is the significance of Kennedy. I am not saying there are not other aspects. Human affairs are very complicated. All I am saying is to begin with what Marx said. You could have specific historical circumstances and climate and all sorts of things. I am concerned with the ideal average. And anybody who is in Kennedy's position will evoke that astonishing influence and have the concern of vast numbers of people. That is point number one.

And now, the other side. Marx said, socialization of labor. He goes on to say that the proletariat is united, disciplined and organized by the very process of capitalist production itself. That is what is happening today in the world to a degree far beyond what Lenin saw in *State and Revolution.* When Lever Hume and these others form a factory in Accra and these other places and they mine bauxite and oil—they are socializing labor. You will see for example, in Trinidad, the insignificant island where I come from, that the leader of the largest trade union in the country, speaking to the country as to why his people have had a strike, goes into great length as to what production is in oilfields elsewhere, in the United States, in the Middle Eastern countries, what their production is, what their wages, what are their profits, their methods of management, etc.; he holds forth at length about it. Last year he was a worker. But he is now the president and he holds forth on world production. He is, by the way, a very fine fellow. The mode, the process of production all over the world has united the population as never before. It is being united, disciplined, and organized by the very mechanism of the process of production.

In addition to that we have a special development of the means of production today, the tremendous means of communication, between government and people. Poor short-sighted Marx did not see that. Radio, television, movies, telstar, the world previously did not know these things. And these things bring a man in Kennedy's position right into actual contact with the proletariat of various countries and make them understand that their fate is bound up with what he does and happens to him. He went to Germany the other day, and he told the Germans, "Now, look, this situation in which you are in Western Germany, that depends on us, and you can depend on us." So that when Kennedy is killed what has happened to him immediately becomes the center of world-wide concern and interest in what he had been doing and what would be likely to happen now. That was quite impossible before, but it is natural and native to the kind of existence that we live today. Centralization of the means of production and socialization of labor at last reach a state where it is impossible for them to be contained in their capitalist integument. It is obvious that society has overstepped the boundaries of the national, political, i.e., capitalist state. And the working class is united, disciplined, and organized by the very process of capitalist production. That is where I begin to talk about Kennedy. That is what he signifies.

Now I don't mean to say that people will not find out all sorts of things about Kennedy, and about Jackie, and his father, his Catholicism, and about Ireland. That is quite all right with me. But I am saying that if you are going to begin seriously to continue a great tradition, you have to begin where I have indicated. Further, you will find Freud and Jung, Durkheim and Malinowski and Pareto and even Croce, all discover questions of psychology and sociology, etc., which can refine and develop and improve the Marxist method. I don't say no. But I insist that before you begin to refine, and before you begin to develop, and before you begin to add, you better find out what it is you have at the beginning. This is where we begin, and from where we go on. But we don't wander about in general, being generally for the working class for all sorts of moral reasons. Marxism is not only a method, it constitutes a philosoophy of life, a way you have to live.

Sir Julian Huxley is what is called a humanist and he propagates humanist doctrines. And another one, Professor Ayer, and these other fellows, Logical Positivists, they propagate philosophical profundities. I say, well, all right, that is fine; so what? I believe that philosophy has to tell you something, come to some conclusions about life. I read some of these books every now and then, and their great point seems to be that philosophy can tell you nothing except about Philosophy. Ordinary men cannot live that way. And we have to find a life to live. That Marxism does.

There is another function which we have to perform. In addition to making clear and driving forward the Marxist conception of society, we now face the fact that the world revolution today can take place within seventy-two hours in all essential parts of the world. We have to be aware of that in the same sense that Lenin wrote *State and Revolution,* when at the same time he was saying: we don't know whether we will see the world revolution within our lifetime. That is the Marxist conception of history, the historical tendency of 1963. And we do not ever know what the proletariat is going to do or when it is going to do it.

Thirdly, we have concrete things to do. There is an examination, a serious examination, that needs to be made of automation. The Marxist movement has not done that. And I tell you point-blank it will not be properly done unless it is done in the tradition of *Capital,* Vol. I, "The Historical Tendency of Capitalist Accumulation"; Lenin on *State and Revolution,* Lenin on *Imperialism,* and the works of Lenin on the Russian Revolution and others. Then we will be able to take up automation and place it. Otherwise you will just gossip all over the place and say you like it or you don't like it, it is valuable or it is dangerous, or you think or you don't think. . . . That is *not* what a Marxist organization worthy of its name is going to do. It has a method and a tradition, and these it preserves and continues.

But in addition to these general tendencies of capitalism as it is and of the role of the working class, the increasing practical unanimity of the activity of the working class, what it thinks and the information it gathers and its conception of itself and other people, which distinguishes 1963 tremendously from 1953, in adddition to all this, every Marxist of every nation has a particular national function to carry out. Lenin's greatness as a revolutionary and the greatness of what he did for the rest of the world was specifically based, as I've tried to explain, on the conditions in Russia, a special situation in Russia, and he very rarely and only at odd moments allowed himself to forget that. I could give you quotations and quotations where he made clear: we are doing it here this way; you all out there will do it your way.

In the United States today some Marxists I know will publish soon the finest study I know of the development of the Negro question as part of the development of the United States.[18] Because it is only by a close examination of what is before you that you are able to understand what is taking place on a world scale. (Some of you may have read today in the *Sunday Telegraph* an article by Claud Cockburn. It is the only serious article I have read on the crisis in the United States. All the rest is a lot of nonsense, fit only for the wastepaper basket. The country is on the verge of a violent civil commotion similar to what took place in the Civil War 100 years ago. And that has been as obvious as daylight, but these, most of them, do not know that.)

In Britain here, if you will allow me, there is something at which I am daily astonished. I have written and am trying to get published a work in which Shakespeare plays a central role. But in my opinion, I am an outsider, I am a stranger. I am absolutely astonished when I read the history of the seventeenth century, when I read of the development of the Leveller Party, when I read that brilliant journalist, Ovington, I think was his name, and John Lilburne, and Thomas Walywny and these others. I am amazed to find that these men are so much Englishmen and what they did so illuminates what is taking place in Britain today and the condition and the mental attitude of the British masses of the people today. I am astonished that the average Marxist revolutionary living in Britain seems to live quite cheerfully without bothering about that. There is one, Christopher Hill, who writes a lot of stuff about the Puritans. He is an expert. That is not the business of experts. That is the concern, and it can only be properly treated by a revolutionary who is looking at society as a whole and who is bringing Marxism as a whole to bear upon the history of his own country, not only its past, but its present, and the relation, as Mr. T. S. Eliot has said, of its past to its present. The Marxist movement does not touch the English revolution. A very grave error. The history of the United States is absolutely un-understandable except as traced from a knowledge of the Civil War and its roots in the upheaval of 1776. The key situations in Britain are between 1800 and 1832, and before that the Civil War in the seventeenth century. There modern Britain began. A lot that began there still continues. That is what the Marxist has to trace. And it can only be done by a Marxist.

So there are four points. You have to continue to study Marxism as a special group because fortunately today a great deal of the conclusions of Marxism are seen by everybody. You haven't to do what Lenin and Marx had to do, to preach and teach Marxism so that people could understand. The world has objectively moved to where people only have to look and listen to understand Marxism. That is what Marx pointed out that capitalist production would do, make all the people understand their conditions of life and their relations with their kind. The objective world has reached that stage. That makes it all the more necessary for Marxists to master and learn from and continue the great tradition. We have to do for 1963 what Marx did in "The Historical Tendency of Capitalist Accumulation," and what Lenin did in *State and Revolution* and his further works. In other words, to be able to draw the necessary conclusions for the advancement of the socialist conception in the world in which we live. It is a very different world from the world of 1938. Nobody has done that. We have to deal seriously with automation, and it cannot be done except in the Marxist tradition. It cannot be done otherwise. I've seen people try to do it and they have made fools of themselves. And you have to pay attention also in a Marxist manner to the historical situation in your own country. That is what I recommend to your attention. Thank you. I've said enough to begin with.

Notes

1. *Hegel's Science of Logic*, tr. by W. H. Johnston and L. G. Struthers. New York: The Macmillan Company, 1951 (1929), vol. 1, pp. 53–75.
2. Marx and Engels, *Collected Works*, vol. 6, p. 487. Moscow: Progress Publishers, 1976; *Capital*, vol. 1, Moscow: Progress Publishers (undated), p. 457.
3. Ibid.
4. *Capital*, p. 458.
5. Harold Wilson was the Labour Party Prime Minister of England at the time.
6. *Capital*, Vol. III, pp. 879–81.

7. Lenin, *Collected Works*, vol. 23, London: Lawrence & Wishart, Moscow: Progress Publishers, 1964. "Lecture on the 1905 Revolution." "We of the older generation may not live to see the coming revolution," p. 253.

8. Ibid., vol. 33, "On Cooperation," pp. 467–75.

9. Ibid., "Better Fewer But Better," pp. 487–502.

10. Tchernychewsky or Chernychevsky, *Capital*, vol. I, pp. 25, 746. See note 16, Chapter 1.

11. Ibid., pp. 27–28.

12. "The Development of Capitalism in Russia," *Collected Works*, vol. 3.

13. See, "What Is To Be Done," ibid., vol. 5, pp. 347–529.

14. Ibid., vol. 33, pp. 418–32, esp. 430–32.

15. Dennis Healy was the leader of a Trotskyist sect in Britain.

16. Leon Trotsky, *The History of the Russian Revolution*, New York: Simon and Schuster, 1937, (3 vols. in one) vol. 3, pp. 168–69.

17. Trotsky, *The Struggle Against Fascism in Germany*, New York: Pathfinder Press, 1971, p. 125. "Germany, the Key to the International Situation" is on pp. 115–31. The Third Period was the period in the late 1920s and early 1930s when the Comintern opposed all alliances with other socialist parties and organizations and called socialists "social fascists." It was replaced in 1935 by the policies of People's Front, involving alliances with liberal capitalist parties and governments.

18. *Negro Americans Take the Lead*, ed., Martin Glaberman, Detroit: Facing Reality Publishing Committee, 1964.

Letters on Organization

December 3, 1962

My dear Marty,[1]

I have to write you a series of letters. They will be one a week unless you ask me to make them two. In them I shall be taking up fundamental problems of our movement, both in a general and a specific manner applied to the specific American situation. I shall send you two copies of all these letters. Whether you will hand one out to others will depend entirely on your judgment. Personally I am inclined to, that is all I say, inclined to that they should be for general circulation not only to party members but to friends. That, however, is a matter which you and those whom you wish to consult will decide upon. In the course of taking them up, I shall refer to Marxism in general and our particular situation. Today I will deal with two subjects only, first, the breakup of our organization, and secondly, Trotskyism, or the movement from which we came. If at any time I write in too concentrated a manner or there is a particular point which you wish me to develop further, I shall do so if I can.

1) Our organization has practically gone to pieces.[2] By saying this, I mean no offense to those who remain behind. But the movement with which we started has been broken up almost to bits. I don't know if you have paid the necessary attention to this. I have been doing so. Without that I would have continued to be in a complete mess. But that is now clear. I would like you to note that I am not concerned with the qualities, in particular the weaknesses, of any individual. We had, or we started with, the best possible people whom one could expect. If we had to choose a set of people now, I am pretty sure we could not choose a better bunch. Let me go through the list with you. There was Rae [Raya Dunayevskaya], an old Bolshevik, very highly trained and very devoted. The thing to note about her is, apart from political weaknesses which will emerge, that in her book[3] she does extremely well up to where she broke from us. After that the book simply becomes nonsense. Next on the list is Grace [Boggs], a very highly educated and capable person. All

that Rae gave to us in political experience and knowledge of Bolshevism, Grace gave in philosophy and a general high level of education. I cannot forget, not only what the movement, but I personally, owed to both these girls. We as an organization could not forget it either. If we forget it or ignore it or pass superficial remarks about it, it means that we don't know what we had and therefore we don't know now what we are without.

Ike [Saul Blackman] was a pretty poor citizen but he did a great deal of useful work. Tobin, who started with us in 1941 was a very tower of strength both in devotion and political understanding. Bessie [Gogol], with all her faults, was a very devoted revolutionary. Louis [Gogol] is one of the most remarkable men of high character whom I knew. Freddy [Paine] was absolutely priceless. Everett [Washburn] was also a very fine type. Filomena [D'Addario] was a junior who we had from the very beginning, had a fine background for Marxism and for years did very well. William G[orman/Morris Goelman] is one of the ablest men and the most brilliant that I have ever met in the movement. That is enough to go on with. I must not forget Jessie [Glaberman], not T[om Quock]. I may leave out one or two people. Above all I must not leave out someone whose name I shall not mention but I leave it to you to fill in, one of the very finest and most valuable types that we had; not only valuable but most precious, all things taken into consideration. The fact remains that we had these people, we had ample opportunity to train them; to give them all we had, and one by one, or sometimes more than one, they have all left us, and left us not for anything but just to fade away, either into some sort of political nonsense or just idleness. We have failed to hold them. It was not due, we have to make clear, to the fact that they were bad people or weak people. That is a lot of nonsense and would only prepare general disillusionment and also personal degeneration.

Now for the breakdown of the organization. (I must not forget [John] Zupan who, with all his weaknesses, was a most intelligent man and meant well.) I have to add that if a man like Zupan was unable to be integrated into our movement there is not the slightest sense in denouncing him. We had ideas, theories, organization. If there was a failure, we have to accept the responsibility. Now why did all this take place? I am no believer in the doctrine of many reasons. In most of these matters I believe that there is a fundamental reason and any number of subjective and individual causes which acquire importance and often do a lot of mischief because they are functioning within the basic organizational structure. This does not mean excusing personal or individual weaknesses. But emphasis on these or looking upon these as the origin of our troubles and weaknesses is the surest way to disaster—intellectual confusion and organizational disaster. I am laying great emphasis on the particular method I propose to use in the analysis of the matter, because it is a method which we shall have to be using for everything, the general analysis of society and Marxism and our own particular problem.

The more I am able to work and think, I find that today in 1962 we have already reached one world. After five years experience in the West Indies, a very intensive experience, I find that on my return to England, my view of Britain and of British politics and my studies of the French and the Russian Revolutions, are immensely deepened and clarified. I want you to pay close attention, very close attention, to the passage I have just dictated. It would be very easy to go wrong here, very, very, easy. But I believe that fundamental to our failure is the fact that we were Trotskyists, that we did not purge ourselves completely of what Trotskyism represented, that it is not only our difficulty but it is a difficulty that runs through all the problems that we face. Trotskyism was not a mistake of Trotsky. Trotskyism was Leninism carried over into a period unsuitable for it. Trotsky fought Leninism for years. Then he found that Lenin was right. He turned over and adopted the Leninist program and policy and by the crude, absolutely unrestrained manner in which he took it over, he was as responsible as anybody else for what the Bolshevik Party finally became under Stalinism. That is where we have been stuck and, my dear Marty, we have to get out of it. But to get out of it we have to know it for what it is.

The Leninism that Trotsky taught was essentially the doctrine of the party. I hope I haven't to go into the fact that this doctrine of the party was concentrated and crystallized by Lenin only after 1917. Before that it was a special product of Russia and he regretted that the Tsarist police state forced Bolshevism out of the more democratic and easier modes of social democracy in Western Europe. I believe I have gone into it pretty clearly in *Facing Reality.*[4] That is what Trotsky took over. The basis of the Fourth International was the First Four Congresses of the Third International. Absolutely and completely wrong. One of the great disasters of the American movement was Cannon. He was a man who accepted completely and brought great personal force (and a solid amount of ignorance of Marxism also) to the development of a Marxist party along the lines of Trotsky. To this day he has been totally unable to adapt Marxism to the American scene. And to the particular age in which we live. This doctrine as it came to be developed laid emphasis on the special group of advanced leaders, intellectual or labor leaders, who had adopted Marxism or the party line. You will note that over the last thirty years it has been a complete and disastrous, a total failure. The only place where Marxism has had any success is in Communist China, and there it was an original doctrine, created by Mao Tse-Tung on an entirely new basis and out of the reach of official Stalinism.

That is where we have come from. We started breaking with it and I will go into my particular role in so doing, how we all broke away from it. But that is what has held on to us and which we have never placed behind us. It is no use pretending or fooling ourselves. When we broke away in 1951 and we put our hands upon some money, it is perfectly obvious that we set up in Detroit another little Leninist or, if you like, Trotskyist grouping which was different in theory, very sharply different, from the Trotskyists, but in reality had no seriously different organizational approaches to the problem of developing a Marxist movement in 1951. We can't blame ourselves. New ideas and new people do not fall from the sky. But it would be a great mistake not to recognize that that is what we did. We had no idea that something else should be done. If we had, it was only in opposition to what was going on. There was no positive doctrine and definite conclusions to be drawn from it so as to orient us and the people around us along a new road. Later in these discussions I am going to carry on with you I shall go into more detail about individual contributions, mistakes, etc. But we can't do a single thing until we get fundamentally clear what has happened to us and why. *That* is what has happened to us and *that* is why. If you look at the labor movement as a whole all over Europe, and even the smaller Marxist organizations, they, none of them, are getting any place. As a matter of fact, the Labor Party and these others are getting closer in their organizational structure to the old-fashioned Leninism than they would like to think.

I hope that this will be reflected upon, absorbed and commented upon by you without it becoming a burden and something on which you concentrate to such a degree that you put aside everything else. This does not represent on my part any sudden light from on high. Sometimes it is only after you write something that you fully understand what you are driving at. *Facing Reality* was an attempt to break out of the stranglehold. That is pefectly clear to me now. The weakness of it was that I had to do it at second hand and thousands of miles away from the living contact which could have made it some road to reality. I expect that it is some years now I have known the American organization is not getting anywhere. That I could tell from the paper. I very often found it very hard to read, and that is an infallible sign. It is an infallible sign in general and particularly in the U.S. — the U.S. being what it is — to believe that any such paper was possibly getting among the working class or among any class in society, that was a form of insanity. If you read *Facing Reality* carefully you will see that it was directed against what was being put forward as Marxism. During the last year before Grace and Jim went their way I made some attempts, not very highly organized, nevertheless some attempts to shift them in another, a definitely different direction. They paid no attention. And what is important is that they could not pay attention because they didn't know what I was talking about. They were people with one cast of mind, one form of development. That had to be broken down and cleared away before something else could take its place and begin to develop.

Next time, which I expect to be next Monday, I shall go into the role of individuals and particularly my own. However, I could not possibly attempt to do this and do it right or make the impression I want to make and draw the conclusions I want to draw, unless we had at the basis of our conclusions the pervading evil from which we, in common with the rest of the labor movement, have suffered. Okay Marty.

J.

December 4, 1962

My dear Marty,

I am sending you two copies of this letter, one for yourself and one as usual with this type of letter, for circulation or as basis for circulation. The details of that, the organization of that, I shall take up with you at some time later.

I am waiting anxiously for the official report of the conference. By official I mean the report that goes to all the membership and (this is my opinion) to all the people whom you think are interested or may be interested. I intend to send you, as I think I said before, an official (so to speak) statement on the report. This in my view must be immediately circulated. Closely connected with the report that I shall make is the letter which I sent to you yesterday and the letters which I propose to continue during the next period. As far as I can see now, although this is by no means certain, the next letter will deal with my personal experience and political developments not, I assure you, in regards to my psychological needs, but in strict regards to our political development. At all costs people have to get to know who we were, what we have been doing, what we are, and what we must be. One of the most useful ways in which I can make that clear is to deal with my own political development. It is something that I understand better than most things and that other people will be able to follow more easily. After that I propose to take up, in the light of the previous letters, a general survey of the basic political problems that face us in the world today, both on a general scale and in relation to our specific problems. Then fourthly, I propose to take up in two letters the political and organizational basis for the preparation of a paper and other publications. I have said a few things about that in the recent past. But I wish to take that to the membership. This is my view.

We have had a disastrous and complete failure. The only thing that is really encouraging is that some people and some good people still remain and obviously have a strong inclination to action and the continuation of Marxism. But I want to make this clear and I want all who are reading this to understand: if people plunge once more into doing this and taking action without knowing exactly where they stand and precisely what they propose to do, not only organizationally (with precision) but also in the most profound political sense, then it is my absolute certainty that the consequences will be another failure even more rapid than the last one and this time complete. I suggest now definitely that the previous letter be circulated to all members and friends and this one also. What I see before me, I do not like.

J.

December 17, 1962

My dear Marty,

Thank you for your letter, the one replying to mine, and the notice of the public announcement of the conference. I am glad that you approve so strongly of the letter I sent and the letters I propose to send for the organization and, I hasten to include, all persons whom you think (or the others may think) are likely to be sympathetic, or to become so from a reading of the letters. I shall reply in detail, I expect, tomorrow or the day after. Meanwhile, this afternoon I shall not hesitate to bring in contemporary or organizational matters. But I shall do so always with the idea that what I am saying is intended for the whole organization and, I insist, for sympathetic friends or people likely to become so by contact with us and a reading of the letters.

I am very much concerned to draw the lessons from the confusion and failures of the last period. Unless we do that, unless we build ourselves on that, we are not only not Marxists, we are not people of ordinary common sense. I define our weakness, our failures, in the past period within two categories. 1) We failed entirely to make any serious consistent analysis of the political situation in society at large. We failed also to do it for the U.S. But that failure was based upon the failure to maintain a constant Marxist analysis and appraisal of civilization as a whole, of world society. That is the epoch in which we live. We did not do it at all. We have to understand that and set ourselves to do it and to do it steadily and consistently, to look upon it as something that we have to do or we shall be doing nothing, merely exasperating ourselves. 2) The second point is that we failed, not only failed, but never attempted the analysis of our function and our personnel as a small Marxist organization. We never estimated, within any organized view, what we were doing, how far we were succeeding, how far we were meeting the needs and necessities of people like ourselves.

That I propose to do and keep on doing.

Let me be very clear again, particularly for the sake of those who for the first time will be tackling problems of this kind and orienting themselves to it. I propose in these letters and afterwards in my political relations with you, to constantly bring before the organization (and actual and prospective friends): a) the analysis and perspectives of modern society as a whole, within which to place the American. That particularly, the American, will be your business, but it can only be done within the general analysis of capitalist society. b) Within the same context and for the same purpose, I propose to analyze and to give directions and perspectives for the proper development of a small Marxist organization, particularly to deal with the experience that we have had and with the actuality such as I see it. The actual working out, instruction, education, drawing conclusions from experiences of the contemporary group in the U.S., you all will have to do. I cannot do it; I cannot attempt to do it. But the general political analysis and the political line, that I propose to keep constantly before you, both in relation to our past and to our future. In this letter I propose to take up the issue of the organization and its personnel. I expect that if there are any problems or observations which anybody wants to make to me *after discussion in the U.S.,* please note that I will be only too glad to hear them, to be able to explain something and as well to learn something. I shall be taking up personnel because we have avoided that all through. I am not going to avoid it any longer and you have to decide, as I shall most certainly have to decide, where the serious political analysis of personnel degenerates into gossip and psychology. You will have to decide that there. I know I shall decide it without the hesitation and without uncertainty.

Let me begin with the leadership of the organization as we have known it. I said in my last letter that Cannon, despite his virtues, was quite unfit to be the leader of a Marxist organization. He was an uneducated person. He had nothing to bring to Marxism, nothing at all. When the organization got into trouble with the failure of Trotsky's analyses, Cannon was quite incapable of even posing the question. The best he reached was that the satellite states of the East were degenerated [workers'] states. We have to understand and to appreciate that. Not only was Cannon unable to do it — Shachtman also was totally unable to handle that question. These were big questions. We put ourselves into a very grievous exemplification of the same.

J[ames] B[oggs] undoubtedly had virtues, remarkable virtues. But he was an ignoramus as far as Marxism was concerned, and so gross an ignoramus that he hadn't an idea that there was something about it that he ought to learn, or at least recognize as his ignorance. I did my best to let him know that there were dangers and difficulties in what he proposed to do and that he should let me see the document so that I could point these out and he would be able to put forward his ideas without doing violence to elementary points of Marxism. You have to take people as you meet them. Not only did he not see that, not only did he not realize what I was talking about, but his ignorance of Marxism and the role of theory in a working-class movement was such that he was dominated by the idea of stating his own views in opposition to what he never considered it necessary to become acquainted with. It is quite clear. The leader of a Marxist organization must himself be a well-educated Marxist and be able, if not necessarily to work out the fundamental problems, at least to know what they are and seek some sort of answer with some sense of historic continuity and the perspectives of a socialist movement.

I am perhaps stating the obvious things in a somewhat elementary and pedagogical way. But we had better get these points clear. Marxism is above all the leadership and, if not the material, the ideological leadership of the working-class movement and of those who consider themselves Marxists. We have to lead. That does not mean being placed in a position with an army or body of followers behind you. In what you do, in the way you pose your problems and your solutions, you show that you recognize your role. In that way you not only attract people to you but you make clear what the role of Marxism is.

You see, the main point in this as in everything is not merely to say what you think is, or what you think ought to be done, but to represent it by your activity and the very way you approach it. That we have lost entirely in the years that preceded our downfall. A lot of babbling about automation, speculations as to the condition of the working class, a quite hopeless treatment of what should have been the very essence of our Marxist approach, *The Invading Socialist Society*,[5] the New Society. Later I propose to write with my own hand the preliminary basis for a discussion of what our paper must consist of. But I can say here that the paper to be a Marxist paper must make clear the decline of capitalist society, its decay, its putrescence, and the rise within it of the new society, distorted sometimes, twisted at times, but nevertheless containing the germs of a new society.

The Chancellor of the Exchequer in Great Britain has announced that Britain will henceforth plan the economy. France is now on its third plan for the French economy. That is merely one example of the way that capitalism has to twist itself within the forms that strictly speaking belong to the new socialist society. The European Common Market is another, a capitalist form, a bastard form, of the United States of Europe. Russia and the satellite states form the other half. That is what we have to do. That is what in 1962 we have to show. Because if we don't show it now, and if we do not have it in our heads now, and if we do not by our conduct and our attitude show that that is what governs our thought, when in the name of God will we be ready to do that, or when will we consider that the public is ready?

Our leadership, our organization, did not have these ideas in its own head. Therefore it could not convey them to any audience in the paper. When I say we failed, the failure begins with ourselves. I fooled around not doing what I should have done. I had no good excuse, but I knew instinctively that to do it I would have to tackle the question from the ground up. I would have had to make our noble leaders understand that they were leading nowhere because they didn't know what was happening. And, quite frankly, I shied away from that immense and difficult task.

Now I want to get a little more closely into the personnel we have had.

There is first of all Rae. If a Marxist enters the Marxist movement and is devoted only to the building of a party and looks upon that, or proof of progress in that, as the proof of the validity if not the success of Marxism, then that Marxist is headed for a personal disaster. It can take, we are able to see, one of two forms. In the case of Rae, it has taken the form of developing the ideas of Marxism, an absolutely valueless concern with theory, running around and babbling about this or that that has been picked up in books which the general public does not read, or from investigation on the spot. It has nothing to do with Marxism really. It is a form of literary escapism. It means nothing and Rae knows that it means nothing. Or, on the other hand, it may take the form as with G[race], of heading back to the intellectual section of the bourgeoisie. I draw attention to these because the worker in the Marxist movement must be helped to realize, and the original impetus will help him to realize, that he is a Marxist, is a member of a Marxist organization, and is doing work at it that is not to be judged, that he himself does not judge, because his organization has two hundred members today whereas it had only one hundred members yesterday. It is necessary, it is possible, to be a Marxist and to continue to be a member of a small Marxist organization, because that is the way in which you live and after a time, from the way the organization in particular and Marxism has developed you, that is the only way of life which is satisfactory to you. If, however, you have the Leninist doctrine of the party and your activity is aimed at building the party, large or small, and you judge, rather you lived with the expectation of this small organization of yours becoming larger and larger, and do not have your eyes on the essential development and disintegration of capitalist society, then you and what happens to you is only a matter of your personal stamina and time. I hope that what I am saying is clear. It can easily be misinterpreted. But this is what I know.

It looks as if I shall have to continue this letter tomorrow. But there is one point I wish to get clear at once. Rae was a very good Bolshevik of the old school — first class. I wish to refer to two things about her. She, after a certain time, came to the conclusion that the revolutionary movement in the U.S. was not getting anywhere in the sense that it was not building a mass movement. Therefore from fairly early under my leadership and direction (note that please, and note it well: under my leadership and direction) Rae saw an opportunity to develop her individual talents and instincts. Cannon did not give her that. No one in the U.S. ever thought of giving that to her. She, however, fastened on to it, and inasmuch as the development of this was, as far as I was concerned, and my leadership of the organization an integral part of the organization itself, Rae was able to combine both. But when I was about to leave and she was put in charge of the organization, and she felt that the theoretical work which had formed so essential a part of her existence was now in danger from organizational responsibility which she had to undertake, Rae changed. You will have to work that out. But I remember well being profoundly concerned at the ferocious fury (that is the only word I can use) with which she began to view the people around her. The thing reached so far, and Nettie [Kravitz], I think, has a copy of the document, that one of the last things I did was draft a resolution, I think with Nettie and G[race] warning Rae about the possibilities, the dangerous possibilities, of this fury and antagonism to people around her which seemed to be raging in her. What it meant was that the personal satisfaction, the personal involvement, which her membership in the Marxist movement had given to her, after she got to know me and to work with me, she now felt was slipping away from her; and her future development is very clear to me. It is not worth going into.

With G[race] we have another exemplification in a related sphere of the same type. G. was a highly educated and very well organized person. In our movement, and I want to emphasize that again, under my leadership (I am not playing any nonsense about what that signified, under my leadership) G. was able to bring into use her large capacities and energies. It was not only that they were directed towards the building of our movement. It was that she as a member of a small Marxist organization found a means of expanding and expressing her best self. When I left that was lost. For a time she came to Europe and we worked together on *Facing Reality* and other work of that kind. But under the influence of J[ames] B[oggs] she became devoted to automation, the trade union movement, what Reuther was doing, all very important and very useful, in fact, very necessary, but what G. had done for both the movement and for herself from the time she came near to it in 1940, that disappeared from her activities and consciousness of development. The result was, among other manifestations, an expression of the same fury which I had seen in Rae before I left. This time it was directed against Constance [Webb] during the few days that G. spent with us in Trinidad. At a certain stage she was unable to command herself and not to give expression to what she herself must have known was indiscreet if not actually stupid. J.B. did his best to pull her out of it but the rage was similar, although not so all-embracing, as that which moved in Rae.

I want to draw special emphasis to the fact that while we were acting and taking part in what were not large and expensive features of the class struggle against the bourgeoisie, what was in reality small and rather narrow political, even though practical, activities, those girls were comfortable, and not only comfortable but happy, those two in particular, because the organization was not only carrying out an objective task demanded by history, but it was to them personally a source of development.

Now I want to end by making this clear. Unless a small organization is doing that for its membership, in the numerous and various forms in which a development takes place, as sure as day two things will happen to it. First of all, it is only a matter of time before its membership begins to drop away under the disappointment at the goal not being reached (or being within reach), and also, as so often in regard to small activities as the expression of large ideas, the small ideas begin to show, and equal bankruptcy with the large. To sum up once more, to be able to do your practical activity to whatever degree that is possible, you have to be functioning within an organization and in a manner that develops yourself, gives you a consciousness of yourself meeting the problems that capitalist society poses to you as a person. To sum up again, the practical activities and the personal development go side by side. In my next letter I shall take up the development of our own organization from the time I took charge of it and trace its course up to the present time. We have to study history and it is time to study our own history.

J.

December 18, 1962

My dear Marty,

This is a continuation and, I hope, a conclusion of the last letter. The two should be sent out together if that is possible and convenient.

A leader is not merely a gifted or effective man. He often is. What a real leader is means that he has brought something distinctive into the organization; this which he brings is characteristic of him. It may be good. It may be bad. Or he may be, as often happens, someone who is in charge — I am not speaking of those. What did I bring to our organization? I not only brought something to the organization. I founded it. We have never tackled this. It is obvious that G. and J. never had any idea of what I signified to the organization; in other words, plain words, what the organization was, what it had been and what it was intended to do, that not only for its effect on outsiders but for its development of itself. I brought something new, something that was required and that can only be judged by its effects. The organization must know that, particularly now, or go to pieces, rapidly or by degrees.

I came into political activity in 1931. Up to that time I had been interested in literature, history, sports and general reading. I got interested in politics, local politics, suddenly, and my first decision was to write a biography of the local political leader, a biography, note it well, based on the history of the West Indies and of Trinidad, and including an analysis of different sections of the population, beginning with an analysis of the mass of people. That was thirty-one years ago. All that I have done since has been along those same lines.

Enough to say that since that time, and as far as I know before that time, no such work or biography has ever been done in West Indian politics — none whatever. The next thing was to get it published. And now I want to emphasize a certain experience which was the result of the political initiative. Please note this because it will mean in the end whether you will sink or swim. I read some of the biography to a friend of mine who had some money — he was not rich. He was a West Indian, interested in the development of the West Indies, and a man who could be stimulated by ideas. Now, note this. To my astonishment (at the time, but not now) he offered to print the biography and to pay for it. It came from the blue. Not only was the biography a great success — I took it to an English publisher. He read it and together we arranged for a smaller publication in an important series which included pamphlets by the British Labor Party and, truth must be told, one by Benito Mussolini. I hope that these letters will be carefully read. When I used to read, and up to now I read seriously, I examine what the writer is saying and examine it carefully in my mind. I don't only just read it or listen to what somebody else who has read it says, and immediately start to shoot off my mouth with opinions, agreements and disagreements. The brief notice that I have written so far of my first entry into political activity sums up a great deal of what you have to do.

After two years in England I came to Marxism, and how I did so is quite a tale, which I might in a private letter briefly outline to someone. The Marxists, they were Trotskyists, were in the Independent Labor Party [ILP]. I joined the party with them and forthwith took a certain step which pitchforked me virtually into the position of a party leader. The step was this. There was a lot of criticism about the weekly paper published by the ILP. They had been publishing it, I believe, for some forty years, and it was a well-established paper in political circles in England. Some of us were criticizing the paper, note this particularly, please, not only because we differed from it politically, but we criticized it as a piece of political journalism. I got together some of my associates, particularly two girls. We took six [issues] of the paper and I made a comprehensive analysis of them, pointing out what was wrong with the paper as a paper, and indicating what should be done to improve it. After we had done that we mimeographed it, sent it to the editor of the paper, who was Fenner Brockway, and circulated it all over the place. In other words, we expressed not our political differences directly with the paper, but we brought to it a criticism and technique of improving it as a political paper. The document went to a convention. The votes on it were even—which was quite an achievement for the Trotskyists who were usually in permanent opposition on political issues. A convention split into two equal parts on the party's weekly paper was quite a problem. Brockway solved it by stating that the paper had already incorporated many of the suggestions made in the document and would bear the document in mind in the future development of the paper. That satisfied everyone. Please note that this in the immediate sense was not an expression of political difference. It said what after all these years I still have to say about our own paper. The paper as a paper was bad and there were steps that should have been taken to improve it *as a paper*. I would not say that politics were not at the basis of the difference. But nevertheless, politics expresses itself directly or indirectly.

I have to continue the miserable story, miserable as it is. After two years in the Trotskyist movement I came to the conclusion that what was needed was a published book summarizing the whole Trotskyist position. I had this very clear in my own mind. A publisher asked me to do a book on socialism in Africa or socialism for Africa. I told him no, that what was required was a book on the crisis in Stalinist Russia. He told me to write a synopsis of what

I intended. I was all set and in less than a week I gave him a synopsis of twenty-thousand words, not only clear in analysis, but full of quotations. He expressed his astonishment and told me to go right ahead. That is the way in which *World Revolution*[6] was written and published. To this day no such book has ever been published in the Trotskyist movement. Nowhere, in Europe, in Asia, in Africa. Nowhere. The book was also published in the U.S. I cannot help drawing your attention to the fact that these things I repeatedly do. They were never done before. They have not been done since. The reasons for this I cannot go into. The fact, however, is of vital importance.

At about the same time I produced *The Black Jacobins*[7] which, if you please, was a book of general historical interest written especially with a view to the elucidation of the African revolution. The point about that book is that it kept an even balance between general history and Marxist policy. I may be wrong. I know of no other such book, at least inside the Marxist movement. They either are on the one side writing general history or they are writing an exemplification of some particular theory. The general public has read that book with interest. On some other occasion I shall tell you the use that is being made of it by revolutionaries at this very moment.[8]

I come to the U.S. The disturbance over the Russian question breaks out. During 1940 I spend some serious days wondering whether I should return to Europe or continue to stay in the U.S. It is very hard to be precise on matters of this kind, but I know that Rae had a great deal to do with my deciding to continue although I doubt if she knows it up to this day. My problem was this. I understood from the very start that when we had broken with Trotsky on the defence of the Soviet Union, we had broken with Trotskyism fundamentally. I understood that it was no question of agreement on everything and difference on one important issue. Being the person I was, I had to decide first that this question had to be worked out, and secondly, where it would be the most convenient for me, at any rate, to work it out. I decided to stay in the U.S. Thus it was, and very specifically with this question of the break with Trotskyism in mind, that on the day in 1941 Tobin, Rae and I met and decided that we would devote ourselves to the investigation and elaboration of the theory required for clarifying the matter. We didn't stumble into it by accident. We decided to undertake it. Rae was to study Russia and she began from the very beginning of the Bolshevik Party. Tobin was our organizer, activist and, to a substantial degree at that time, our financer. I was concerned with Marxism, politics in particular, *Capital* (to which Rae also devoted a great deal of attention), history and the coordination and exposition of what we arrived at.

You will please note that there was not the slightest possibility that this was going to bring masses of workers to the WP or to ourselves. Nevertheless, with immense energy and devotion we applied ourselves to this work, the three of us, in a manner that cannot be excelled to this very day. You psychologists, America has many of you, here is some psychology for you to play about with—although I must ask you not to write to me about it—there were the three of us addressing ourselves to a colossal task, not only against the bourgeoisie, but against the leaders of the movement of which we were members, and by which we lived. But we were doing something. We were doing something that mattered, at any rate it mattered to us. Is there any such spirit in the organization today? You know best. For my part it does not exist among us. In 1941 we couldn't teach anybody anything, because we recognized and tackled the fact that before we could teach we had to learn something. How the movement developed is a story that in my opinion ought to be told. But here I have to say only two points which are of direct and immediate, and life-or-death application—not two, in reality three, although two of them were very definitely ours, our achievement.

1) What we were doing, our activity of this very special kind, our apparently purely theoretical perspectives so impressed Lyman [Paine] that he began then and continued for many years to make my existence not only financially possible, but financially feasible. Understand, please, that it happened because he got interested and soon felt himself completely involved in what we were doing and thus was impelled to give all that he had to the work. I can assure you that I have no idea where we would have been and what we would have done without it. All I have to say is this, that a revolutionary group which cannot win such support has only itself to blame.

2) The same range and profundity, although apparently abstract and remote from practical results, from immediate results, won another of our greatest victories. I remember going to Chicago and meeting G[race] for a discussion. A woman of immense qualifications, great abilities and great energy. There was a little difficulty at first but in the end we won her for ourselves. An immense addition without which we would not have been able to do the things that we did.

3) The third point was not so much our decision but nevertheless we carried it through and it was in its way as valuable as the other two. We sent a number of our people to Detroit, and being what we were, we made a contact with the vanguard of the American labor movement such as none of the workers who went to Detroit were able to make.

I want you to note those three as integral part of our movement's development. I do not mean to say that we met this or that individual in Detroit who joined us. That was important. But I mean something else. I mean that being what we were, and training and educating ourselves as we were doing, [we] made a contact with the labor movement in Detroit far deeper, more profound and more educative than the others who came from New York.

The climax of this work came in what is the central production of our movement, *State Capitalism and World Revolution.*[9] I shall have in time to take up with you what that document means, why we ought to republish it, and more importantly, how we ought to republish it. This, however, does not concern us here except to say this: other political movements have gone to pieces. They don't know where they stand. They are in immense confusion about the attitudes to take to the tremendous and urgent political issues of the day. We are not. We know where we stand and no events that take place, however great the scope, are able to upset us or confuse us. That we owe to that document. People who leave us have to find all sorts of personal or subordinate reasons, or they have to break with Marxism altogether, but *State Capitalism and World Revolution* remains a rock of stability and the basis of progress and meeting new developments. You should know the mess which modern European thought finds itself, and American thought as well, that *State Capitalism and World Revolution* settled.

It is in my opinion the finest document, Marxist document, on the development of modern politics, world politics, that I know. What matters to us is how we were able to print it.

If you work hard you will find in that document a) the Hegelian dialectic; b) Marx's *Capital*; c) Leninism; d) the history of our movement; e) the history and development of the world working-class movement and particularly the American working-class movement; f) a view of Western thought on the whole, in its relation to Marxist and particularly Stalinist thought.

That is a comprehensive preparation for the writing of a comprehensive document. In other words, it was the result of ten years of serious work at the fundamentals of Marxism in the most comprehensive sense and of the closest and most intimate contact with the American working-class movement.

Now along with that and as a matter of fact as a preparation of ourselves we published the following:

a) a complete study of the Russian Question, the most comprehensive that had been done to my knowledge in the Marxist movement so far;

b) the economic-philosophical documents of Marx. Some of you will notice that of late years Moscow and a number of philosophically or politically minded people have published these and are rowing amongst themselves in analysis of it. We, a small group of people within another group, published that document;

c) I wrote for our education and understanding, including my own, some eighty thousand words on dialectic applied to Marxism. Among ourselves we call it "The Nevada Document";[10]

d) *The American Worker*,[11] one of the first serious studies of the actual life of a worker in the plant. This you will note was not the politics of "Plenty for All." It showed the deep and profound comprehension we had of what constitutes Marxist politics;

e) made a fundamental analysis of our politics in terms of social forces in the country. Those in reality constitute the essence of the two *Balance Sheets*;[12]

f) an analysis of world politics in *The Invading Socialist Society*.

Not a single one of these could have been considered as aiming at winning over any trade unionists or workers in the plant. But it was by means of these that we were able ultimately to produce *State Capitalism and World Revolution* and everything I have listed appears in that work. If you look you will see. And at the same time we were constantly winning over to our side a number of intellectuals and workers. In other words by our concern with the most fundamental premises of Marxism (and this, mind you, includes the kind of contact we made with Detroit) we added to our forces and to our original political strength. I believe I have established the basic principles sufficiently to move rapidly on. We split from the SWP and we went our own way.

During that period we organized ourselves and we published:

a) *Mariners, Renegades and Castaways*[13]

b) *Indignant Heart*[14]

c) various pamphlets dealing with the working-class movement in Detroit.

In all these we broke new ground. We continued along the lines that we had started in 1941. Now I want to tell you in two paragraphs what has happened to us.

If I had remained in the U.S. free to work and move around, if only in the limited fashion in which I was allowed to move by the U.S. law, by now we would have had the following:

a) a serious book by Rae on the development of Leninism, its historical origins and its relations to the present day, not that nonsense that she has published.

b) a book by G[race] on dialectical materialism for the ordinary person, politically profound, and nevertheless able to be grasped by the ordinary reader.

c) a book by William on the Civil War that would have been ready by 1960 to celebrate the beginnning of the Civil War, and certainly a book by 1963 to celebrate the one hundredth anniversary of the Emancipation Proclamation.

d) I had intended to lay the basis for a comprehensive and penetrating work on the Negro Question in the U.S. by myself.

e) We would have had a large pamphlet or a book on the Negro Question along the lines *Correspondence* has been working.

f) we would have had a pamphlet on the Woman Question.

g) we would have had a comprehensive work on the situation of the working class in Detroit.

We not only would have had them—we would have been able to break through and get bourgeois publication of some, if not all, of these. You will remember I began by saying what I was oriented to almost instinctively as far back as 1931. There has been a consistent line and development along the line up to 1951 and during the last two years that I remained afterward. You may think what you like, and I don't mean to be rude, but I know that if I had been around, and able to move around the U.S., that is what our organization would have achieved; and as sure as day we would have continued to win over people, workers and intellectuals, in the way that we won them over in 1941, and followed the course that we followed. That is our movement. That is the past of our movement and that will be its future or it will fall apart.

The second paragraph is to tell you what you know. From the time I left, what we did between 1941 and 1953 disappeared from us. We were unable not only to start something new and to do what we should have been able to do within a new sphere and by means of our independence. We never even were able to continue what we had done for twelve years with such immense success. Think it over. Discuss it. Work at it. Because on your understanding of this depends your future success or total disintegration. I contributed substantially to the failure. After I came to England in 1953 (God how it tires me to think of it) I spent my time quite often wrecking my right hand writing letters (with carbon copies) to Lyman and Rae, trying to guide them toward what seemed to me the proper leadership of the organization. Even now when I think of it, of the work I used to do, I feel distressed. It is perhaps the only thing in my life to which I look back not so much with bitterness but with regret, with recognition of the fact that I wasted my strength, my time and my physical health on something that was absolutely useless. That I shall never do again.

For what I should have done, it is now as clear as day to me, from the very moment that I landed in England, was primarily to analyze the world political situation, the place of America in it, and the functions of a small organization dealing with our own organization as a center. Instead I committed the tremendous mistake of trying to correct and develop individuals without relation to what had made us what we had arrived at, the fundamental politics of the situation. I hope that what I am saying is clear. That is what I am and that is what I propose to do. You all are only about a dozen or less. It has never at any time crossed my mind, never, that you all were not worth my paying the kind of attention to you which, if I devoted it to something else, would bring results. Never. I have just spent five years in the West Indies and, owing to an illness chiefly, I have been able to penetrate and develop my conception of Marxism in a manner that was behind me when I left Europe in 1957. I mention this because that is the way I am, that is the way years have developed me, and I am trying to tell you that is the way in which you have to develop yourselves in order that your own organization should develop and you should attract people to you. There is no other way.

The last thing I have to say is this. It is a result of my practical experience with what was no more than bourgeois nationalist politics, that I shall be able to write I hope the best and most fruitful analysis of Leninism that has yet been made. I have it all set. It is only time and opportunity that I need. I started in 1931 by instinct. After thirty years it is now stronger than ever, more comprehensive, more developed. I wish you all the same. I wish at any rate that this will help you to realize yourselves. I shall write again tomorrow but this letter is finished.

J.

January 3, 1963

My dear Marty,

This is the first letter of the new year. The holidays have intervened in our sequence. But I hope from now on to keep this series (and whatever may follow it) steadily going perhaps four or five days a week.

They are very difficult to do. The temptation is to go into the long needed and much overdue analysis of the general economic and political situation and then draw the political conclusions which become necessary to us in that general situation. That is where I know we have gone wrong in the past, particularly during the last few years, and I haven't got to preach what ought to be done. That is not the main task. The thing to do is myself to do and to show by example and definitive procedures outlined, what we have to do in order to recover our fundamental basis and our fundamental perspectives (I wonder how many people will read the above and understand it; or if they do not understand it, take the necessary pains and troubles to fight with it until they do.)

Over and over again through the years that I worked with them I had to tell Grace and Rae, "You both of you will spend hours, days and weeks on a section of Hegel or on a chapter of Marx, sometimes on a single paragraph. But what I can never get you both to do is to pay the same attention to the problems of the organization as an organization." I have said that to them twenty times each if I have said it once. It is that that we have to break.

1) The first thing the organization has to do is to be active and to know what it is doing and why. At the present time you have to do the following, now at once.

a) You have to see to it that these letters are promptly reproduced and distributed. I don't know exactly how that ought to be done. S[elma] and I have been wondering if it would be worthwhile to type them straight on a stencil. She is doubtful if the typing will be accurate enough, hard enough in every line to allow you to reproduce at once. At any rate now without delay that is what you all have to do, to decide and take steps to work out a way of rapidly reproducing all these letters in an accurate and presentable manner.

Now I want you to note particularly that I believe these letters should be distributed not only to members but also to friends and people whom you think will be interested. They are going to form a pretty complete series. Part of your preparation also for distribution must include having a certain number of them in reserve so that everyone at short notice will be able to get some in sequence and hand them over to someone to whom they will be, or may be, of some use. Some you will ask to return these documents. Others you will decide to let them retain them because they may be of some use. This is a matter that should be taken in hand at once, and worked out quickly, accurately and neatly. This is what is new. We are not going to ask people to join us because we are going to instruct the proletariat to be the vanguard of the revolution. Our general purposes are clear. But today we have to get back into our heads what I always had in mind and the rest of us, particularly the leadership, following me, always had in theirs. We attracted well meaning and socialistic people, workers above the average and serious intellectuals, to our organization. This is one step. We cannot continue to drift along as we drifted along during the past few years. We have to pull ourselves together and restore what we have lost and in addition do what the general circumstances of the age require. That I shall come to.

2) The second point is that the account of our conference should have been treated in the same way. I have not yet seen any account of the conference. I have been waiting anxiously for it. I have seen instead a document intended for the general public. Very good. But the organization, the members of the organization and friends and people likely to be interested (I am sticking to the formula), have a right to know immediately what the conference did and our report of it. We have no secrets. If we quarrel, well then we quarrel. We put it in our report and to hell with those people who think less of us because we quarrel at a conference. Have a certain number of copies available for friends and contacts. When you talk to a new contact be able to let him know what you have been doing by putting in his hands an account of your latest conference. People are won over it is true by conversation and (this is most profound and I shall have to go into it in some detail) the kind of person they see you are, because by that they are instinctively judging your organization and what it will mean for them. But prepare the document. Prepare it in time (you all are terribly late with this one), prepare it accurately and so that it looks well, pull the organization together by a rapid preparation and distribution of it. Keep your friends and contacts informed. And put aside a reasonable number of copies so that when you meet people and talk to them about the organization you will be able to hand out a copy of what you have been doing.

3) Work. I sent you a draft of a pamphlet. I consider that pamphlet very important. I asked also for any view, long or short, or material which might be useful, etc. I have not heard a word. I don't know what you are doing with it or how you have decided to deal with it. But please understand that this is the political work of the organization. In the old days that never happened between those of us who were responsible for the documents and programs of the organization. We took these matters seriously. You all are few in number. You have had a bad and a hard time. I am merely telling you now what with utmost certainty and confidence of success I would do and see to it that those who were nearest to me would do in order once more to restore to the organization what it has lost. I am not writing any private encouragement or wise instructions to Marty to tell him how to lead. I have no more time for such nonsense. If I have something to tell him that I think he alone should know or should know first, then I shall do so. But what I have to say in regard to the rebuilding and development and experience of the organization and its members I have to say to everybody.

4) Please get in contact with William. I would suggest that three or four of you, or two or three, go to see him, that is to say, make an appointment with him to have a talk with him. I suggest that you place before him the possibil-

ity or the urgency of his doing a pamphlet which you all will print in, I think the time is November 1963, a century after the Gettysburg Address. It should come out about a month before and it should be well advertised even before that. The title should be something along these lines: first line, Gettysburg; then the second line should or could be something like this: The Negroes, the Battle and the Speech, or, The People, the Battle and the Speech; dedicated to the Negro People.

All the critics and the babblers can have a fine time pointing out what they would entitle it instead, as if they had been thinking about this and nothing else for the past two years. The point is to organize a proper approach to William, let him know that you think him perfectly able to do this, that you want him to do it and you undertake the responsibility of publishing. That is what we used to do. That is how we used to make people aware that we were alive, the correct people, and that is how we used to know that we were alive.

William may probably give some trouble. That is part of the difficulty of building an organization. You have to have patience and determination. You watch him closely and you go back and keep on going at him. Unless something has happened to his mentality I can't think of anyone in the U.S. more capable of doing that than William. You will have to be adaptable and full of resource. William may not be in a situation to do a lot of work of the specific kind required. That does not trouble you. You maneuver and try to get him at least to give three talks, or any number that you can on the subject. He will probably be able to talk. Take what he says on a tape. Type it out and then give him the scripts to work on them. That is precious stuff if you can get him to do anything at all. The copy of any scripts that you may give him or that he may do send immediately to me and I will comment on them. But that is the way to get down to business, for the organization being the kind of organization that it is, to set out to do the kind of work that it can do and which will be effective. You can't wait till the month before or two weeks before the date of the centenary and then expect to rush to whip up something. What happens is that you and not the thing gets whipped up.

5) I gather from evidence that I will not go into that there are a lot of young people around nowadays who are looking for something to which they can attach themselves, something which looks as if it means something. Not only have I got evidence to that effect, but in the U.S. in particular (and I shall be going into that, the specific position of a small organization in the U.S.), there are people not only waiting but anxious to get themselves involved in something more than day-to-day. I give you one example which I

would undertake and feel that unless there were all sorts of cantankerous people or objective obstacles in the way, I and my group of associates would succeed. It is this. I understand that you have not got to look for but you actually have someone who knows Russian or is able to translate it. Even if you don't have, get somebody. In the same way we translated the economic-philosophical manuscripts years ago before the present philosophers of alienation discovered it and began to draw their ridiculous and untenable conclusions, there is now a document in Russian that is crying to be translated and which would have been translated before if we had continued along our own natural road. It was a document published in 1927 in Russian, the account of the first meeting of the Shop Stewards in Russia. I cannot go into their history now. Deutscher in one of his books has made a reference to the volume, and a very superficial reference it is.[15] That Shop Steward Movement actually wanted to take over control of industry or the running of it entirely, even before the union movement had established itself. This was too much even for Lenin and the Bolsheviks. The Trade Union movement as an organized social force was barely in existence. But since the Hungarian Revolution in particular, this movement of the factory committees in Russia in 1917 and the course it followed afterwards has assumed enormous importance. This importance is bound to grow. In time it will be of far more historical significance and contemporary application as the beginning of the road that is facing the working-class movement, of far more importance, historical significance than these economic-philosophic manuscripts. Get somebody to find the thing, to read it, and not to translate it in full but to prepare what will amount to an accurate pamphlet giving the essential details of the problem. Let me inform you what you have to do. You can get somebody to undertake this upon one basis only. You have to convince them and impress them with the conviction that you and your organization, the people whom you represent, feel that this is a vital document and that you want to get it out. You show that you have something, or represent something, which you communicate.

We live in peculiar times. Before I end this series I shall go into some outline of the fact that never before has the need and at the same time the possibility of a completely international socialist order been so near and so urgent as at the present time. That is a matter not of feeling and desire but of strictly objective analysis. Those are the facts of the case, the obvious facts. Nothing but a tremendous effort on behalf of hundreds of millions of people can check the drive to inevitable disaster to which capitalism has led us. This is the time when those who were working with us, this is the time that they choose to rush off into all sorts of individualistic and petty-bourgeois adventures.

But this is the time that we have to work, to do what is before us, what we can do, what nobody else is doing, what has to be done and what we will not be able to do if we do not pay attention to what is in front of us. The plans that I outline above for you are strictly within your competence. I shall now tell you a few things about the way you ought to conduct yourselves and carry out your business. The points are three in number. Sometimes I shall be very brief in the points that I make. You will please to study them over carefully.

1) We used to meet at the decisive periods of our organization at 629 [Hudson St., New York],[16] about a dozen of us, week after week. All I have to say about that is that I do not remember a single instance when I was late for the meeting. Few of us were late. If anybody was late, it was only about five minutes at most. I do not remember ever having been late. To that I will add that one weekend, I think it was at the time of our split, we had prepared a document of some sixty pages in length. I think it was the day before we were to hand it in, our people looked at it and said that it didn't look good enough and it ought to be done over. Whereupon they sat down and did the whole sixty pages over. That was an organization. Build one of the same kind.

2) James Cannon, in accordance with his experience of the revolutionary movement, an experience lasting over many years, expected that when we joined him in 1947, that we would give trouble. We did not. We were serious people, well trained. What we represented, what we were, is symbolized by his telling Bessie one evening, "What I can't understand is that the Johnsonites don't provoke." We didn't provoke. That is not because we had studied good morals. It was because we were people with a solid past and wide perspectives of our own. Contrary to all the people whom he had known in our position, our behavior was different. I haven't the slightest doubt that if I had remained by now we would have been a very powerful organization touching American life, American political life at many points and attracting many of the young people to us. This is the time when Shachtman chooses to recommend to the young people joining the Democratic Party. That that can happen is due to the fact that we have never believed for many years and do not believe that the single person will make the difference between building the organization and not building it. In the world in which we live, it is not one person but several people together who will build. You will see that in the last chapter of *Mariners*. It is policy which matters. Today the world is one. I find that the essentials of politics, the essentials are the same in Britain, the United States, in the West Indies and in Ghana.

3) We therefore have to pay attention to what is in front of us but at the same time we have the whole world and particularly the history of our movement behind us. I am certain, as certain as I have ever been of anything, that I will write my book on Lenin and present him in a manner and with a reality and conviction that he has never been presented before. I thought I knew. It has taken me many years to find out what he was driving at. It also took him many years to find out what he should drive at. Nevertheless I shall in the course of these letters make some references to him. If our organization did not provoke, if it finally became what it did, it is because even to the extent that our limitations allow we followed as far as we could the principles, the principles, mind you, established by Lenin. One of the most important that guided me and which I recommend to you was the principle established in the "Testament."[17] To me at least the idea there that most impressed itself on me was not the analysis of the differences and the probable explosion between Stalin and Trotsky, although that was profound enough. It was what he wrote about Zinoviev and Kamenev. He had worked with them, or rather they with him, for some twenty years. In exile together they had written some of the classic works of Leninism. It was said of them that they imitated his handwriting and laughed at his jokes before he made them. Their history in Boshevism, particularly after 1917, is something that I may tell you one day. It is very instructive, that history. But what stamped itself on my mind, never left it, and which I hope you will do also is this. On his death bed and only then, Lenin wrote for the Politburo the following observation: Z and K had behaved very badly in the revolution at the time of October. That, he said, should not be held against them. But, he added, note the careful phrasing, their behavior was not accidental. In other words, highly placed as they were in the Soviet State, and they occupied the very highest positions, on his death bed he thought it well to tell other members of the Politburo that in any similar critical situation, Z and K would behave in the same way.

It is not only the acuteness of the observations. It is not only the fact that under those conditions and knowing them as he did, he was prepared to keep them in the highest posts. What matters most is that he kept his mouth shut about it and said the words only when he knew he was going and he thought that who remained behind in charge should know these things. Note finally that he did not say it to one or two behind the back of Z and K. He wrote it to the committee of which they both were members. You all are as you are. But the best that you can do is to guide yourselves by the best of your ancestors.

J.

January 7, 1963

My dear Marty,

As a matter of fact, I don't know whether I should continue to address these letters to you, that is to say, as a matter of form. I think that the address should be: dear friends. Comrades is a little too narrow. Forgive me if I keep on saying that these letters (and later when they become a somewhat integrated sequence) are a sort of permanent manifesto as to what we are, what we are doing and what we have been.

This represents work.

The specific work that we, more particularly you, all have to do at the present time. Remember that I suggest first of all that you work out ways and means of reproducing them in sufficient numbers. It seems to me, although you all have to decide that, it seems to me that typing in sufficient quantity is out of the question. I want a certain number of everything. To put it crudely, I want to have *here,* to begin with, at the very least a dozen copies of every letter, of every document. Each member over there, as I tried to develop in my last letter, must have some. Included must be the report of the conference. (I see that that work is being done. I find it pretty slow. As I see it from here it has been placed upon one person. I don't see it that way. In addition I shall have to write to you as part of these letters a serious response, critique, to the report of the conference. This too must be reproduced in sufficient numbers to become a part of the material by which we make ourselves known to people and by which we get to know what we are, what we are doing, and our individual response to it.)

Let me continue with work, work that is to be done now.

I see that two of the comrades are busy working out a statement of what we are. I see that you all have decided what its length should be. I had thought of giving my ideas as to the form and content — more or less of a draft. I think that would be wrong. You all are the persons best fitted to orient all ideas intended for the people of the United States. I shall await the draft and give my views on it. That is a very different thing from my giving ideas of a draft and you all working on it there. That relation we will have to work out properly. But it is one that we shall always have to be on guard to see is most effectively done. The important thing in my mind is that anything that is to be effectively done in Britain (and on the Continent, a very important business to which I have already referred: do you recall?) I see as having its center in the U.S.

Still in regard to work. I believe that your next step, in fact immediate step, must be some work on *Facing Reality.* What I suggest is this: two of your members or your members and a friend should get to work upon a four-page, perhaps an eight-page summary of specific aspects of *Facing Reality*. At least six of an eight-page memorandum should deal with what small organizations aim at in regard to the publication of a paper, and in general. In fact that is what the little pamphlet should be about. However, included in the pamphlet, preferably at the end, should be about a page of what the rest of the pamphlet deals with and a statement, or rather an indication to purchase. I hope you have in mind what I am driving at. This document too will be one of our standard things for handing out. I shall need a few, with some copies of *Facing Reality* so as to be able to propagandize the idea of the book, what we are, what we are trying to do and also with a view to sales. Please don't bother yourself about this having to be done by some highly experienced person. That is not so. Give the work to two people who will discuss what is to be done and then prepare their draft. I believe there should be a number of quotations from the book in this pamphlet which will not be necessarily printed but will be done according to the particular means of publication which you all have worked out.

Still in regard to work. Quite recently I have gotten into contact with someone very learned about the theory of the Russian Revolution and its development to the present day. I have learned that in the course of the past thirty years, and probably more, there has only been one reference made in published material, that is to say, in material widely known, to the account published in Russia in 1927 of the Russian factory committees. I knew that there was only one reference I had seen in English.[18] I had been looking about for this for a long time, and the particular reference, the solitary reference, that I know, and that which this man knows, was of quite a different order to what I wanted to know about it, and to what I believed should be published. My view of the significance of those factory committees is entirely different from his. I learned, however, that as far as is known, there is only one copy in England, at the British Museum, although there may be another. There are two volumes, very small. I inquired if it was possible to order copies from Russia. I was told, no, they are long out of print. I was told also that the task of translation would be quite easy because the volumes were not very extensive.

Now I know what that volume will mean to the Marxist movement today and still more what it will mean tomorrow. I can only tell you this much. At all costs, in your place, I would make every effort a) to find out if these volumes are in the U.S., and where they are, if any can be gotten, you never can tell what you can pick up in some bookshop, some Russian bookshop; I shall certainly make some sort of attempt to find out if there are any lying about in Britain. b) I should find somebody who will be willing to translate them. They are of much greater importance than the Economic-Philosophical Manuscripts. In my opinion, if properly translated, and properly introduced, it should not be too difficult to find a bourgeois publisher for them. But if even a bourgeois publisher cannot be found, then if the translation is good, the introduction is good and we are able to make some people understand what is the significance of the publication, we can publish ourselves by finding someone who will stand the expenses; in these cases you often find a printer who is ready to go along with you. That is one of the things, the sort of thing that the working class movement needs and that we can do.

I will be quite astonished (if we have made our activities and perspectives known along the lines I have indicated) I would be quite astonished if we ourselves will not be able to get rid of at least one thousand copies, not only to some intellectuals but also to workers who will be profoundly interested. If I may say so, this is the proletarian counterpart (the modern historical symbol of our problems today, the practical concrete problems of the working class) that the Economic-Philosophical Manuscripts represented in theory. (You begin to understand now, I hope, the mess that those two girls have made of us and of themselves by adventuring off in the way that they have done.) Nevertheless we know what we want to do, what we have to do. Work at this please. It is essentially a matter at present of seeking for the necessary information. You will find a page or two on the matter in the book of Deutscher on the Russian trade union movement.

This ends the section in this letter on the work, the practical work, that you have to do now. In preparing these letters in some organized form and in a connected way with other publications, we educate ourselves and we inform people of what we intend to do and we touch chords among various intellectuals and interested workers as to the kind of people we are and what it is and who it is that they can join up with. I am saying it over and over again because I know how many times and how often these things have to be said in order that they can be absorbed and accepted and in order, this is the essential part, that they drive out the false ideas and the particular types of outlook which those false ideas bring with them and which have sunk deep into our organization. It will not be easy, I assure you, to get rid of those and to get the new ones into our heads so that the discussion and the imagination and the organization of what we have to do become a normal and regular part of our activity and our discussions.

II

As I go on, I am learning what I have to do in these letters. First of all, as you see in that earlier part and in the previous one, I am making it clear that we have certain types of work to do and to do now, and that we get into our heads that we are not a special vanguard group of people, but that from the beginning, in all our activity, we not only *declare* that we are not the embryo of a vanguard party but that we do something f? more important, convincing and revealing to us our own way: *we act in that way.*

I now have to tackle the preparation for a total clearing out from our minds of the Trotskyist heresy of opposition to socialism in a single country which is no more, as time has gone on, than a section of the Stalinist bureaucracy. That I intend to show very clearly but with the necessary brevity (brevity is indeed the soul of wit. But it is a very hard soul to arrive at, much harder than the Christian soul.) I have found that Trotsky's ideas are now the standby and the source of radical and would-be revolutionary activity among all sections of the radical bourgeoisie and the leaders of what should be the revolutionary proletariat. That is not going to be a simple matter to get rid of. It is, I believe, what dominates the conceptions of millions of workers, for example, in France and Italy. Trotsky began it, and undoubtedly he saw it (and when he started) it did have elements of the socialist revolution in it. But a false policy inevitably moves in a certain direction and ends up being the weapon, and the most effective weapon, of the counter-revolution. It will take quite a few sessions or letters to get this clear. We need it because we need to know what we are doing and we need to know what we are up against. There is every sign, by the way, that this is beginning to break in the quarrel between Russia and China. You will appreciate how difficult it is for me to write to you about this instead of being able to speak to you. But I have to do the best I can and you have to do the same.

The fundamental problem of the revolutionary movement today is that by the vast majority of people, the world is viewed as a conflict between two blocs. That is the problem. On the one hand, the democracies led by the United States; and on the other hand, Russia and China and the satellite states which all in their different way represent the break with imperialism, and still continue in a corrupt degenerated way to represent the revolution, the unleashing of the revolutionary forces, which began in Russia in 1917. That is the problem: the corruption of the revolutionary movement in Russia, the tremendous evils, the mischief, the straightforward political mischief, that it has accomplished and is still accomplishing, all that we have to put up with and do our best to correct, even in time to break with it, but nevertheless to establish ourselves with it now because that represents the opposition to the imperialism and capitalism which we have known for centuries and which Lenin and Marx and all the others fought against.

That is the essential corruption of our day and though I may not be able to do much with it in this letter, I shall continue one aspect of it in a second.

Just for a moment get your minds out of the problems of Marxism in the United States. Just realize that you have to think in these days as international socialists, as Marxists. Marx and Engels always did that. Lenin founded the Bolshevik Party and the Third International on that basis. You have got to get that into your heads and to make everybody whom you meet understand two things: a) that that is how you are seeing the world and politics, national and international; and b) get hold of this please, get hold of it, this letter is an example of it, that while that is the basis of your thinking and the particular method which you apply to all fundamental international and national problems (there is not much difference between them today), while that is how you think and that is how you approach problems, nevertheless, you have concrete, immediate, practical tasks to perform which you are performing and in which they can participate. That is the vision, the mental conceptions, which I am trying to place in your minds, to get you not only to know but to feel, to live by.

Now once more to this question of the blocs and to your situation as Marxists. What is constantly in my own mind is that in 1945 three million people in Italy joined what they considered to be a revolutionary Marxist party devoted to the idea of overthrowing capitalism by socialist revolution. The Italian Communists were also in complete charge of the Italian union movement. There was not a dissimilar situation in France. People keep on talking about how Marx was wrong, about how he foretold the revolution in the advanced countries, whereas it has only happened, or only been made possible in the backward countries. Get it into your heads, please, (and this is only the first of a few fundamental points, without which Marxism is nonsense, that have been entirely lost and which we have to restore first of all in our own heads) that the bourgeois regime, or whatever regime is in power, breaks down and is obviously unable to continue to rule or to keep any order in the state. That is what happened in France and in Italy in 1945. In addition the outburst of the population with the aim of replacing the rulers of the old society with the new, took place on a scale which both Marx and Engels, and Lenin would have been (perhaps I do them some injustice) absolutely amazed at. That is what we have to know and to study, not what Marx meant by alienation and what he didn't mean: these people not only corrupt themselves but they corrupt everybody who pays any attention to them.

In other words, the socialist revolution in the modern sense actually appeared, showed itself in 1945, far more powerfully, far more concretely than in 1917.

The idea that the American army was able to suppress this revolution is a lot of nonsense. An American army could not have suppressed a revolutionary movement of which the would-be leadership consisted of three million members of the population, and in addition, the backing of the whole organized trade union movement as was the situation in Italy. The details I shall go into with you some time. But what happened was not merely that the Communist Party misled the movement, etc. The critics of Trotsky who have pointed out that to keep saying that the Stalinist Party under the leadership of Stalin misled the workers in Germany, in France, in China, and everywhere the revolution came up, to which Trotsky devoted the last years of his life, was merely to say what amounted to this, that the working class was unable to lead its own revolution and therefore allowed itself to be fooled by a party led by the Russians. That argument is unanswerable.

What happened was that the great masses of the working class were themselves dominated by the conception of the two blocs. You don't fool three million people. The revolution of 1917 was a tremendous event in the development of modern history and modern people. And the masses of the workers everywhere did not merely follow the Communist Party, being merely stupid and misinformed. They saw essentially Russia and all that it was doing (and now there has been added to it China) as the opposition to the imperialists and the capitalists whom they knew for hundreds of years and whose crimes and mistakes had sunk into their bones. The Communist Parties did not so much fool them, the Communist Parties themselves were dominated by the conception of the two blocs. We cannot attack them too severely, without understanding. Trotsky himself to the end of his days, despite all his attacks upon Stalinism, was dominated by, and in various ways propagated, the conception of the two blocs. One has to get rid of the conception of masses of people as stupid, misled, corrupted, and so forth. The Russian Revolution was so tremendous an event in human history and in modern history that it affected the conceptions and attitudes of a whole generation of people. And when after the war there was the possibility that people would begin to understand (and it takes a new generation to grasp the essence of what is happening), the Chinese Revolution came in 1950. Mao Tse-Tung joined up with Stalin (although Stalin had been opposed to the Chinese Revolution and had told Mao so), and fortified and strengthened in popular conception what the Russian Revolution had done and what people still believed it was doing in its opposition to Marx's capitalism and Lenin's imperialism.

Now I have to go on in this letter to make two points on which you will have to work and which I shall develop later. But it is essential that you get in your mind these two essential points of the political situation today.

1) The first and *immediate* point is that there is taking place a split between those two forces, Russia and China, which together in historical se-

quence and by their unity, have re-enforced and developed this conception of the two blocs. About the split I have to tell you only a few sentences for which I hope you are prepared and are able to work out yourselves. It is not a split between counter-revolutionary or opportunist Russia and revolutionary China. It is no more than a split between two branches of the bureaucracy of the bloc. Mao and the Chinese Communist Party are no more revolutionary than Stalin and the Stalinists were revolutionary during the Third Period. This is a bureaucracy defending itself and, when it is convenient, I shall be able to go at some length into the position of the Chinese Communist Party and not only to go into it but to indicate how you yourselves or some sections or friends of the organization, can go into it and make it clear.

This is profoundly important for you. Exactly for you. The reason is this. While you are doing the practical work which I have outlined and which undoubtedly you will develop, while you are doing this and you draw and attract people to take an interest in what you are doing, and to one degree or another participate and actually join in with you, you absolutely have to be able to do a) what is your duty, otherwise you have no cause for existence; and b) what people of the kind who are attracted to you have a right to expect from you. In this Russia vs. China business in which China is masquerading all over the place as the Marxist-Leninist revolutionary wing of what everybody calls "the socialist states," it is vital, a necessary part of a Marxist movement in the U.S. to be able to show and to explain what is really taking place. You do this and you keep on doing it so that after a time people learn to expect it from you. That is your task and it is a pretty urgent task.

However we can't do everything. We are a small group of people and we have to spread out our tasks. But it is at any rate good and necessary to know what is the function of a small Marxist organization. I hope in time to assist you or some friends of yours in taking up this question. You see, by the way, what a fool G[race] has made of herself by runnning off and supporting the Marxism of J[ames] B[oggs]. When I speak sharply and with a certain contempt of his determination to expose Marxism, etc., it was not any personal or subjective attitude, I can assure you. It was obvious to me from the very start that of these and similar problems he knew nothing but I hoped first of all that he would know that he knew nothing and that G. would help him. That is point number one. That is what we have to do.

2) Point number 2, however, is of tremendous scope, and the first thing we have to get in mind is to understand it ourselves. We claim that we have broken with Leninism and the conception of the Vanguard Party. We claim that the Trotskyists have continued with that and that is the reason why they have failed to get any distance. We must understand that their conception of the

Vanguard Party is the continuation up to today of the Russian Revolution which was successful by means of a Vanguard Party. In other words, these so-called intellectuals, theoreticians and Marxists, with Trotsky at the head, have all been and are still carrying on a conception that is now nearly fifty years old and which the world has entirely outgrown. Follow me closely here, please, because I can't go into it with the fullness and detail that I could if I were speaking to you. However, I shall try my best to do it briefly because if I do not do it now, all that I have been saying before in this particular letter will be somewhat abstract and therefore be something mental, intellectual.

I have to treat it historically. The Second International represented a certain stage in the development of capitalism and the organization, experience and consciousness of the working class as a part of capitalist society. Marx first and Engels after, were more or less satisfied with that organizational expression of the stage of development of the proletariat. What happened in 1917 was that Lenin broke with that. What he substituted was the necessity for a vanguard party. That I shall have to go into with you. I have touched upon it in *Facing Reality*. But the vanguard party represented a certain stage of development of the working class in Europe and the advanced countries; but particularly it must be seen in relation to the fact that the proletariat had not only to organize itself in regard to the new stage of capitalistic development but it also had to fight against the well-established and well-rooted Second International. Now I have referred to France and Italy in 1945 — the significance of those two movements and their repercussions all over the world was this. There was no longer any need for a vanguard party. The proletariat itself became the vanguard and therefore one of the subsidiary necessities for the vanguard party, the fight against the Second International, was solved in action by the proletariat itself. We live by what happened in 1848 in France and what happened in 1871 in Paris. Let us realize that the whole vanguard party conception was rejected by the proletariat itself, and the proletariat in Italy and in France, although differing in form, is in essence the world proletariat of post-World War II. We therefore can arrive at this, that the whole conception of a vanguard party has been rejected by the proletariat itself.

The Second International has been rejected also. That it appears to flourish in Britain and other places is just a lot of nonsense and fakery. The proletariat has no more fundamental belief in it, even to carry out parliamentary procedures than it has in its capacity to establish universal peace. The Second International is dead. Politically speaking in regard to changing society, it is dead. The Third International is on its way out. It is my opinion that China saved it. Now there is the split with China. These Communist Parties everywhere are in tremendous confusion. They have to make a choice. And they are being made to face certain realities. The fundamental reality is that they are no longer needed. A political party of that kind is no longer needed. The proletariat will have to find out its own ways and means. It has always done so. Every class has always found out its own ways and means. It took a long time at times. Usually it waited for quite a while and then with great violence did the work of a century in two or three years. Today, however, and I leave this with you to work out and I shall take it up some time later, the proletariat has got two obvious problems to settle. The first is the problem of atomic war and universal destruction. The second is the relation with the revolution of the colonial territories, with which we have to include, for example, the situation in Latin America.

Let me tell you what are the points that I will have to develop in regard to these things in the near future, the lines along which we have to think for our own salvation. These are the lines. The bourgeois state is totally unable to bring world peace. Take that literally please. They cannot possibly do it. Such is the economy, such is the scope of world politics, that any solution, even a temporary solution, is beyond them, all that they can do is to fail. What is required is that the world proletariat and the colonial peoples in the world themselves become convinced that war and all the things that go with it, the national safety, etc., must come to an end. The mass of the population, led by the proletariat, has got to believe that that is the way it has to live. The problem can no longer be left in the hands of a political grouping whether bourgeois or proletarian, with whom it is a matter of political policy and political arrangements. That is finished. Vast numbers of people in the world today know that that is no solution whatever. It is very hard to understand that the population has not to follow a correct policy but to think of life in different terms. This has not got to be a policy to be carried out but accepted as a way of living.

We have had one example of it before. In the Thirty Years War, Germany was reduced to pieces and the European people fought to a bitter end the last of the great religious wars. After that one, the masses of people, bourgeois, landlords, proletarians and peasants, accepted as a way of life, that people could have their own religions and there was no necessity to have any religious wars. It was possible to live that way.

We are now on the edge either of a pit of disaster or a total conception that we have to live differently, not depend on leaders who will work out a policy that will prevent national and international conflicts and war. This is very hard to explain, but I shall go into it some time later. However, the colonial revolution is intimately connected with this conception of the proletariat. They are tied up in this business of the two blocs. They say that they are non-aligned.

But in reality they are stuck with the choice of one or the other. Look at India today. Here is my last sentence. Only when the proletariat breaks completely with the conception of the two blocs, and all sorts of party politics, will the advanced countries be able to involve with them the hundreds of millions who are making the colonial revolution. Grapple with this. For when you have it and you do the work that is before your eyes, you will not only be going somewhere but it will be impossible for you to be shifted.

J.

January 20, 1963

My dear Marty,

First of all I want to emphasize to everybody the imperative need for a rapid and immediate reproduction of letters, etc., and their quick and organized dispatch to whomever is on your list for them. I also need to have a certain number with equal rapidity. It is absolutely impossible for any one set of people to carry on discussions by themselves. In every respect, fundamental and particular discussion and everything that flows from it, is international. And with all those who are not licking Khrushchev's boots, the center of such discussion is the U.S. Furthermore, the sending to you of these letters, or rather the mental and physical organization of them, is a heavy — not burden, nothing is a burden that you want to do more than anything else — but it demands an increasing effort. In a short time it will demand, as I see it, a very great effort indeed. It means that I must have, and almost automatically, a number of old and new ones as they come out. There are people here already whom I talk to and whom I know would benefit immensely and help me tremendously by having these, expecting them, and knowing that they will continue in some sort of order. I notice that you say someone is delaying with photographs of the material. I would be very glad if you see about that, if anything can be done about it, as rapidly as possible. You all there have to decide. You have to decide. But from here I am nervous over everything having to be typed over and then stenciled. Maybe that is the only way. I hope not. You see, I constantly see in front of me, or come across, long extracts, from books and from the British and French press which I could usefully, very usefully indeed, include in these analyses. I feel an inhibition about sending those extracts, etc., to you, an inhibition even towards incorporating them into these letters. I want you to understand, therefore, that I am handicapped and will continue to be handicapped in what I am doing until I know for certain that you all have worked out a fairly simple, quick and unburdensome method of rapid and consistent dispatch. It may ultimately come to nothing but typing over and stenciling. Maybe, I don't know. You have to decide. I hope not to hear from you very soon about what you are doing. That will mean very little to me. I hope to receive results.

I am very glad that you all have been thinking about me and have decided to send me all the books, papers, etc., that I need from the U.S. There is one thing that I want to express about this profoundly important matter. People who have something to send that they think of special interest should send it more or less through one person who will be in charge of it. All I can say is that I have been thinking about it quite a lot and am profoundly glad that you were all thinking about it too. It is these things that matter. I shall refer to that attitude, to an organized and disciplined attitude, very often.

Until I begin to hear from you regularly and consistently, and by you I mean all of you, I have to depend upon myself and my instincts to know what precisely I shall deal with and how it shall be dealt with. As long as one letter is circulating, or rather one copy, that is bound to go on. However there are one or two points that I, trusting to my instincts, my previous experience of the organization, my conversations with people here, and my general analysis of the world political situation (I make that list purposely), I am deciding what I shall take up and how I shall take it up.

I think that central to the existence of people devoted to socialism at the present time is the question of the vanguard party. Primarily I am concerned with what those people who are devoted to Marxism think about the vanguard party; not think, that is a mere phrase, but what they feel in their bones. Now I believe I have said, but I don't mind saying it again, and it is being said all over the place, that Lenin's great contribution to Marxism was the theory and the practice of the vanguard party.

I have made it clear, or rather we have made it clear, that we in 1962 or, beginning in 1951, repudiate that conception. When I get my books and papers together I shall be able to send you some extracts, especially when I know that the distribution of my ideas will be prompt and without burdening the group of you. Nevertheless, I want to insist on two points in regard to the vanguard party:

1. These are the negative points. Lenin as late as 1914 built his whole conception of the vanguard party on the violent repression of democracy by the Tsarist government. There are many things that I say in these letters which some of you will have to work out and prove in detail. I keep on saying, spread these letters around because I know what is troubling a lot of

people. It is absolutely certain that you get responses and interest at various levels, sometimes on a high level and sometimes on a lower level, from all sorts of interested people and groups. Let Shachtman take the youth that he can find into the Democratic Party. We will teach them, and confidently *teach* them what we know. There are things that we as Marxists know. To repeat, therefore, Lenin's conception of the vanguard party was a reaction to specific Russian conditions. He made quite clear that if Russian conditions allowed it, he would have been very happy to have what the British and the Germans and the Belgians, etc., had, the same type of party.

2. Now the second point, another negative point, is that when he formed the Third International, the Second International was a very powerful organization and an organization that by means of clever maneuvering was able at times to present a very leftist front. Nevertheless in all essential matters they continued to be the left wing of capitalism. Under these conditions and because of these conditions, Lenin was forced to transfer the conception of the vanguard party from the specific conditions of Russia to the world at large. It was for the purpose of creating an opposition to the Second International and its continued domination. I want you to note as an example to be followed that when the Second International broke its principles and supported the war, Lenin, while carrying on all sorts of opposition, violent denunciation of his opponents, and organization to the extent that he could, he was away from home (note, please, that that did not bother him; he did what he could wherever he was; and he organized those around him; I ask you to note that, please), Lenin himself worked out why this had happened. He wrote *Imperialism* in order to satisfy himself as the reasons why the Second International had behaved in this way. And in order still further to get his mind clear he studied the *Phenomenology of Mind* by Hegel and did a re-study of the Hegelian *Logic*.

What I am saying is that he settled down to get his mind clear, and the minds of his associates, on the basic issues of the day, one of these being the betrayal of the Second International and, therefore, the need for transferring the ideas built up in Russia to the world working class as a whole. Note please, that while he worked at the *Phenomenology* in order to get his mind clear, in order to write *Imperialism*, he did not hold forth on *Phenomenology* to everybody and anybody. We find out these things afterwards from his private notes. We have to follow along the road, the intellectual road of our ancestors. We start off fortunately from where they left off and we deal with the problems of the day according to the intellectual development of the day. What Lenin did by himself and for his own clarification, that is finished. We are a group of people and can do that in a world where knowledge, procedure, information, have become more and more a matter of association and organization in common. Let me remind you that we believed, at least we thought, that the Third International was finished in 1933. More of that later.

That is dealing with the vanguard question in a negative way. A good organization will itself read up the necessary documents and have itself well fortified in these matters. Now you will be asked the question by Trotskyists poisoned by their doctrine and by other people who are dominated by Stalinist conceptions, not only their theory but practice: what do you propose instead? That is not, I warn you, a very easy question to answer when sitting and talking in a friendly conversation, especially with some unfriendly people. In time I shall be able to send you the exact quote by Lenin in his early writing: that the party in reality reflects the most advanced stage of the working class as an organized body under capitalist production. Not only does he say that as if everybody understood that. It is work for some devoted Marxist to show that, at every stage, that governed his conception of the party, and of the country as a whole with which he was dealing: Russia is the finest example of that. We have to use the same methods. I have already referred, I think, and have no hesitation in referring a second time to the fact that the Bolshevik Party in Russia in 1917 had some seventy-eight thousand members. In Italy in 1943 three million people joined the Communist Party to make the revolution, and the Communist Party had complete control of the trade union movement. That is the situation in the world at large today.

I want to refer particularly to one of the primary questions. International war, hydrogen bombs, and the other types of universal destruction weapons that are being frantically sought for by the whole organized force of government. There is no vanguard of special people who are the most advanced, the most devoted, etc., on the one hand, and the mass of workers and general citizens who have to be educated by this vanguard, etc. That is entirely out of the question today. Negatively, the circumstances which prompted to the formation of a vanguard party have disappeared. Positively, the whole world situation has produced a new perspective towards a new solution. Some time or other (that depends on you, on the way you organize yourselves, and on the way you help me to organize myself and to draw into association with me people who can help me), sometime or other I would like you to note the polarizaton which is taking place in modern society. Lenin once stated with his usual insight and precision the difference between the Soviet *type* of state (note that the word "type" is underlined) and parliamentary democracy. He said that it was the division between legislative and executive functions.

Now what we are seeing today on a world scale is an exemplification and development of that division. The whole Stalinist experiment, the whole Nazi regime, are not the result of evil men. They are the result of the drive towards the unification of the executive and political organization of all aspects of the state. In the democratic countries today you can see a notable example of the same process, taking a very striking form: De Gaulle is the master of France. Find all your reasons — due to the specific situation of French capitalism and the French revolutionary and military tradition and De Gaulle's great services to a beaten France during the war, find them and please find them, because it is necessary to find them. When you have found them, you will find yourself in an awful mess trying to explain how it is that Adenauer occupies and has occupied the same position in Germany. You will then have to explain how it is that Kennedy in the U.S. occupies in regard to these international problems of war, etc., a position that Roosevelt never had. You will find also that Macmillan is master of the Conservative Party in a way that Churchill never was. And what is more striking than all these is that Gaitskell, who has just died, was recognized by all as the center and organizing leader of the Labor Party and represented what psychological journalists and investigators like to call "the image" of the Labor Party in the public mind.

These things are not at all accidental. The very structure of modern society, particularly of contemporary society, compels democratic babbling to subordinate itself to a leader. The issues that have to be decided, economic, political, social, governmental, executive decisions, are not things to be discussed in Parliament. They have to be decided upon, from their very structure, and complication, by a single person in charge of an executive organization. So that democracy itself is today subordinated as far as possible to the executive. What is most striking is that the public, the mass of people, seem to recognize that instinctively, and lean more and more towards supporting a particular individual leader as head or the decisive factor of a political organization, of a government, and at the same time, mind you, recognizing that these are absolutely unable to control, or to have any control over these tremendous issues, some of which are a matter of life and death. Under these circumstances, which can be demonstrated by severe analysis, all the talk or conception of a Leninist vanguard party is the most utter nonsense. That is to be demonstrated by a strict intellectual organization of economic and other objective facts and theories and also by a collaboration and organization of the experience of workers and all other types of people in the economic organization in which they function — you will find that everywhere.

The polarization lies in this, that on the one hand the structures and the objective facts of the world in which we live are driving us, have driven us already, to this concentration upon a single person in charge of the executive, and are responsible for it. On the other hand, all that the politicians of the left can do is one of two things: a) in the democratic countries by vote make one of their men the head of the executive, or b) in the totalitarian countries make the head of the executive outright head of politics and call it socialism. That is the world in which we live. The opposition to it is not the substitution of your man to be head of the executive or the creation of an executive which is the master of politics and in which politics consists only of a cutthroat internal struggle. The solution, not only from abstract theory, but basing itself on the political representation of the proletariat in the very struggle of capitalism, the solution is a *type* (note that "type" is underlined), a type of state based upon "workers' councils in every department of national life." Here we have again an example of Lenin's fundamental dictum that any fundamental change in political thinking and organizational representation of the proletariat or of society came and could only come from the working class.

I want to get this point clear. Khrushchev only a few days ago said that the first interchange of hydrogen bombs in a war would result in the destruction of seven hundred million people. I am not concerned with the number. Maybe it is only seventy million. Maybe it is seven thousand million. I don't know. I don't care. What I am concerned with is that that is the conception which is now in the minds of the vast millions of the world's population and that conception is not subjective but it is the result of economic development and the social and political structures which this economic and scientific development imposes. We now face the necessity not of opposing or substituting a correct policy for a wrong policy. We have to substitute a different structure which will produce an entirely new type of political thought and political action.

I now have to move to a conclusion of this letter. I hope I have destroyed or at least laid the basis for the destruction of all conceptions of the vanguard party. That is finished. What do we do instead? Realize that what is going to be done, what will have to be done, by the great masses of the world's population, will not be done through their being taught by some special group of people. That is out. And the disastrous failure of the Communist International to do anything else but make mischief is sufficient proof of that. There are other examples which I can give you and will give you later when I have got all the documents. What it means is that the population itself to a substantial degree has been educated and is being educated by the march of capitalistic development themselves. We, therefore, as any other group of politically minded persons who realize the situation for what it is, have merely to do what we are able to do, to see to it that we organize ourselves properly to do what we are able to do and what nobody else can do, and a) to make contact with and keep contact with, and develop contact with all those within our immediate or our distant circle, to show them and to demonstrate in fact that we have something, and in this case it so happens that we have the best that one could possibly wish for; b) to make contact with and work sympathetically with all other types of organizations, our own and others, recognizing and getting them to recognize that while we are going to insist upon our own past, our own outlook and our own organization, and nothing will ever move us from that, nevertheless, we realize that where the whole community, so to speak, is involved in direct opposition to one degree or other, the idea, the very conception of a vanguard is unbelievable stupidity. There simply cannot be a vanguard where the whole of humanity is involved and the whole of humanity knows that it is involved.

Of necessity, inevitably, in the mass that is in opposition, there will arise an innumerable number of groups, organizations, people, and individuals even, who are expressing their opposition to this or that but what is in reality an opposition to the whole perspective of universal disaster which is part of our existence today. The Marxist alone can bring all of this into some sort of total perspective. The Marxist alone can do that. But he has to realize that in such a vast environment and such an immense and massive movement against what is going on, he must respect and realize for what they are, the movements of various types of groups and people, whoever they are, whatever they are. His only claim to recognition is the fact that more and more people, these various groups and organizations, will learn that in the immense confusion there is a center which seems to have a grip on what is going on and is itself up to the eyes in the concrete struggle.

I hope you will grapple with this. It is not very easy, I assure you. I look forward to the time when I will get within a few days at least a dozen copies of the latest letter and also receive from you letters on particular points to which I shall be able to reply briefly and of which a selection shall be published. Order, dispatch, discipline, precision. An outstanding example of how this was not done is the absolutely shocking report, or supposed report, of your conference which I have received. The next letter will be devoted exclusively to this and its importance in relation to what I have been saying in this one. I think I can say confidently that it is the worst conference report that I have ever seen. Everything in its place. Till next time. Meanwhile study it to be able to appreciate what I will have to say about the conference report.

J.

January 20/26, 1963

My dear Marty,
   Will you do the following for me, please, immediately?

   a) Get this letter typed and mimeographed (here I suggest only) a hundred copies.

   b) Circulate it to members and friends far and near. Here, of course, you exercise along with the other comrades, your discretion.

   c) As soon as the letter is circulated and there has been some time, call a meeting and discuss it. It will state what is to be discussed, at least there will be no problem for serious people to arrive at decisions in regard to the various points raised in this letter. The letter is not going to leave it vague as to what is to be done.

   d) As soon as the meeting is over please send me, and be ready to circulate along the same lines as above, the minutes of the meeting.

   e) You will send me copies of the letter and copies of the minutes. I have suggested about a dozen copies.

   The letter is, I consider, profoundly important, because I am pretty certain that you all are vague upon matters upon which you should have no doubt whatever. I shall divide it into three parts: A) which deals with the public; B) which deals with the organization; C) which deals with me — you know me, I wouldn't tell you my name, although this question of my name will have to come into what we decide.

A. The Public

   In my last letter I dealt with the public. I said that we have reached a stage in modern society where, on the fundamental problems, the whole of the general public is involved. There are not advanced people in regard to atomic war and backward people who have to be educated into the realities of atomic war and what it means. That division in advanced and backward elements of population is now destroyed. We in our organization have laid it down years ago that today there is no difference between theory and practice, that the public is ready for an understanding, probably understands the realities of the political problems that are placed before it. I think we said that unless that is so, to talk about the necessity for socialism on a world scale is a lot of nonsense. We said that years ago. It is more than ever true today.

   Here is a quotation from a woman high in public life in Great Britain, a woman who occupies a key position in one of the most decisive phenomena of our day, the phenomenon of mass communications. Modern mass communications have altered the mentality of society to a degree that has not been equalled since the invention of printing. This is what she says:

> I have a great belief in the intelligence of the audience. When a producer fails with a programme and says it was because it was over the heads of the audience, I tell him it is he who has failed.
>
> There is a confusion that the informed are mature and the uninformed are immature. Often it is quite the opposite. I like to think our audiences are mature people who want to be informed.

This woman is the person responsible for a new set of programs on the BBC television. The program to which I refer is a Saturday night program which is being seen obviously by millions of people. It is a program which is satirical about people and about things in Britain including and most violently including, traditional things. I can only give you a few examples of the subjects on which the performers have poured their unadulterated scorn and satire. One of them is the various religions into which Christianity (and the other religions) are divided. I would not have dared either to write or to publish such a thing in a revolutionary paper. Another point that they have taken up, and made the most improper remarks, is illegitimacy. Needless to say politicians, businessmen and all public figures, and I am informed even royalty, are treated in the same way. This, please remember, in a country that is so deeply soaked in tradition as Britain, and this in a public means of communication such as the BBC, which is run by a corporation under government control and paid for by the government. This is not some isolated station in Kansas or California with an exceptional talker or little company. This, as far as Britain is concerned, is official and universal. I mean to say that it is a national program; all the stations in the country get it, and there is no choice. The woman whom I quoted obviously had a certain conception and that conception, if not shared, at least is not opposed by the people who are in general responsible for a procedure of this kind.

I want to say, and I say it without a tremor, that I have had these opinions for a long time. There is, however, one point she makes on which I would like to make a clarification. Read the quotation again. What I would like to add is that the people who are informed are supposed to be mature because they have the information which bourgeois society uses as a means of educating certain sections of it. The virtues of the so-called uninformed are that they are not educated in the education, and particularly the advanced education of bourgeois society, but are educated by their daily life in an advanced society, their contact with the fundamental realities and the human relations imposed upon all who live and who are subjected to and experience the educative realities of an advanced society. In later discussions I hope to bring before you that this relation, I am now satisfied, exists in every part of the world to one degree or another.

In the previous letter I went into what we must expect in the way of instinctive and organized resistance to the abominable crimes of which bourgeois society today is guilty. I made it clear that we have to have a certain attitude to the public in general, based upon our general understanding of what the public is, in 1963, not what it was in 1933, or still worse, in 1917. I hope in time we shall be able to make clear and concrete the objective and subjective qualifications of what we know today as the general public and our particular concern, the great mass of people.

I hope that is absolutely clear and accepted. That means that we have to have a basis upon which we are all agreed and which is the basis of our view of society and *therefore* of the work we have to do.

Let me end this section by stating this. Unless we have that in our bones, devote ourselves as time goes on to making that as clear and as concrete, and as effective as possible in our own minds, and in the minds of those who listen to us or read what we have to say, we are just wasting time and, I have to say it plainly, we would be better employed elsewhere. That is where we begin, we must never forget it, and it must be so much a part of our minds that it appears and governs everything we do, everything we say, and is an indelible part of the impression we make on people.

B. The Organization

We come now to the organization.

We have repudiated the conception of the vanguard party. That conception ruined the socialist movement, and the movement of the proletariat, for a generation. I believe only two sets of people in the U.S. believe in it. The first is the State Department. The second is the Trotskyists.

Nobody else believes it, at least in the U.S. The conception, the belief that you are setting out to form a vanguard party, a party which will lead the socialist revolution in the U.S., is the utmost nonsense. It has no relation whatever to the existing social situation, to the world in which we live. In a previous letter (to understand this letter you will have to read and study the previous letters), I dealt with the mentality which a generation, on a continental or on a world scale, arrives at, and maintains, after a tremendous event like the Russian Revolution of 1917. But not only the masses of people absorbed this conception and mantained it, were bound to maintain it until they received another violent shock, either on a national or most probably on a world scale, for that is the way populations think and move. The intellectuals and political leaders not only encouraged the people to think along these lines, despite all the evidence to the contrary. They ruined themselves, these informed ones, they ruined themselves by their sticking to these ideas, flattering themselves that by sticking to them they were carrying out some sort of opposition to decaying bourgeois society.

I have to make this quite clear in a very concrete manner. And when I use the word "concrete" in these letters, as a general rule I have in mind a mode of expression, examples, etc., which can carry the conviction to the ordinary person.

The vanguard party conception ruined all attempts to form a Marxist party in the U.S. and contributed substantially to the catastrophes which have befallen it. What the vanguard party conception did to the U.S. Trotskyists was to make them think and act primarily of themselves and in opposition to other organizations which were challenging them for the position of embryo of the coming vanguard party. This means that their whole conception of who they were and what they had to do was governed by the necessity of establishing themselves, and in some way or other educating whomever they got into contact with, into the validity of their claim and the denunciation of the other rivals for the coveted position of leading the American masses to socialism. Look back at what they have done and what they have not done. It was between the limitation of making people understand that they were the vanguard party and the other people were not, that they lived, and this mentality governed every single thing they did. You all know them. Some of you have experienced them, you will be able to tell. I can only give you the most striking example that immediately comes to mind.

Look at the publications of the SWP.

They published a number of books by Trotsky, about the Comintern, about his conflicts with Stalin, about the Chinese Revolution, about the Spanish Revolution, etc., etc.

Cannon himself wrote on the building of the proletarian party, an internal party quarrel. He also published some supremely superficial reprints of some talks (he called them lectures) on the U.S. proletariat. After some forty years in the U.S. working-class movement, he has published absolutely nothing which gives some kind of view of the development of the American people or of the American proletariat. Absolutely blank.

As far as I know, Dobbs is the same. The whole lot of them. When an intellectual among them left them and thought of writing something, Mr. Burnham held forth on the Managerial Society.[19] The American people, the younger intellectuals and the workers interested, as they were bound to be, in the life around them, in their own lives, in the lives of their own people, in the lives of those in their own country, learned from Marxism absolutely nothing.

I would be glad if you all in your discussions gave further examples and perhaps made lists of these publications. For the time being I merely wish to add that after a number of years, Max Shachtman is about to write his great work — upon what? The Communist International. I remember by chance that an American Marxist, his name was Weisbord, wrote two large volumes on the history of the Communist International. There was another, a Lovestonite intellectual [Isaac Deutscher], who wrote on Lenin, Trotsky and Stalin. Harold Isaacs produced his great work on the Chinese Revolution. And most instructive, Sister Rae wrote her book on Leninism and then I gather went to Africa and has been holding forth in Britain and in the U.S. on the African Revolution. There are other examples, I am sure, that we can work out. On the American Revolution, on the American people, they have nothing to say. Some of them are people not without ability. What has happened is that their whole outlook and mentality have been dominated by the concept of the vanguard party which had to teach the people about Marxism, and other such matters which would make the people understand that they, the preachers, were the ones who should be followed as they were the leaders of the socialist revolution. I have been through this thing myself from start to finish and I know these people; I know what they think and why they think as they do. Please pay attention to this and get all traces of this poisonous mentality out of you.

I give you another example. First of all let me say that in a previous letter I pointed out how from the very beginning we have been different. Our total orientation was different from theirs. The list of our publications shows that. Whenever I think of what we were preparing to do on the Civil War, I feel, not bitterness, but the greatest regret for anything that was planned and didn't come off, more than I have ever felt about anything in political and mental life. (What would be very valuable is a list of our publications. Send it to me, please, and I shall be able to make notes on it.) This, if you please, is not only a clear example of the difference between us and them. It is also closely connected with activity undertaken by the Trotskyists and ourselves. They came to Detroit, and to the working class in general, in order to teach the working class and to make it realize that they were the vanguard party, and the destined leaders. We came to Detroit, and we did the work, as the British prayer book has it, in the sphere of life in which it had pleased God to call us. That we did. And we had certain successes to our credit. That you have to do and we have never failed in doing that, and I hope we shall never fail.

Not only because the working class needs the assistance we can give—but because we need it for the specific functions which we have to perform. Our entry into the proletariat was governed substantially by the recognition of the fact that without this contact with the proletariat, and, to put it plainly, without being able to learn from it, all our Marxism and therefore our Marxist organization was doomed to futility and failure. In every sphere you will find that this conception of the vanguard party dominated the Trotskyist movement, affected every single sphere of its activities, has ruined it and keeps it ruined.

I shall now go to the building of the organization and I shall do this in differing sections so that you will be able to discuss and if need be to postpone decisions or to vote, according to whatever circumstances you propose and decide. All through I hope there will be present the two points I have already made, first the state of the proletariat and the masses of the people, secondly, and this is very important for you to bear in mind, the demoralizing effect of the vanguard party.

The Building of the Organization I

An organization of this kind is built first of all and will long continue to be built by the accession of individuals, a group of two or three, and at times a dozen or a score. We must never forget that today, at one time, twenty people can join us; if you forget that, you don't know what you are doing and inevitably you are doing the wrong thing. I had intended to take up what I shall now say under section C; but I think you should bear it in mind in everything that follows. I haven't the slightest doubt that a proper Marxist organization which well before 1939 or even as late as 1939 had broken away from Stalinism and put itself on the correct road would today have at least five thousand members and, much more than that, be a powerful center for socialistic propaganda and organization. I haven't the slightest doubt of it, and what is more, we can apply those ideas to our own selves. If we had had our mind clear and I had not been sent away as I was, our own organization today would be a few hundred strong and a center, a known and accepted center, of Marxist theory and American and general analysis of society. I want you to understand and I shall go into it under section C, that that is what I had in mind. I am working with you all with that clear perspective and absolute personal certainty, that, particularly at the present time, we can aim at pulling together dozens and then scores of people. I shall go into that and my personal reasons for this, and the reasons for my personal certainty under C. But I am confident that most, if not all, of you are not aware of this and of this objective perspective. That is why I have asked for special attention to be paid to this letter and why I am dealing with the specific subjects in the way that I'm doing.

To this must be added that today outside of the Stalin-Khrushchev monstrosity, the center of the world outside of that is in the U.S. You all have not only a moral responsibility but an objective necessity and advantage of being the center of Marxism and the Marxist application to all aspects of society today. Nobody believes in bourgeois society any more. Nobody. I repeat that. Nobody. There are some people who have positions and are holding on to those. There is a great mass of people who are going along from day to day. But one thing we shall have to do, and I am in a position to begin it at any rate, is to make clear the complete degeneration which exists today, everywhere, even within the bourgeoisie itself.

That opens the way to a Marxism which is not only intellectually comprehensive but objectively effective in what it attempts to do. That is what I am going to deal with in some detail now. But I tell it to you at once and do not reserve it, as I intended, so that you may be aware of this in various points that I now take up. You have to beliee that you are going to build an organization. Unless you believe that, you will be nothing. You will need a lot of money. Very soon you will have to have not only an office but a typist and organizational secretary combined. As soon as is reasonably possible you will have to make your political leader, secretary or whatever you call him or her, a full-time person. Without that you can build nothing. I know that at once you say, that is all very well but where will we get the money from? The money; you believe, or, I shall not be rude, I prefer to say that people believe that you get money in order to carry out good politics. They are absolutely wrong. You carry out good politics and that brings in some money. All the money you require you will be able to get, in relation to your political activity and your political effectiveness. Let us now go into some details.

The Building of the Organization II

In view of what I have been saying, and particularly in view of the total rejection of the vanguard party conception which must be the basis of all our activity, I have now to deal, briefly, but I hope effectively, with activity, and union activity in particular, of the organization.

Nothing that I have said and nothing that I will say is supposed to be an obstacle or a deterrent (fine word, isn't it? good modern word, deterrent), nothing must be considered as a deterrent to active participation in the work of the proletariat or those who are carrying out some attack against one of the crimes which bourgeois society is imposing upon the mass of mankind.

I can best illustrate this by two examples, and I have no doubt that you all will be able to supply others.

a) In France in 1936 the French Trotskyist organization was very small. But one day, in the upheaval that took place, one of them in an organization of many thousands of workers put forward a very advanced program and stage by stage took it through, the organization accepted what became, for the time being at any rate, a national policy. Now note this please. A good Marxist can individually and with the help of his organization carry through such practical work, build himself deep into a mass organization, in fact, wherever possible members of a small organization should be doing that. That is not at all the same thing as asking to build a vanguard party. I hope the difference is clear.

b) The second example I shall mention in general, although I believe that we ought to have among our papers a copy of the action. I shall only tell you in general terms. One of our people some years ago found himself chairman of a small branch of a tremendous mass organization. The leader of the organization was carrying on a great national struggle against the government. The whole nation was interested. The leader, in the capital, came to the conclusion that he and his organization were defeated, and he sent a message around to the innumerable branches telling them that defeat was inevitable and they should quiet down and take it. He had his boys in the particular little unit I am speaking of, and they, of course, were prepared to put through the policy of the boss. Our man in the chair moved quickly and proposed that as the matter had come up late it should be postponed until next time. It was a defensive maneuver, to give some time to the workers to think over things a bit. As far as I remember, there was nothing more or very little more in his proposal. The proposal was accepted — with national consequences. After the branch meeting one of the members said that he didn't see why they should accept defeat. They would see about the struggle themselves. Next morning at, I think, about four o'clock, he and some of his friends got into a car and went around the district telling local leaders not to work, to come out, not to pay any attention to the decision of the national leader to accept defeat. Tens of thousands came out. Within a day or two hundreds of thousands had come out. A tremendous victory was won and when the national leader sent around to give the final news he made it clear that he had been defeated and that the victory was due entirely to the independent activity of the rank and file. I am not saying that nothing at all would have happened if our man had not taken the steps which he did. The fact remains, however, that in branch after branch and there were hundreds of them all over the country, the decision of the national leader had been accepted. He, however, was in a position to do something about it and he did, with the consequences I have indicated. I shall be glad if anyone has among his papers a copy of the report that was made to our center.[20]

Finally, I will add that after a certain amount of contact had been made in Detroit with two or three dozen workers by an intellectual who had never been near a factory in all his life, but showed not only sympathy but a grasp of what was going on, many of the workers were prepared to discuss their situation with him and his opinions of the various policies that occupied them.

Finally, I want it absolutely clear, and I am sure that with Marty holding the position that he does with you, that aspect of a small Marxist organization will continue and nevertheless be in no way confused with the conception and practice and theory of the vanguard party.

The Building of the Organization III

I have now to deal with the question of theory very briefly. I have got merely to list the chief points:

a) There is first of all the foundation on which we rest, *State Capitalism and World Revolution*. This is an unshakable base. First, you will notice that those persons who have left us can find no political objection. They scurry around and find some phony reason. You will remember that Bauer[21] and company, for example, left the SWP on some basis of the attitude of Pablo.[22] Pablo also found the SWP position on Stalinism wrong, and then came back. I don't know where he is today. The story of the Trotskyist movement and of the revolutionary groupings on the whole is full of such political splits. Personally, I shall tell you in the next section, I don't believe in them at all. But the political position they wish to leave was vulnerable and they took the opportunity. We stand unshaken and unshakable. All sorts of political organizations, not only small ones but larger ones — political personages like Roosevelt and Churchill — even the various Communist Parties, particularly the Italian Communist Party — in passing the Social Democratic Party of Italy; vast numbers of politicians and people in Russia itself consistently show that each and every single one of them gets into obvious confusion and insoluble difficulties as to what Stalinism is. Their mistake and their confusion fill the atmosphere every day. With that document written in 1951 we remain unshaken. That is our foundation. When the time comes and we do the work on that document that has not been done in ten years, you will be able to understand and absorb its basic strength and, you will see in time, its range.

b) I have already asked you to do what we did with the Economic-Philosophical Manuscripts. We were years in advance. Now all we have to do is get the Trade Union debate and the general debates of the Congresses of 1921 and, of course, the account published in 1927 of the 1917 activities of the Russian Factory Committees, and once more, and this time we will do it properly, we shall do what the Marxist organization has the right and the privilege to do, be a genuine vanguard of the socialist movement. That is merely one stage. There are others ahead.

c) I want you to go through the list of our previous publications and to realize that alone of the Marxist groups we were establishing the premises and getting ready for a Marxist analysis of the people, and the relations connected with them, of the U.S. All that is no accident. It is because we laid the foundations never forget, and always had the perspectives of doing what a Marxist organization should do. Not playing at being the vanguard party, getting ready, all sixty of us, to lead nearly two hundred million people in the U.S.A. in the socialist revolution. Let the Trotskyists and the State Department share that illusion between them. Note by the way that the Stalinists do not share that illusion, not they. You will be able to see in time, I hope you know it already, that they are depending everywhere upon the Russian army to defeat the bourgeois armies and to install them in power. That leaves the State Department and the Trotskyists in complete charge of the theory of the vanguard party.

d) Bear this in mind and know that if we continue with those ideas that I have expounded, and seriously absorbed what is correct and thoroughly reject what is wrong, we cannot fail in producing a paper which will represent those conceptions and that policy.

All that I have to say about theory and its practical effects is contained in the above. To all that I have to add only this, and you ought to know it by now. In the increasing demoralization of bourgeois society and the approximation in political activity of the two blocs, vast numbers of people are looking for something. I have heard only recently from someone in a position to know, from someone who knows them intimately, that what is noticeable among the functionaries and leading elements in the Labor Party organization in Great Britain, is the total absence of any political ideas. That was not always so. They are forced into that emptiness and bankruptcy today. What political ideas can they build? On what political basis? This vast emptiness is around on every side. For example, you will know best if I am correct in saying that this emptiness is most repulsive to you, and that there are in the U.S. today on the campuses, numbers of youth who are looking for something. From all that I have heard and the little that I have seen, that is taking place everywhere. Even the American government itself is aware of what it calls the lack of national purpose. These people are there. Please do not make the mistake of not knowing that there are more people of that kind among the workers than there are among the intellectuals. They (the workers) are harder to get because they are people accustomed to dealing with serious and fundamental matters and they have their own experiences of facts and ideas which correspond to them. What they will have nothing to do with is people who come to them telling them to join those who are about to lead the socialist revolution. The proof of this, in so far as it can be proven (for to be able to see this, to recognize it, requires some knowledge of theory) will have to rest with you. You will have to know this, you will have to be convinced of it. Otherwise you can't work seriously.

I am writing in sections. You discuss section by section and say what you think. It will take two, possibly three, discussions. It does not matter. The problem, as I see it, is to know what you are going to do and what are the prospects you have of doing something effective. The theory is sound and has all the elements of progress. The people we have to deal with are there. You must be as sure of that as I am. There is, however, another aspect to this matter of the small organization, and that I shall deal with now.

The Building of the Organization IV

People can be impressed with a theory, especially if they are informed of it often and are able to judge of its validity. They are also anxious to join something. But they will only join something that seems to be going somewhere and that seems to have the correct people. The idea that they will join only a huge organization that is leading the working class is a lot of nonsense. It is a stupidity which is the direct result of the theory of the vanguard party. But people, and particularly Americans, must feel that what they are joining or what they are being asked to join is not only active but effective and businesslike.

That has been entirely missing from our organization since I left it. You all have not the slightest idea of how to act in a way and how to make your presence felt in a way that will attract people, the kind of people who are interested in what you have to say. I shall spend some time on this. We had better go into it so that we will know what we are doing and what to expect.

You sent me the other day what purported to be an account of your conference. I know more or less the weaknesses, the feebleness of the organization; but that conference report made it very clear to me that I had to take it upon myself to get down to business with you. Whom do you think would be encouraged to join an organization or consider joining at some time, with a conference report of that kind?

Let me begin at once by telling you what form that report should have taken.

First of all it should have had the summons to the conference and the proposed subjects on the agenda. That should have gone out, and have been printed in the report. Then you should have stated how many people came to the conference and from where they came, etc. Then there should have been the appointment of a secretary who would draft a report. That, if you please, is the report of a conference, the kind of report that you need, you, yourselves, and the kind of report that people who know about your theory and like it, will recognize as a report coming from serious people for serious people. Then must come the first session. You will say in the report (you will pardon me if I have to go into these elementary things) when the first session began and if you were late. You will then give an account of the discussion. These can be very brief, sometimes three or four lines and in certain cases ten lines. Then you come to the decisions that were taken at the morning session, the time you left and the time you appointed for the afternoon session. If you change chairmen in the afternoon, you put that in. You also give a concise but full report of what took place. You state the motions, you state how many voted for, and how many against. I hope I need not go any further. At the end of the report you ask when the conference report will be ready. If there is a party, then note it.

This means that there is a full report of the activities and temper of a certain set of people. It is important for you to know what you did, how you did it and at a later stage you have an executive report maybe, which will start from where the conference left off and rigorously deal with the decisions, proposals, mistakes and omissions of the conference. You know that, you live by that. That is the structure which holds you together. But there is far more to it. I keep telling you to print one hundred copies at least, of all you print, all your documents, including the report. Some you distribute to your contacts; you keep the others. In time to come you distribute those to new people. For example, I am very much concerned with what activity I myself shall carry on. I simply am depending to a substantial degree on what you do, on your reports of activity, on your publications. If anybody asks me who you all are and what you are doing I shall be able nine months or a year from now, to hand over a set of reports, documents, etc., and say these are the people. Never be afraid that you will not find people who will respond to such disciplined and organized activity.

If I am proposing to do that here, what about you in the U.S. and the people whom we shall impress by the excellence of our ideas and the political and journalistic skill with which we expound them? I repeat, that conference report was a complete disaster. It could mean nothing to people who are of a serious turn of mind and are ready to commit themselves but only to something serious. I think that I have said enough about conference reports, reports of executive committees, etc., the more important organizational meetings, and the way in which you publish them for yourselves and for people who are attracted to you in one way or another. Unless you take yourselves seriously, others will not. Here again you have the opportunity to discuss, to decide and then to vote if need be as to how you are going to carry on your business in the future. There may be people who are interested in what you are doing and will take six months or more before they finally decide to come in with you. Do your reports properly and have them waiting, along with your political analyses and your popular statements, for your own sake, and for an increasing circle of people whom you will meet. Have them ready. I am asking you for a dozen of everything. I will need, I am certain, that many and as time goes on I will need more. Please discuss, decide and function in that way.

The Building of the Organization V

The precision and the effect that you give of concentration and a serious attitude to whatever you may be doing is absolutely necessary, particularly in relation to the breadth and scope of our general analyses. People will only take those seriously, the general analyses I mean, when they see that whatever work you put your hand to, you do it with utmost seriousness. Otherwise, inevitably the general analyses assume the impression of just being a lot of talk.

Now the beginning of seriousness of activity starts with yourselves and with the work you do for yourselves. At the present time, and maybe in the future also, although in a different form, what is decisive is what you do with these letters. I received a letter from Marty recently in which he gives me details of the organizational steps you have taken to reproduce your own material. These things you know best and have to decide them yourselves. I am glad you have reached as far as you have done. Now these letters have not been circulated as I have suggested they should be. That must be corrected at once. Everyone must have his own copies of the letters, all of them, from the very beginning because they constitute a sequence. This letter is fairly long and I aim at more or less a complete statement of general attitude that we should have to our business.

Closely connected with this letter I shall do what is not so urgent for a decision on your part, but which must be read in relation to your plans. As soon as possible after this one, I shall go into organizational relations and the personal attitude of an individual to the organization. I paid the most scrupulous attention to every aspect of this question when I was with you. But it was a question I know is most dangerous to talk about and personally I was disinclined. However, I did it. It is obvious that all of you must from now have an idea of this. Therefore, as I say, I shall send you another letter on which you will not have to vote but which is very necessary in order for you to have a comprehensive conception of what I am trying to say.

After that one, I shall stop. I shall stop until you have gotten all of your affairs in order, have been able to read and discuss these letters and discuss this one in an organized manner and express an attitude to its different sections. That is going to take you some time. Just do it quietly and systematically. However, when you have done it, we will have to take up the question of future letters. This is what I shall now suggest and of course you all decide and let me know.

I believe that the next set of letters should deal with fundamental economic problems and related matters in the period of what I shall call the Sixties. In addition to what I have observed and what I think necessary for the small Marxist organization, I shall insert some important quotations and passages from the classics and from contemporary newspapers, etc., which I think relevant. What I shall be doing is this. I shall be stating the basic economic developments of the day on a world scale. Then the objective results in the development of the proletariat, the capitalist class and the intermediate classes. Next I shall take up politics in the nineteen-sixties and by politics I mean Marxist politics. I shall refer specifically to Great Britain which I know best, but also the U.S. Those will probably take three letters, no more than four. Understand what I am doing. I am preparing us for a mentality and an attitude to the fundamental Marxist approach to the problems of the day. I don't know that I have ever seen this anywhere within recent years or for a long time. The SWP and the WP, which must be our main terms of reference, at least the terms of reference that I shall make to you, periodically at a convention made some general statement in which what the party had to do was immediately and vulgarly related to what was supposed to be the general economic and political situation. Politics today is fundamentally different from what it was in the nineteen-fifties and still more different from the nineteen-forties. We, that is to say, people in general, have made tremendous advances: either the socialist society on a world scale, please note that, on a world scale, or destruction, a total descent into barbarism. That is where we are.

Now the next set of letters after those three or four will deal or rather raise the question of how and what we shall produce as a weekly newspaper. In this second set of letters I shall go into detail as to the kind of material, the range of material, the method of treatment, the development of the comrades' writing ability and all that goes into the publication of an effective newspaper. But in order to be able to do this, the members of the organization and all those people who are around us who may be interested today or who may become more interested tomorrow, they must have certain basic conceptions and attitudes to society which they must share, if even in places they have serious disagreements. You share the disagreements. So that, to repeat, first our general analyses of world economics and politics, and then after that, with the previous letters and that in mind, a statement of how we should approach the question of the paper. That I shall go into in detail. Without that, without some such approach, we do not know what we are doing. And not only we do not know, but we are unable to convince or convert people, and we shall be given to much idle squabbling among ourselves about unimportant things.

There is now something which I must say at once. To the organizational aspect of it I shall refer in the letter which is to be attached to this one. But the fact itself is something which you do not know and which expressed your total incapacity to have understood what was required of you. I refer to the split with J[im] and G[race]. Look at that document which I wrote immediately and the letters accompanying it.[23] I realized early that we were in for a very serious break with Marxism and it was best to meet it head on and without pulling any punches. But that we had to do it was our fault and our responsibility. What the split should have come on, what any split in the small organization should always come on, is a program of the kind which I have outlined in these recent letters, against another program or no program at all. I say this because I am convinced and I want to show you in the letter that is to be attached, that in these small organizations when splits take place, despite the profundities of the political analyses that were made, in reality they are due to one thing and to one thing only. The people are tired of the kind of life they are living and the activity they are carrying on, and they wish to get out of it. That is not an easy matter to illustrate and learn. Fundamental attitudes of this kind can easily be expressed and something of them will be expressed in serious political terms. To be able to distinguish between the personal attitude and the political attitude leads you into psychology which is the ruin of everybody concerned.

Nevertheless, the political organizer, the political leaders, and in the small Marxist organization everybody is a political leader, must see to two things and two things only. First, his basic political position must be sound and must be able to meet with events and remain sound. Secondly, his program, or I should say, your program, your method of procedure, what I am doing now must be, for example, as clear as a political analysis. Nothing was clear, no program, when J[im] and G[race] split. I who had to write the document realized that to have a split in a small organization and be talking not about what you were doing or what you proposed to do, but of the fundamentals of Marxism, was a disaster. That discussion, that difference, could mean nothing to the people who were around us, nothing from which they could learn and around which their activity or their developing need for an activity could center. As it was, we could claim, and legitimately claim, that they, the opposition, had broken away from Marxism. OK. They had broken away from Marxism. So what? Many thousands of workers had broken away from Marxism. The world had not changed thereby. We were just what we were before. Only we were worse. But I hope you realize the immense difference it would have made if we could have faced them with a program of this kind and perspectives. They would have had to put forward theirs. Or they would have had to realize that they wanted to go elsewhere. I want to repeat. The fact that the split took place over the letter I had to write, and it is only now that we are mobilizing ourselves with a comprehensive firmly based program and perspective, that shows me clearly what we did not do. I hope it is as clear to you. Unless it is, you will merely repeat the same mess as before.

Let me get back to what I have been talking about in this section.

I think that the new series of letters should be one per week. I think that you should more or less organize yourselves so that everyone knows that he will receive his letter for his own use and the letters that he has requested to be able to hand out at such and such a time. I believe, in fact I know, you will have to work out as accurately as possible the kind of paper you are going to use, how much it will cost, which will mean you will then know how many copies you will be able to make every week. I have been saying one hundred copies and asking for a dozen of everything. I don't know how much it will cost to have one letter done. I believe that you might very well have three or four lines printed on the upper part of a page and every copy will have that as page one and various advertisements of our material, etc., on the inside of that page. You see what I am trying to inculcate. To begin now and to begin with yourselves and your circle a systematic preparation of ideas and organization of material. It may be that you can only afford fifty copies of each. I would like to know that you could do a hundred. I want to say again that you must have many in reserve, and it is by this systematic exposition of your ideas and your organization that you attract the attention and ultimately the cooperative activity of people.

One last word on these proposals and even the analyses of the next two series of letters. And what I say now refers to the past letters also. I can only indicate a line of approach. On that matter, as I shall show in the next section of this letter, I am very clear and firm. If you don't do more or less as I am proposing to you, you will get nowhere. Of that I am absolutely certain. But at this distance I can only give you as clearly as possible, even in theoretical questions, the general direction. You will have to work it out yourselves. I am not laying down laws. That is why I suggest a careful circulation of the letters, careful and systematic, and also bringing in of other people. You will have to decide. But what you have to decide, as I see it, as I know it, is how you are going to carry out after full and complete discussions what I am proposing to you.

C. Myself

This is going to be tough. I have been thinking about it for a long time. But you can't easily get rid of the attitudes and practices, successful experience of many years. But I have to tell you a few things about myself and its relation to what we are doing. I have to write it down because I am not there in person, not to tell you instead of writing it, but to carry it out and to convey what I wish to convey by actions and proposals and theoretical discussions and slight but quite important personal relations. I shall not write it down but the personal relations by which G[race] finally became integrated and effective in our organization I shall deal with in the letter which I say shall be an attachment to this one. The other day, quite by accident, I came across a brief note which I wrote to her at a certain time, and that made up my mind. I said, to hell with it, I shall tell you all about it, not to learn about G. but to learn about yourselves. I shall try to be as brief as possible, though I know I should be as lengthy as possible. However, here goes.

a) I have now had about thirty years of working in small organizations. I have worked in the Independent Labor Party which was a small organization that had four or five members of Parliament. I have worked in the Trotskyist organization which was inside the ILP. I worked in it when it came out. I came to the U.S. and worked in the SWP; then split from the SWP and worked in the WP. Inside the WP I organized a small organization of my own. I took the organization into the SWP and then split away and started independently. During the last five years I have been engaged in functioning with what structurally was in essence a small organization beginning at the beginning. During some of this time I was in the leadership of the international Trotskyist organization and took part in its various conferences, etc. I have been a member of and worked in close association with the British Labor Party.

Now during this period, I am able to say first that I was extremely successful in building the kind of organization and in making the kind of effect I aimed at. Never was that more clear than when I, a Marxist of the small organization, went to work in the West Indies.

Within the scope of what was possible, particularly in regard to the effect on the people whom I aimed at, or whom it was my business to aim at, I have no complaints to make, nothing to be ashamed of. Please do not forget that I worked with Padmore, Jomo Kenyatta and the others who built up the organization from which was launched the emancipation of Africa. That, too, was a small organization. And there I saw both in theory and in practice one of the greatest organizers of a small organization I have ever seen, George Padmore.

In addition to the above, I was able to draw to myself and my perspectives and policies some of the best people it was possible to get. I have made that clear already. You do not pick up people like the people we had up to some years ago, you do not pick them up and be able to develop their very great capacities except you have something to offer them. In other words, unless you have something that develops them. Bear that in mind, please, we shall come back to it often.

b) However all that is merely background and very necessary background for you to read over and to study and study and discuss, to what concerns us here today. The facts of the case that are relevant are these. When we split from the WP I wrote after discussion a balance sheet which in reality was a treatment, a study of the small organization inside the Marxist organization. Note, please, that except for Cannon's building of the proletarian party, I don't know anywhere else where that has been done. When we split from the SWP another analysis was made of the functioning of the small organization in a previous Marxist organization and the necessity and perspectives of breaking away. Nobody else that I know, certainly not in the U.S., so consistently and seriously related the small organization to its particular environment. I had to leave the U.S. unfortunately, most unfortunately. However, in 1957 in *Facing Reality* I addressed myself fully and completely, I believe for the first time in the Marxist movement, to the analysis of the small organization. And the analysis of the small organization as such meant a certain attitude to the ways and means that now faced us in the building of a large organization, a mass party. There for the first and only time the thing was done. I went to the West Indies and there from the very start I initiated a certain line of approach. The result has been the book, *Party Politics in the West Indies,* in which I treat of the building of an organization in an undeveloped territory and also, as must be done, relate the organization to the general social situation of the country in which you are building it. So that over the years, in addition to the political analyses, etc., I have paid special and consistent theoretical attention on the basis of practice, upon the building of the small Marxist organization. In relation to what I am trying to do now, it is, if you will allow me to say so, a very impressive background. I know what I am about; it is the result of many years of Marxist and Leninist theory and practice centering around this particular objective, the building of the small Marxist organization.

I am aware that something is happening now which makes the task I am attempting of peculiar difficulty. When I was with you all, I was pursuing the same objectives in the same manner, but because I knew where I was going, among other things, and always judged by the empirical results of a theory, for that and for other reasons, I had authority. I had authority with the organization and I had authority with persons outside the organization: more than any of you can suspect the authority that I have had with people far removed from the organization, and am to this very day able to exercise is due not merely to some exceptional personal qualities which I have alway had (it is no use shirking a plain statement of fact), but due to the fact that such qualities as I possess are disciplined, stimulated and organized by my contact and relations with the organization and with the time and with the people with whom I have functioned. That authority of which I speak goes far beyond what even the best of you may think. It was not only an authority which allowed me to maintain order and discipline inside the organization — it was an authority which allowed me to make the necessary empirical observations, and propose the necessary empirical activities for the organization, by which a theory is made real and effective and by which it is also strengthened as a theory.

That form of authority is now beyond us. There is only one way in which it can be effectively renewed and strengthened. That way, both in regard to yourselves, the people whom you have to deal with and in regard to me, is the most careful and systematic doing of whatever you think has to be done to carry out what I am proposing. This is easy to express. It is not too easy to understand. But we have one advantage. You all are people who I think have reached this stage, where the Marxist outlook on life has become a part of your conception and experience of existence. We will now see what we will see. I merely repeat that I constantly had to bring to G[race] and R[ae] that they were ready to spend weeks on a single sentence of Hegel and of Marx but did not spend the necessary time on the analysis and procedure of the organization. I have given you the evidence that has been from start to finish my primary concern. I am trying to transfer not only the results of my experience but also to transfer to you the habit of thinking and of working on Marxism, always with the perspectives of doing what you have to do and that, in this case, is the building of an organization. I can go no farther with this.

c) The last point I have to make is that personally I am more than ever engaged in building the organization and in earning my living. The earning of my living to me would be a comparatively simple matter, except that I always try to combine it with some effective manifestation of what I am strictly concerned with, the building of the organization. For the time it looks as if I will be able to manage. Nevertheless, the strain is vey great. You would hardly guess the amount of time and, in the future, the amount of time and actual investigation and collection of material which I will have to spend in doing for you those two series of letters. I appeal to your good will, your sympathy, your humanity, your Marxist aspirations, etc., etc. But I also appeal to your determination to do precisely and with organizational attention and concentration what I propose. There lies the solution of all the things I have been talking about. I now have to send you a letter on organization on which you will not have to vote. But on this one, as I have outlined it, you have something precise to do.

Till next time,

Yours,

J.

PS. I have asked you to make a list of all of the things we have published from our very beginning. I want you to know that at this time I am working on Lenin and on Shakespeare. Also I have had in mind for some time an article or a letter to you on Whitman in relation to some work that one of you is doing. We have been very deficient on American history and also on modern science. I mention these things because there are people around us, and there will be, people who will bring qualifications and faculties that we have not been able as yet to touch. We must make up our minds to deal with them all. We shall be able to do that. But only if we do with the necessary care and concentration and discipline what lies before us to do. The rest will follow.

PPS. Please carefully work out the space between the lines of your publications. These letters, for example, are closely spaced. For the public, even our small public, I feel certain the space should be wider. I draw it to your attention. You will decide.

[Three meetings were held to discuss these letters. Minutes of these meetings were included in the mimeographed publication of the letters. They seem to be too abridged to convey an understandable record of the discussions. There were differences between members and non-members, with members often in the position of being defensive about James's letters and non-members being more critical. There was general acceptance of the need to work on certain pamphlets — on Leninism, on China, on Cuba, on Negroes and the Civil War, on automation, etc. A committee was formed to approach William Gorman to lecture on the Civil War and there was an attempt to begin the necessary work on the Russian factory committees. Most of the assignments bore only partial fruit. The work on the factory committees and on the Civil War was only partly done.[24] Ultimately, a mimeographed bulletin called *Speak Out* was published for a few years. In 1962 and 1963 the resources of the group were extremely limited. There were about a half-dozen members. There was no office. The chairman of the group worked full time in a factory, etc. A sign of the limitations of the organization was the inability to do a decent, legible job in mimeographing the letters. Another sign of a problem was the fact that most of the non-members dropped out of the discussions after the first meeting. — *editor's note.*]

Notes

1. These letters were addressed to the Facing Reality Publishing Committee through its chairman, Martin Glaberman. This text is taken from the mimeographed version, transcribed with modifications from the original letters. The typing and mimeography were less than adequate. Corrections are indicated where necessary without being too pedantic and making the text difficult to read.

2. The previous organization, known as Correspondence Publishing Committee, was decimated by a split led by Grace and James Boggs and Lyman and Freddy Paine. Earlier, in 1955, there was a major split led by Raya Dunayevskaya.

3. Raya Dunayevskaya, *Marxism and Freedom*, New York: Bookman Associates, 1958.

4. C. L. R. James, Grace C. Lee and Cornelius Castoriadis, *Facing Reality*, Detroit: Bewick Editions, 1974.

5. C. L. R. James, Raya Dunayevskaya and Grace C. Lee, *The Invading Socialist Society*, Detroit: Bewick Editions, 1972.

6. Atlantic Highlands, NJ: Humanities Press, 1993. First published in London in 1937 by Martin Secker and Warburg, Ltd. A Kraus reprint was published in Liechtenstein in 1972.

7. New York: Random House (Vintage Books), 1963.

8. Activists in the struggle against apartheid in South Africa were circulating copies secretly, using them as weapons in the struggle.

9. Chicago: Charles H. Kerr Publishing Co., 1986.

10. C. L. R. James, *Notes on Dialectics: Hegel, Marx, Lenin*, London: Allison & Busby, 1980. It was initially called "The Nevada Document" because its original form was letters sent by James from Nevada.

11. Paul Romano [Phil Silver] and Ria Stone [Grace C. Lee], *The American Worker*, Detroit: Bewick Editions, 1972.

12. *The Balance Sheet* published in August 1947 by the Johnson-Forest Tendency, was subtitled *Trotskyism in the United States, 1940–47; The Workers Party and the Johnson-Forest Tendency*. It was signed by J. R. Johnson [C. L. R. James], F. Forest [Raya Dunayevskaya] and Martin Harvey [Martin Glaberman]. It should be noted that Glaberman was not in New York when the document was prepared and took no part in the preparation. Adding his name to the authors was a collective political decision. *The Balance Sheet Completed* was a mimeographed document, published in 1953 upon the departure of the Tendency from the Socialist Workers Party.

13. New York: C. L. R. James, 1953. An edition without the last chapter was published by Bewick Editions in Detroit in 1978.

14. Matthew Ward, *Indignant Heart*, New York: New Books, 1952. Later editions were published under the alternative pseudonym, Charles Denby.

15. Isaac Deutscher, *Soviet Trade Unions*, London: Royal Institute of International Affairs, 1950, Note 1, p. 16, *Oktyabrskaya Revolutsiya i Fabzavkomy* [The October Revolution and the Factory Committees], Moscow, 1927.

16. This was the home of Lyman and Freddy Paine, and provided a home for the Johnson-Forest Tendency.

17. Lenin, "Letter to the Congress," *Collected Works*, vol. 36, pp. 593–99, esp. p. 595. This was often referred to as Lenin's Last Will and Testament.

18. See note 15, above.

19. See note 14, Chapter 1.

20. The organization was the United Mine Workers of America, led by John L. Lewis, involved in a battle with the United States government. The individual involved was in a small branch of our organization in Morgantown, West Virginia.

21. Erwin Bauer was a leader of the SWP in Detroit and was active in the UAW.

22. Pablo was Michel Raptis Speros, a leader of the Trotskyist Fourth International in Europe.

23. See C. L. R. James, et al., *Marxism and the Intellectuals*, Detroit: Facing Reality Publishing Committee, May 1962.

24. The book on factory committees was not found. However, working on the present book triggered a new search and a copy of the Russian book was located helped by the interest and help of University of Michigan Professors Deming Brown and William G. Rosenberg, so that the project is once again a possibility.

Perspectives and Proposals

Leadership

Ladies and gentlemen, I want to make clear that there are particular reasons why I have asked you to come to this particular meeting. First, you must be clear about one thing: I don't propose to ask you to join anything. I have nothing which you can join. Secondly, I not only do not propose to ask you to join anything with which I am associated, I am not proposing to you to join something else. That is entirely away from what I have in mind. I will tell you precisely what is the origin of my inviting some of you here.

I have been, for over 20 years, in touch with an organization in the United States. We have done a certain amount of work, very good work, and I have accumulated in the course of those years, and by taking part in politics in England, a certain amount of information which I want to exchange and which I have to a large degree kept to myself. Now I have found it necessary, I think it urgent, to make it known to my friends in the United States and elsewhere, those who are interested. After 20 odd years it is the first time I am going to speak about these matters.

I believe, however, that today a circle of people such as you would be interested in them. First of all you may have some political perspective of your own. And if even you haven't, what I have to say will be of importance to you in judging what is a great preoccupation of any civilized and active person today, the politics, if not of his own political organization, then of other people and the world in general. You may know some of the people of whom I will speak and may have been very much concerned with the events. But I have thought that it would be interesting to me, and it would be helpful to us that it wasn't concentrated so narrowly but should be broader. And I can't imagine myself in your situation where it wouldn't be interesting and valuable to me to listen to something of this kind.

There will be two more meetings. This one deals with Leadership. The second one deals with Membership. And the third deals with what I call "McNamara,"[1] that is to say, the political and economic movement of the world as it exists today. There are many things I am going to leave out, but the things that I say will form a whole. And they are particularly directed at those people who have had the experience that we have had over the past years.

Now the fundamental question today in all politics in the West Indies, in Ghana, in Britain, in Russia, and everywhere else, is what is taking place in the world today, and what position have countries, political parties, and individuals taken towards the general activities of the political organizations and countries. The people of underdeveloped countries, their political leaders, have taken fairly clear positions. (About this I have spoken before and will speak again.) They are non-aligned. They are neither with the West nor with the East. Unfortunately, although they say that and politically try to carry it out, some of them lean to the West and some of them lean to the East, because they have not got clearly in their mind any different road that they can follow. But that problem is a problem that now occupies everybody in the world. Everybody. The world is now more than ever one. And I think the first thing I would like to do in talking about leadership is to get clear what is the basic position today of any political leader. Wherever he is, if he is ruling a country, if he is leading a private political group, or if he is leading a political party which is the government of a country, the problems that I will deal with are the essential problems.

The world in which we live began in 1917. It began with the Russian Revolution. You all are young people, you don't know the world before that. I knew it, I actually lived through it, a good bit of it, and I know the history of it. I have had to study it, and I have known people who lived then and have read their writings a great deal. This world in which we live began in 1917 and has continued up to the present day, continued steadily.

Now what took place in 1917 was this. There was the Second International formed by Engels,[2] following Marx, and it consisted of millions of workers in the developed countries. Millions of them. For the first time since the Crusades, in 1889, Engels and the Marxists had formed a mass movement of European peoples. The underdeveloped peoples were outside of it. There were not too manyAmericans. This organization went into the war of 1914, a war which everybody foresaw, and which they had sworn they would never enter into; but they went into it. One man, however, with some others, said that this Second International, the International now of Harold Wilson and all of them, this International went into the war. Lenin & Co. said: "This International promised not to go into the war and it has betrayed." And they plotted and planned so that in 1918, by the time the war had come to an end, a whole set of European peoples, led by the Russian people, revolted against the Second

International. And there was formed the Third International, with the Russian Revolution at the center.

This is what took place beginning in 1917, 1918, 1919. So then there was formed the Third International and the massive working class movements of the world were divided into two — the Second International and the Third International. But something more happened which had not happened before. The colonial peoples, not only the working class or the peasants, but colonial political movements as a whole, began to take a great interest in, and some of them to join, the Third International, or to at least be affected by it.

So you had first the Second by itself with the colonial peoples out of it; then the Third International and the formation of a new revolutionary organization consisting of millions of people with Russia at the center; and now the colonial peoples beginning to take part, some taking part in the Second International, but a good many of them sympathetic and very interested in the Third International. The world had changed entirely.

Now I want to go for a moment into a new figure. He had taken part in the old revolutions, and then he had been expelled from Russia. But he seemed to be a man who would form a new organization, mobilizing all the revolutionary forces in the world as they hadn't been mobilized by Lenin in 1917. That was Trotsky. A very great man. A very fine intellect, and a great revolutionary — a man devoted. I knew him well, I know his work well. Trotsky during the thirties built up an organization based on what he knew had happened to the Second International and the formation of the Third.

Trotsky believed that the Third International would go the way of the Second. You remember my telling you that the Second International had sworn that it would not go into the war, but when the time came, each one joined up with its own ruling class. Trotsky believed that the Third International would do the same. He believed that the leaders of Russia, when the time came, being a bureaucracy, would give up the Russian Soviet state and join with the capitalist states. He believed that every Communist Party in every single country would join with the ruling class in that particular country and give up the struggle against the war, just as the leaders of the Second International had done in 1914. So that Trotsky's idea in building what he called the Fourth International was this — the war would come, and when the war came, the Third International would disappear into its component parts, just as the Second International had disappeared, and then the Fourth International would take the place in political life that the Third International had taken when the Second International joined up with their own bourgeoisie. That was his belief, that is what he wrote, and please remember he was a man of extreme ability, of extreme devotion, and vast experience. But that is the conception that he worked on, particularly from about 1927 until he was killed in 1940.

Now this is the first thing that I want to bring home to you—he was an able man, he was a devoted man, he was a man who devoted all his life and his extraordinary powers to this idea of the development of the revolution of the advanced peoples and of the colonial peoples. But he was wrong, he was wrong as nobody else was wrong. Because, as you know, when the crisis came in 1939, the Third International did not join up with the various sections of capitalist society, the Russian bureaucracy didn't join up with the bourgeoisie, as Trotsky expected. The Russian bureaucracy remained and fought on behalf of the Soviet state, and the different sections of the Third International remained completely devoted to the Russian state. Trotsky's policies and what is left of his parties have not recovered from that blow up to today. The world in general believed that when the Second World War began Russia would remain in the center of the revolutionary struggle and the revolutionary Third International; but they believed that they would be supporters of Russia and they would fight for the revolution as Lenin's International had fought for the revolution in 1917 and 1918. And the problem that is facing us today is, is that so or is that not so?

Some of you here are colonials; you would understand, I am sure, that if people were absolutely certain that the Russian Revolution and the Third International were going to lead the revolution in every country and would help the colonial peoples toward freeing themselves and leading towards an international socialist society, they wouldn't be non-aligned. Do you think they would be? But they are not quite sure of what is happening there. So the world today is balanced between some who say, they go with America, some say they go with Russia. But now Russia and China have split to pieces. They don't quite know what is happening, and people are not sure of Russia. The colonial peoples are ready to go with Russia, but they are not too sure that going with Russia they are going to get all they want. You know the situation of Castro—he was uncertain, he didn't know whether he would or not, and then Khrushchev told him, "All right, come with us," and everybody knows that to get him over, the Russians have promised a lot of aid and so forth.

That is the situation. Now in this confusion there is a road that certain people want to follow. I, for instance, am a member of the Labor Party. I have been for years. When I went away I was. But I still continue to say what I think. And I am going to get up during any election and speak on behalf of the Labor Party, and I am going to say vote for them instead of voting for

Macmillan. But I am not going to tell anybody that the Labor Party is going to change fundamentally the system — the condition of society in England today. I am not going to do that. And what I am talking to you about today particularly is this general situation in which the average person cannot make up his mind on which side he is going to go, and some say, "I am non-aligned," and some, particularly the colonial peoples, say, "I am in favor of the political organization of my own country, but I don't like what it is doing, I am not satisfied."

I don't want to ask you your private affairs, but I know any number of colonials, people from India, from Africa, and the East, who are absolutely fed up with what their own political leadership and organization is doing, but they don't know what else to do, and for the time being they give the same support to it that I give, more or less, to the Labor Party. But I believe that in the world today you have to work out your own way, and although you may give general support to some political organization, and see to it that if they are attacked you defend them, and any assistance that they want you give it to them, nevertheless you have to go your own way and try to work out ways and means of coming to some conclusions and some effective activity in the circle to which you belong.

Now one of the first things I have to do is to tell you about a similar organization and a similar person. It may seem strange to you to talk about a small group of people acting together in the midst of the vast confusion that the world is in at the present time. But I have had some experience of one of these organizations, and it ought to be of particular interest to most of you here, and particularly to some of you. I had an experience with George Padmore in an organization that he called the African Bureau. I don't know if you know anything about that organization. It consisted of seven people. Five of them were West Indians. It was run essentially by West Indians. Padmore published a paper. We had a man named Makonnen who got all the money to pay the rent for a big building we hired, and got the money to publish the paper. Padmore got some money, and so forth. I was the editor of the paper. One of our members, whom we educated, and who educated us by his militant African nationalism, was Jomo Kenyatta. It was a small organization — seven people — but it was to have a certain weight in the world. I haven't talked about this over the years, but I'm going to now.

Another day I was in the United States, and a friend of mine came to me and told me (she always used to go to all the Negro meetings), "I have been to a meeting by Du Bois and I met a young African there, and I asked him if he wanted to meet you, and he said, yes, he knew of you, he had heard of you, and he would be glad if I would arrange for him to come and see you." I said,

"Fine." She turned up with a young African, and his name was Kwame Nkrumah. He was a student at the University of Pennsylvania. Now Nkrumah in those days didn't know very much. But he told me he was coming to England to study law. And I wrote a letter to George Padmore telling him this young African was coming, and he is not very bright, because Nkrumah knew very little, but I said, one thing there is about him, he is determined to throw the British and all of them out of Africa. So meet with him and take care of him, discuss with him. Nkrumah came, and a year afterwards they held a big conference in Manchester at which Nkrumah made one of the leading speeches, and I read a pamphlet that he wrote about one year after he came to England. And when he left the United States he couldn't have written that pamphlet if his life depended on it. He had learned that *here*, in the African Bureau. Now he didn't come and only learn from the African Bureau. He contributed a great deal to the African Bureau also, but there was an organization of which he became a member. So I want you to remember that.

Of that small organization, George Padmore in time went to Africa with Nkrumah and organized — Nkrumah sent for him when [Ghana] became independent — and organized the first conference of African states that had ever been held in the world. Second of all, later Padmore organized the second conference of African freedom fighters that had ever been organized. He had organized the first one in 1931 — in the Kremlin, they had helped him — and he had organized that conference. And he had to wait until Nkrumah was established in Ghana, and in 1958, twenty-seven years afterward, Padmore organized the second conference of African freedom fighters. Jomo Kenyatta wasn't there because Jomo was in jail, but he came out and is today Prime Minister of Kenya and what is going to make you laugh is, at the next Prime Ministers' Conference Jomo is going to call on the Queen to be invited to have dinner at Buckingham Palace. That's good and I'm going to be very happy about it and laugh like anything.

I want to make it clear, when you get together and you form a small organization in the world in which we are where everything is topsy-turvy and things are falling apart, you needn't be afraid. You form your organization, and you go ahead. You don't know what will come out of it. That wasn't so in 1914; that wasn't so in 1890; the world was very stable. But after the Second and the Third International, and the present condition that the world is in, ten people could get together and begin to organize and form something, and you don't know what will come out of it. You have confidence and courage, but also you have to have a proper political line. I have made clear that Trotsky made a false analysis of the world at large. He was a gifted, able and devoted man. I could tell you, there are not many born like him every day, you know—not many like him; apart from what he did in the Russian Revolution, and so forth—that was a tremendous man. But he went all wrong on the fundamental issues, so that all he did went to pieces, and the organization that he formed is nothing. You have to get the correct analysis, you have to get a proper view of how the forces in the world are moving. But once that is so, get that clear, you form your organization of a few people and you are not afraid. You are not scared as to what is going to happen. In the world in which we are and the confusion and the mess, you don't know what is the perspective, what you will meet, how your people will develop, what is going to be the result of your work, what persons you will meet to whom your ideas will matter.

I would like to say that there is a country today, an area, which is quite important in its way. And I have made the acquaintance of one person who is interested in it, and I wouldn't be surprised if ten years from today he is completely master and head of an organization of many millions of people. I am not worried about it; it has happened before. And I know how it happened. I have talked to him. He has the possibility. It may come to nothing, you know. But the possibility that it can happen—it can happen at any time. And wherever you are, that is the attitude that you have to have to politics in the world as it is today.

Well, this organization in the United States—we built it up between 1941 and 1953. It takes time, you know. Now there are those here who may be a little bit upset at what I am going to say. An organization must work out what are the proper relations and forces of the fundamental forces in the world today. You heard, by the way, how Paul Robeson, at the age of sixty-something, has made up his mind that he can't follow the Russian people any longer? Have you read about that? Yes, that appeared in this night's paper. Now that is really something, to be sixty-something, and have given up all your career to go over to Russia, to leave the United States, etc., only to find out that it wasn't so good. That can be an accident, but you can't do that. You have to grapple with the fundamental problem, you have to make up your mind. And at the same time you have to be quite sure that what you are doing is of significance in 1963 because the world is in the state that it is.

We formed our organization in 1953. I want to talk about certain things concerning leadership, and then I want to make a conclusion about a particular leader. And I think it would be good for you to hear that. I was the leader of the organization from '41 to '53, when I left the United States. I am not going to go into this, that, or the other, however, except that by '51 we had made up our minds as to what were the forces moving in the world, and we had got that right. By 1963 we ought to know whether what we had worked out in 1951 was well done or not. We have got that right. Furthermore, we were not afraid of anything. We were confident that we were going someplace.

I am talking about leadership, and I want to take up some qualities of the poltiical leader, because at the end I am going to talk very seriously about that. Now about the poltical leader, I am going to speak about myself. There were other poltical leaders and other characters in the United States carrying out politics. As the political leader of a group which began with three, and at its best had some 70 people, I was able to meet all the other political leaders in the country, in our grouping, on equal terms. I had first of all written of, along with some others, what the exact situation was. And secondly, I was able to hold the position against all others. Unless your political leader is able to do that, he will not only fail, but you know what he will do? Violence, putting people in jail, arresting them, because he is not able to hold a position and defeat all opponents, etc., both in speech and writing. That I was able to do. My group's members and youth knew that whatever the occasion, whoever was the person who challenged us or who wanted to get into contact with us, Jimmy, as they used to call me, could hold a position. And in choosing and looking for your political leader, be able to find someone, and look at him and see if he can hold a position. The organization of which I was a member made a choice of somebody who couldn't hold a position, and they have paid, they have paid bitterly for it. It is well if he should have expounded, preferably in print, the basic doctrines, or be a good newspaper man, and expound regularly the basic doctrines of the organization. Otherwise he is leader in name only. I was in a fortunate position; I needn't go into details. I could hold a position with anybody who came.

Now I am going to make a big jump. You know one of the reasons why I was able to do so? I'm going to come to that in time, but I want to start it now. Shortly after we started to form the organization, somebody in the United States took charge of me, and saw to it that I and my wife and my child never wanted for a penny, so that I was able to devote all powers that I had to the organization, to guiding it and representing it. You know, there is a lot more to politics than politics. And I can tell you quite frankly, without that support and assistance we would never have been able to do the things that we did. He took it over completely. He made it his business to see that, within reason, I wouldn't want for anything. And that went on for years. I hope that is clear. Without that I would never have been able to do the work that I did. Never! And I would like to say at this time that he was able to do this, and he was inspired to do this, because he could see, first of all, that we had something, that we had made an analysis of the general situation, as I said at the beginning, and that we were serious people going in a certain direction, and that in the general confusion in the world, and in that particular country, here was something that seemed to matter. So under these circumstances he was stimulated to put his hand in his pocket, and kept on putting his hand in his pocket.

If any organization cannot find, or is not able to make contact with somebody who is able and ready to put his hand in his pocket, and keep on putting his hand in his pocket, it is the fault of the organization. They have not made the impact upon the world in general and upon people in particular that they should make. I have never known it to fail. Never. If you are able to convince a certain number of people that you know what you are doing, that what you are doing is important, that it is correct, and that you are serious about it, you will always find the necessary financial support.

I am not going to go into details about it, but there are a few things I wish to say. This is the first point I want to make in regard to the leader. He must have, and he must show, capacity in general fields. I would suggest, in any case, the writing of some basic book dealing with the principles that he wants to expound. He must be able to win over people, and the organization as a whole must impress people so that the financial support that is necessary for the leader and the leadership to function comes to them. No organization is ever able to build itself by the subscriptions and pennies of the few members who belong to it. That is impossible. Absolutely impossible. Can't be done. If you can't win support, you'd better give up. You will gain nothing.

There is another point I wish to speak about, that I have found in regard to leadership. And this is particularly important in the United States. Not in England so much, but it is particularly important in the United States, and as far as I have been able to gather, in the colonial territories. Lenin — I want to give you an example — in 1923 he was on his death bed. I believe that already he couldn't talk; he had lost the power of speech. He knew that he was going. And therefore he wrote a testament, something to his party committee.[3] And that testament is one of the most important political documents in the education of any group of political people of our day. I want to give some of it to you. It says there is likely to be a split in this party because of a difference of personality and attitude between Stalin on the one hand and Trotsky on the other. And it says the party will split, and the country will be split, right down the center. He saw plenty, didn't he? He foresaw the split between Stalin and Trotsky.

But there is much more in the letter. It's very hard to understand, you know, you will have to spend some time reading it, and studying it, and discussing it with your friends. It says, Stalin has become General Secretary, has concentrated an enormous power in his hands, and I am not sure that he always knows how to use that power with sufficient caution. Ah! He says, he has got a lot of power as the General Secretary, and I don't think that he knows how to use that power—do you get this phrase, please—"with sufficient *caution*." God have mercy, how they can tell people, political leaders! For Christ's sake! You have the power, you are the head, etc. but don't use this power—Kwame Nkrumah is in a lot of trouble with this—Lenin said, "with sufficient caution."

He says, on the other hand, Comrade Trotsky, as was proved by his struggle, is distinguished not only by his exceptional abilities, yes, he says, personally he is, to be sure, the most able man in the present Central Committee, but also by his intense, far-reaching self-confidence. You got that one? Self-confidence. And by a disposition to be too much attracted by the purely administrative side of affairs. You know what that means? Bureacrat and boss, in charge of this, and tell this one and that one what to do. That's what he says. He was the greatest politician, in my opinion, who ever lived. And he says, that fellow? He has a lot of power and he can't use it with sufficient caution. And this other one—great abilities, he is the ablest man here, but he has too much self-confidence. He is too much inclined to fix the matter by administration; bureaucrats, the secretary, the organizer, the this and that.

Now he had two friends with whom he had worked for about 20 years, Kamenev and Zinoviev. And those fellows had, at the time when the October Revolution came, they had been against. You follow? They had been against, they had said no. And Lenin had said, "Expel them from the party!" But they remained. He says, however, I will only remind you that the October episode of Zinoviev and Kamenev, the ones who were against the revolution, was not, of course, accidental. I wonder if you know what that means, or not. He says, they behaved like that in October, and whenever a critical situation like that arises, they will do the same. It is not accidental—I know them. But, he says, don't use that against them. Kamenev was his collaborator on the Committee of Labor and Defence. Kamenev was the editor of his Collected Works. Zinoviev was head of the Communist International. He says, I know these two. Whenever anything like this happens, they are going to behave in a certain way. But he said, don't use that against them. Well, I wish I could stick that into the head of all people with whom I am politically associated.

I will go further. He then took up two other members, Bukharin and Pyatakov—and pay close attention to this, especially you young men who have some education—he said, they are in my opinion most able. He says, Bukharin is not only the most valuable and the biggest theoretician of the party, but he may also be legitimately considered the favorite of the whole party. But his theoretical views can only with the very greatest doubt be regarded as fully

Marxist. Now that is a thing to say about somebody! He is the greatest theoretician of the party, the most valuable and the biggest, but his theoretical views can only be regarded with doubt as Marxist. For there is something scholastic in him, he never has learned, and I think he never fully understood, the dialectic. This is what the Russian party lived by. I wonder if you appreciate the significance of that, coming from the works of Lenin, a man who lived by Marxism and the dialectic.

And then he says, Pyatakov is a man undoubtedly distinguished by exceptional ability, but too much given over to administration — you remember what he said about Trotsky? — and the administrative side of things to be relied on in a serious political question. He had worked with them for 20 years; they never knew what he thought. He didn't express himself all over the place. He couldn't speak anymore, and he knew he was on his death bed, and he wrote down these things. It is one of the greatest political documents that I know. In a party, there is talk all over the place, between this one and that one and the other one. But a political leader, and a political leadership, has got to shut his mouth and keep it shut.

Now Lenin was not satisfied with that. About ten days afterwards he said to himself, I haven't made it too clear. And he knew why he hadn't made it too clear — because he was dealing with a difficult matter. And he put a postscript to the testament. He said, Stalin is too rude, too rough. He doesn't behave himself properly. His attitude to comrades is not good. And, therefore, I propose to the Committee to find a way — follow carefully, please, this is very difficult — to remove Stalin from that position and appoint to it another man who in all respects differs from Stalin only in superiority, more patient, more loyal, more polite, more attentive to comrades, less capricious, etc. I tell you that it has taken me years to understand how profoundly Lenin was concerned with certain fundamental things, of which he himself gave an example. You have to be able to keep your mouth shut, and you have to have a certain attitude as a political leader to the comrades. More patient, more loyal, more respectful, less capricious — to have more character. Now if I were to say these things to some political leaders I know, they would think I was crazy or tell me to go to Sunday School. This is the greatest political leader that we have known. He said, put that fellow out, and put somebody in who is more superior to him in these qualities. Thirty years I have been in organizations and I can tell you I have learned to appreciate those.

That's how a political leader has to behave, that is how he has to conduct himself. But furthermore, he has to be master of the general political movement, otherwise he will be like Trotsky and fall to pieces. He has to be determined to go a certain road. He has to impress the public in general and his own comrades and people, too, to give them some support. But he has to shut his mouth and not be passing remarks about this and that and that and the other. The rank and file can pass remarks, but the political leader does not say anything until, like Lenin, he's dying. And above all he must have character as a human being — more polite, more patient, less capricious. That is the point.

Now I want to break off for a while and speak about three important political leaders. I want to take Napoleon, I want to take another political leader that I have known in the United States, a man called Cannon, and I want to take another political leader who exists in England, a man that I know called Healey.[4] I know some West Indian political leaders. I have written about them, there is no need for me to go into that. I have written about many of them. I have some conception of one or two African political leaders. I am not prepared to talk about them. I prefer to talk about Napoleon, about Cannon, an American political leader of a small organization, and Healey, a British political leader.

You all know Napoleon. Many people believe that he is the most gifted with regard to effective action on the thought and body of human beings who has ever lived. Many people would say, if you asked them who was the greatest, they would say he was. I am going to tell you three things about him. Napoleon had the greatest commander of artillery that the Europe of his day knew. He had the greatest cavalry leader in Europe working for him. The commanders of his armies, the left wing or the right wing or the center — he had the best that Europe knew. As a Foreign Minister he had one of the finest Foreign Ministers that the world has ever known, a man called Talleyrand. And as head of his police he had one of the greatest Chiefs of Police ever known. That was Napoleon's staff. You know what he didn't have? He had no commander when he was not there. In other words, this highly accomplished political leader had the finest staff that it was possible to have. But when he was not there the staff could not function. He made it that way.

The second point that I wish to make about Napoleon is this. It was said by certain people that there were yes men. The most important memoirs of Bonaparte make it clear that Napoleon had no yes men. He didn't want any. When he had a discussion you could say anything at all, any point of view. That's what you were there for. I don't know any political leader who has a lot of yes men. If he has, that means something is wrong with his politics. I don't know any, I mean I know a few, but these are not serious political leaders. All the modern political leaders I have known didn't have any yes men, not one. And I have never known a political leader who, when he has found a man who is not a yes man, but will talk up, wanted him dismissed. No. If a man is in your political organization and he's opposed to you, that's something else. But as long as he has the general line, etc., no yes man.

The third point that I wish to tell you about Napoleon, and this I want you to remember about political leadership, is this: it was known that whenever news came, Napoleon was never upset by it. Never upset by it. But he once wrote a letter. He said, you think it doesn't upset me? He said, but when the news comes and I am in the center of all of them, they're looking at me, and I always take it calmly. All bad news must be expected. Napoleon never showed the slightest sign, but he said, when I leave them, about three-quarters of an hour afterward, I get it in my stomach. When the bad news comes and I am in the center, somebody must be disciplined, ordered, and show no sign, and he says, that's what I have to do. And that also is part of leadership. That is what the leader has to know, and that is what the ranks, looking at the leader, get to feel, and get to understand. It would be good if a leader acts that way by instinct, but it is good if he knows it, and knows that that is the way he ought to behave.

Another political leader whom I know is a man called Cannon, a very distinguished political leader, leader of a small organization in the United States. A great leader of labor, a great master of strikes, and a great man to handle people in an organization. I'll tell you one story about him. Somebody went to see Cannon one day, and when he came back he said, "Well, I've seen him, I've talked to him, I've told him everything." They said, "Yes, and what did he tell you?" He said . . . he couldn't say. "He said nothing." A remarkable person, recognized as such by all. But he was not able to analyze politics in the sense that I have spoken to you about at the beginning. He was not an intellectual type. He had one assistant, therefore, a man called Shachtman. And all historical and intellectual conflicts and all such business, Shachtman did it. And so you had the famous combination of Cannon and Shachtman. And when Shachtman left him, when they split, not only did Cannon go to pieces, so did Shachtman. Now you have famous combinations like that in the political history of the world. I will give you two others. You may have heard of them. Brandler and Thälmann, leaders of the Communist Party in Germany, Brandler had been a butcher but he was a political leader and his principal assistant was a tall, thin intellectual. But the two of them formed one person, the political leader. Luckily in some people, like Lenin, you have both in one man, but the two of them were together. And Cannon and Shachtman were together. When the time came to work out decisions after Trotsky was dead, Cannon couldn't head the organization by himself. He was a remarkable man, recognized as such by all. But there were certain things he couldn't do. He couldn't do the essential thing with which I began, analyze a political situation and work it out. You have to do that. If you can't do that, all the other things that you are doing are going to fail, as they failed with one of the greatest men the modern world has known, Leon Trotsky. He made a mistake in that fundamental analysis—I know why he made the mistake, I can't go into that now—but once that is wrong, no kind of character, no kind of abilities, no kind of devotion can help you.

The last example I want to give you is of a man called Healey. He leads a semi-Trotskyist movement in Britain today. He is an Irishman. He is the leader of this organization, and even his own party members and friends will tell you that he is the nearest approach to a gangster that the political movement has ever known. That's the type he is, but he is the effective leader. And why? Because the politics he is carrying on can only be carried off by a person of that type. Because certain incorrect politics exclude him from the opportunity to develop. When you're carrying on a wrong form of politics, you need violence, brutality, an extreme strength and vigor and a merciless discussion with anyone who opposes you because you can't win people in arguments. The things that Healey proposes and talks about, how can you argue them, they are a lot of nonsense. And that's a different type of leader. You have a political leader who suits a particular type of organization and particular type of politics.

Now, I will speak for about five minutes on some people who worked with me from 1941 to 1953. I told you just now about Napoleon and his leaders. I want to tell you about these people. One of them was a woman named Forest [Raya Dunayevskaya]. I have never known anybody who from outside had such a knowledge of the Russian Revolution and the foundation and development of Bolshevism from the beginning in 1903 and before that, to 1960. I have never known any private individuals who knew Russian who had so mastered that and so lived by it. She had her weaknesses, but if you were able to do something, that was an assistant. That was a member of the staff. I have known nobody like this, nobody. There was another one who knew what to do, somebody called Grace [Lee]. That girl had an important college degree in the United States. A high class women's college asked her to come and teach philosophy there. She had taken a doctorate of philosophy at two American universities, she was very familiar with German, she knew French. She took shorthand and typing, apart from her university degrees, and she was the best that school had ever had. She had general history, French and German, capacity to organize and grasp anything, a profound knowledge of philosophy and the ability to apply it to our own doctrine. I have never seen in all the organizations an individual whom I would exchange for her in her capacities. There was a third person who is still around us, I will not mention any names, who without a shadow of doubt is the most brilliant that I have ever met in all my life and who showed tremendous capacity. I have also met a labor leader who among those labor leaders who have come from the masses is a man with as much education and understanding as any I have known. Now I am going to draw something to your attention, these were four people whom I have never seen surpassed and some of them not equalled at all for the particular gifts that they had, who contributed to our organization and the development of the ideas, some of which stand to this very day.

Now I am going to tell you something now which I have never told anyone up to now. If I had to write a testament, God forbid, I would have to say something about each of them which could be very damaging in the ears and the mouths of stupid persons who do not understand what an organization is. They had great defects and so forth, but you do not judge members of an organization by their defects. You judge them by their qualities. And underline this please, underline it. Two plus two plus two plus two plus two: five twos in an organization does not make ten. It makes one hundred. Kamenev, Pyatakov, Bukharin, look what Lenin said about them. But they were the leaders of the committee, the central working committee, of the greatest political party that the world has ever known. There has never been anything like the Bolshevik Pary before or since. No political party was so clear in its mind and had such a perspective and was built up with such inherent power, etc. But look at what he had to say of each of them. Yet together they formed an organization and he knew that.

Now these people I am talking to you about, I know their qualities, nobody knows their defects more than I do. I was their political leader and together, they and one or two others I can't go into here, formed a group of people which it would be hard to equal anywhere. I know politics pretty well, you know, groups of people. I know the Labor Party pretty well and I know the Independent Labor Party very well and I wouldn't exchange those for any of these others, not any. And your organization, your political leader must be able to attract people of this kind. I have written a few pages and I am going to write a biography about George Padmore and I say that it was the testimony of Padmore's qualities that he was able to attract and keep people in his organization like Jomo Kenyatta and Kwame Nkrumah. That is the testimony of the political leader. If you can't hold them you are nothing and until you win them, you can't keep them. It is all very well to be a political leader when you become a premier or something and you sit down in a big chair and smoke a pipe or something, fine, wonderful, but the test of a political leader is to have nothing, and still draw some people. That is political leadership.

Now, for the last, knowing all this, I want to speak about a particular political person in the United States. It is clear that I attach immense importance to the abilities, character and personality of a political leader of any political organization. I believe that more important than ability is character. It is obvious that was what Lenin thought. Because ability — you can always get ability, if you have the character. You follow what I mean? It comes. You can manage. You mustn't be a fool of course. Character in the sense of broad humanity, capacity to meet with people, to integrate, etc. Shakespeare thought the same. Lenin, it is clear, knew that that, more than anything, was what was required, and that is what everyone he knew had.

Now, there is someone in the United States who should be, in my opinion, a political leader.[5] I think the choice of him as political leader is quite obvious, otherwise I wouldn't talk about him. He has lived in the United States all of his life. To be an international political leader that won't do.

You cannot be a political leader today if you have lived in only one country. Thereore, if you want your political leader to have the necessary breadth, what do you have to do? You have to see to it that he goes abroad, lives abroad and gains the international experience and contact which are necessary. Is that not so? Otherwise you are just talking about it, just talking nonsense, just babbling. That is number one. You sit down and you decide, you discuss the matter, and say, well he has lived in the United States all his life and we have to move him out for a while. For three months he has to go, or six if necessary. That is the political experience all had in the past, until recently. Send him over to France or Paris or somewhere, or do something with him, otherwise what can a person do? That is the first thing that has to be done if you want a political leader to carry out the duties which I have talked about.

The second thing is even more important. He cannot work in a factory, or typing letters, or be an agent for selling shoes or socks and run an organization. The things I am talking about demand constant concentration. Isn't that obvious? You have to see to it and make it clear that this burden is removed so that he can give his complete attention to what we are talking about. If you have 1000 people it is easy but if you have only ten it is not. You have to relieve him from working for somebody, for it demands every bit of ability, every scrap of energy, every bit of concentration and every bit of relaxation time. And he needs some contacts with people to be able to express himself in the way a political leader must express himself, and which I know from personal experience and from what I have seen. You have to do it, to relieve him.

Thirdly, I believe that not only must he be sent abroad to gain experience. (By the way, I don't only mean to go to Britain, you know, or to Paris. Let's say he is a political leader in Persia, you send him to Calcutta, to India; or if he is in India, you send him to Egypt, to Nasser, but you send him somewhere. Let him move around. And every three or four years you send him somewhere. You don't send him to go fend for you, he should fend for himself.) First of all, he should see some people and get to know what is happening and see and get to know them, some of the leaders, that is number one. Number two, you have to remove him from working for all sorts of people, for the work he has to do is plenty. Because he not only has to attract this kind of staff I have told you about, and it can only be attracted by somebody who has power and is exercising power; you have to be able to hold them, which means that he must know what he is doing and they should be able to come to him and know that when they come to him for this or that or the other they can get his broad considered views.

The [fourth] thing that I think about that I will mention now is that he must make an impact on his own people, upon his own public. He must be able to be effective in his relations and contacts with people so that the organization can feel proud of him and not only proud, but know that once he gets up to speak he is going to deal with whatever needs to be dealt with. And it is just as well, if he should produce not only journalistic articles but he should produce some solid work of which people are aware, to which it can be referred, "this is what so and so has done." In the world in which we live people respect that, this thesis or this piece of work or this history or something — so and so has done that. Help him to do that. If he is the man that we think he is he will want to do it. But he may have a lot of trouble. He may have a string of children, or an old mother who is very hard to keep, or a mother and father, I don't know what he may have; but watch him, realize his responsibilities and see to it that some concerted organized attempt is made in order to assist him to fill the post which is to be filled. You can't tell to what extent he may fill it. He may fill it and make of it an extraordinarily big post, far bigger than we thought. But that is the way we must think of a political leadership.

And if the political leader thinks of himself in this way and the people around him think of the political leader in this way, I have little doubt that they will be able to find a way, but if they don't, then they will be living from hand to mouth, and it will be their death and God help them.

Membership

We undertake a very serious examination tonight. It will be rather difficult, even for those who have some experience of the past, our past, some orientation, not merely something instinctive, but who have been practising and listening to the particular way we have been going. But even for you it will be difficult; and in any case it will be new.

What I am going to do is going to demand a great strain from you. I will tell you with some precision the line I propose to take. Number one: I shall establish that we are not only a new kind of people, a new kind of political activist, but our whole orientation, our understanding of ourselves, and therefore how we present ourselves to people, how we think, what we plan, what we propose, and how we carry it out depends upon this understanding of ourselves. Number one, I will have to make that clear. Number two: I will have to show, and this will take some length, why we are as we are, how we are what we are, and the distinction between us and all other political organizations that exist at the present time. I say organizations, not political types, because I hope to show, and you will be able to see for yourselves, that any number of people are thinking as we are thinking today. That is perfectly clear, and once you get clear in your mind what you are after, what we are after, you will be able to see that. Always suspect those who discover what nobody else knows and who have some extraordinary truth which they want to convince the world really matters. That is not valuable at all. So I have to go at some length into our historical origins and our historical perspective, and the fact that what we are doing a lot of other people are doing too. Why we are able to do it in an organized manner I shall touch upon. When that is done, when I give the historical background, the historical perspective, I will go into some detail [about] what we have been, what we have done, so that we will be able to understand what we have to do. I will spend some time on what we have done. And having done that, that is point three, I come to the final point: what I propose that the organization does in the view of what I have been saying and in the new recognition of itself which I hope to make clear.

Now, to begin with, the type of people who we are and the type of people whom politics demand today. That depends on knowing the type of people whom politics demanded yesterday. In *Facing Reality*,[6] on page 86 and afterward, I went into the type of person who was the political activist and the type of person whom the organization aimed at developing before 1914. Lenin was very clear about this. He said, speaking to the Bolsheviks, "Look at the Germans; they have had a hundred times more forces than we have." He understood the backwardness of Russia. He continues: "but they understand perfectly well that the average does not too frequently promote really capable agitators, etc. from the ranks." The average was not sufficient, they have to rise above the average. "Hence they immediately tried to place every capable working man in such conditions as will enable him to develop and apply his abilities to the utmost." You see, he chooses the capable working man, he has him in mind, what we call the advanced worker. "He is made a professional agitator, he is encouraged to widen the field of his activity, to spread it from one factory to the whole of his trade, from one locality to the whole country." Note please that that is a special advanced worker who is chosen from among the average workers and becomes a professional revolutionary, a professional politician making his experience in the country as a whole, he is a specially chosen person.

"He acquires experience and dexterity in his profession, his outlook becomes wider, his knowledge increases," — note this please — "he observes the prominent political leaders from other localities and other parties." That, if I may say so, is a reflection upon the limited means of communication, not only in Russia, but in the whole of the advanced world in those days. There was no radio, motor cars were not as they are today, there was no televsion, there was not the mass communication that makes a country today into one, and therefore you had to have these special leaders on an objective basis who moved around and gathered information that was not available to the average person. "He observes the prominent political leaders from other localities and other parties, he strives to rise to their level and combine within himself the knowledge of working class environment and freshness of socialist convictions with professional skill...."

Take note please of this "freshness of socialist convictions," because in those days it was to a large degree subjective, although based on the actual reality, whether you had socialist convictions or whether you were determined to overthrow capitalist society. It is not so today. Everyone has socialist convictions today in that he has to get rid of this thing which is crushing him down and threatens to destroy the whole of society. What was a subjective matter in those days is now an objective necessity of society.

And "he strives to...combine within himself the knowledge of working class environment and freshness of socialist convictions with professional skill, without which the proletariat cannot carry on a stubborn struggle with the excellently trained enemy. Only in this way can men of the stamp of Bebel and Auer be promoted from the ranks of the working class." It is very clear. Lenin conceived of the working class as people of a certain level, a certain average level, and the aim of the socialist movement, of the Marxist, is to seek and encourage and create a body of leaders. That's what he attempted or wanted do in Russia.

He goes on to say later: "When we have detachments of specially trained working class revolutionaries who have gone through long years of preparation, . . . no political police in the world will be able to contend against them, for these detachments of men absolutely devoted and loyal to the revolution will themselves enjoy the absolute confidence and devotion of the broad masses of the workers."[7] Now that is today *dead.* That does not apply anymore. To the degree that it applies it is reactionary and leads the working class to defeat after defeat.

Now, in 1956 I think it was, we made it perfectly clear already that a new type of working class was in existence. It was having new problems, universal problems, it had universal knowledge, etc., and therefore (a very important part of Marxism), what was advanced and revolutionary in one age had now become reactionary. It happens all the time.

Now I continue with the statement in *Facing Reality:* "Now, half a century later, what do we see? The trained professional agitator, the revolutionary socialist type of Lenin's day is today the basis of the bureaucratic machines of the unions, the political parties, and the governments." Remember that phrase please: "the unions, the political parties and the governments." "Society has moved on since that time, and these elite types have now become the greatest obstacles to that release of popular energy and creative power which has always been the most powerful motive force in the creation of a new society." They were needed before 1914, they built the movement before 1914. Today they are the greatest obstacles in the way of the movement. "Propaganda of the so-called 'Free World' against totalitarianism has obscured the fact that this particular social and political type is not necessarily a Communist. According to the political climate of the country he lives in, he may be a Communist or a rabid anti-Communist. In the United States or in Britain you will find him on every rung of the ladder of the union or the Labor Party. Often selfless and devoted, he is not infrequently engaged in a desperate struggle against a union or political bureaucracy. But his only perspective is that of substituting a more democratic, more capable, more honest set of bureaucrats."

I am speaking about the different types of political activists and leaders of a different epoch, of a particular age. Today we have a new type of political activist: "On whichever side of the Iron Curtain he is, he is the mortal enemy of the shop floor organization, of Workers Councils in every branch of the national activity, and of a Government of Workers Councils as the essence and content of a new society." He is a working class man, he is an intellectual, he is a functionary, but he is mortally opposed to the creative and independent activity of the masses of workers or the people in any community. He wants to overthrow the existing rotten regime, but he conceives of the overthrow as putting himself and his friends into power. He doesn't conceive of it as an extension of democracy. Whether he is a Communist or anti-Communist, for him the working class — and I would add, the peoples of the underdeveloped countries — are incapable of acting successfully without a trained and dedicated leadership. Here is the Marxist dialectic in its most profound content. The social type, the specific personality, which represents the spearhead of the workers' movement at the beginning of the century is today the solid core of the bureaucratic reaction in every section of the working-class movement.

Now I want to refer briefly, and I want to do that periodically, to the underdeveloped countries in their particular relation to this idea. I have stated that this thing, this particular type, was one particular type of leader at the beginning of the century before 1914 and now he is the complete reactionary. The process has moved much more rapidly in the underdeveloped countries. What we are watching in them is this, that the type of political organization which is formed and carries through the struggle for independence does not take years to become a totally reactionary organization. In other words, what took 40 to 50 years to develop in the advanced countries, or 25 to 30 years, now develops with extreme speed in the underdeveloped countries before the independence and after the independence. Most of those organizations which worked splendidly and finely before the independence, as soon as they get in, are immediately in difficulties and are unable to govern the country and have to develop the most reactionary tendencies. It is happening all over Africa today.

Now what faces us is the task of getting this clear in our own minds. It demands, it will require, serious study. I can only outline for you what is the process, the general process, but you will have to study it for yourselves. I can give you a general line: it affects all political people, all political organizations in the world today, all organizations without exception.

Our modern world begins with the Russian Revolution. The 2nd International, which Lenin had believed in fully and completely, had promised that they would not support the war (they had passed two big resolutions to that effect) but they had all gone to support the war. And Lenin set out to form an organization which would be a new International, because the 2nd International had held sway and had been one of the most powerful, dynamic and forward-looking organizations in society as a whole. In 1917, and then afterwards very rapidly till about 1921, perhaps a little later, the mass of the people rose in country after country and they followed the 3rd International or the revolutionaries against the 2nd International. That is what the Russian Revolution caused, it created a new International, millions of workers who were opposed to the 2nd International. The 2nd International had failed to carry out a revolutionary policy at the critical moment and the 3rd International moved into the position that the 2nd International was supposed to hold. Lenin formed the 3rd International. He organized it on the basis of the soviets of the Russian Revolution, the creative activity of the workers. And these two Internationals faced one another, the 2nd and the 3rd International. The 3rd was supposed to be revolutionary and the 2nd played about with it, but became more and more parliamentary as a result.

However, about 1922, Lenin was very ill and he made a statement to the 4th Congress of the 3rd International which has never been fully appreciated and which I advise you to work on, what came before and what came after. He had been ill for about a year and he was only able to come to the Congress to make one single address, and he told them this: he said, now look at the principles on which the 3rd International has been founded and which have been enshrined in the political policies and programs of the 3rd International, they are not suitable for the International. He had written some of them himself, the most important ones. He says, they are too Russian. You all don't understand them. He says, what I suggest to you is that you go home with those resolutions, study them for one year and then come back for us to go through them again. In other words, at the last Congress of the International which he attended, Lenin was already breaking with the concept of the party on which the 3rd International had been founded. If we did not know it at the time, we ought to know it today. He said, now this thing which I have put before you all, I have written the resolutions but you don't all understand them, we can't work on them.[8]

At the same time, or a little later, in 1923, Lenin broke completely with what he had been teaching before. This is what he told the people of Russia in those three last essays, which I have been studying, and that I am going to write about, and which I will go into with you anytime you are ready. He says, we have two things to do. One, we have to educate the peasants of Russia, nine-tenths of the population. And, two, we have to change the government, to re-organize the government, the government is rotten, it is as bad or even worse than a capitalist government, it is not even as good as a pre-capitalist government. He says, two things we have to do, therefore: to educate the peasants and to change the government.

Now I want to make the reference to the underdeveloped countries. Lenin did not say that the first thing which we have to do is industrialize, that we have to do this, that and the other which all these underdeveloped countries are now crazily pursuing and getting themselves into more trouble than ever. He said, number one, we have to educate the peasants, and number two, the corruption, incompetence and inability of the government to conduct affairs in a decent way, that we have to change. Those words are completely applicable to every underdeveloped country today, from Communist China down to the latest one from Africa. One, the education of the peasants, and, two, the change of the government from corruption, incompetence and general inability to govern the country. Those were the two things he said.[9]

He was not understood, because these are difficult conceptions. And there was a notable member of the Russian Bolshevik Party who became a leader of the tendencies which Lenin was dropping behind, and that was Trotsky. Trotsky had opposed Lenin on the question of the party. Lenin had insisted on forming a party, Trotsky had said this kind of party which you are going to form is going to lead the people to terrible cruelties of all kinds. However, Trotsky had said that we cannot have a democratic revolution in Russia, what you must have is a proletarian revolution, you cannot have a bourgeois democratic revolution, you must have a proletarian revolution. And he said that this proletarian revolution can only succeed and continue to succeed if there is a world revolution, a permanent revolution. That is the idea with which Trotsky fought Lenin in Russia up to 1917. In 1917 he joined with Lenin, because now Lenin said that the Soviet had been formed and therefore we will go on to the socialist revolution. Trotsky maintained his ideas about the permanent revolution, but he said on the question of the party I was wrong, Lenin was right, and he became 100% Leninist party type. He remained that way to the end of his days. He created a mass of mischief right through the revolutionary movement, holding on to what he thought he had been wrong on and holding on to the idea that in his theory of the permanent revolution he was absolutely right. He remained wrong on both of them and he has caused an immense amount of mischief, inside and outside Russia, for which all of us are paying today.

You will note that I say in 1923 Lenin was breaking with the concept of the party on which he had educated the 3rd International. He was also breaking with the concepts of the party and the peasantry and electrification, etc., which he had laid as the foundation of the development of Soviet Russia. That was happening in 1922 and 1923. Trotsky was holding on to them as tightly as ever. Lenin died and Stalin got hold of the power. You know how he got hold of the power, what was the basic principle? He also finished up with the concept of the party and he finished up with the concept of the world revolution. He finished up with the concept of the party and he concentrated on what Lenin had concentrated upon — the government. Because what the party used to do under Stalin was just a lot of nonsense. There was no real debate, the thing had already been fixed. They stood up and everybody voted and said yes. He concentrated on the government and the particular section of the government which he concentrated on was the police, the secret police. Stalin was not concerned with any party. But Trotsky kept on talking about the party and trotting out the great debates of the party and calling for reorganization of the party. Stalin just went on fixing up the party by means of the secret police. He saw what Lenin had seen, that the government had to be fixed, although Lenin wanted it fixed one way and he wanted it fixed another way to suit himself.

Trotsky was thrown out of Russia in 1928 and he began to form an organization which was supposed to take the place of the 3rd International at a critical time, in the same way that the 3rd International had taken the place of the 2nd International at a critical time. Trotsky insisted on the role of the party, where he confessed that he had been wrong before 1914. And he kept on insisting on the impossibility of Russia developing without the permanent revolution of all the advanced countries. That was his theory and that was what he educated the 4th International on. In other words, what I began this talk with, the new kind of person and new kind of political activist who had come into existence, Trotsky never understood.

He kept on saying that Russia was going to return to capitalism because the party was not doing what it ought to do and because of the absence of the world revolution. That is why he failed, that is the reason why Trotsky failed. Because the Stalinists or the members of the Communist Party all over the world had listened to Trotsky for years stating that Stalin's policy would end without a shadow of a doubt in the restoration in Russia of capitalism. That's what he kept on saying from 1924 right on to 1929. He said you are going to restore capitalism in Russia. In 1929 Stalin did exactly the opposite. He collectivized the peasants and he put the workers in their place and he nationalized more than ever. Whereupon the revolutionaries all over the world said Trotsky is a very fine fellow, a good revolutionary, but he was telling us the end of Stalin's policy in Russia would be the restoration of capitalism in Russia and now Stalin has made socialization, the nationalization of everything, stronger than ever. That was the ruin of the Trotskyist movement.

Trotsky, however, did not change. He continued to say to the end of his days, all the Stalinist parties are going to join the national bourgeois parties. He continued to say that inside Russia the bureaucrats, under pressure of war and revolution, the majority of them, would join the bourgeoisie, ready to restore capitalism, and as a result the 4th International would get its opportunity. That was Trotsky's policy and that was his conception. It was a continuation of what he thought Lenin meant in 1917, and his policy was a disastrous failure. Why? Basically for this reason. I began with it, the new type of political activist and political leader and working-class leader who had come into existence as a result of the development of capitalism and changes in society.

Trotsky took the position that the party was absolutely necessary. Lenin had been breaking with that in 1923, the role of the party, and that Russia would return to capitalism without the world revolution. Russia never did return to the type of capitalism that Trotsky was expecting. Stalin nationalized and collectivized the peasantry. The Trotskyist opposition, and for that matter, any opposition to Stalin, not only inside Russia but also outside Russia, simply faded away, because they had nothing to go by. On the one hand was Stalin carrying on in a certain direction, on the other hand was Trotsky, of tremendous reputation, pointing out that what Stalin was doing was going to lead to this, and it didn't lead to this, and it didn't lead to it in 1929 and when the war broke out it didn't lead to it. Trotsky completely misconceived the development of a new type of political leader and a new type of society, in which political leaders of the working class would seize the opportunity themselves to establish power and most of them looking to the Stalinist government and army to help them to seize power.

Trotsky's conception that they were going to join the bourgeoisie once more was entirely false, and the result of that has been that the working-class movement all over the world has not known where it stood, what to do with itself, what was its doctrine, what were its perspectives. Nobody was able to tell it anything which mattered. The result was that the 3rd International went along behind Stalin and now that Khrushchev has said that Stalin was a traitor and an enemy they don't know where they are. They are wavering and wobbling about between Khrushchev and China. The 2nd International gave up the revolution altogether and each party stuck with its own particular bourgeoisie, so that the working-class movement, as far as ideology is concerned, has fallen apart. It does not know where it stands. And the underdeveloped countries have not developed any ideology of their own. They don't know whether to go with the 2nd or the 3rd, and they themselves, as the years go by, are neither in one place or the other. They have nothing to teach their people or to bring them up in any way.

This is the question which I am going to deal with now. Up to 1914 the working-class movement on an international scale called itself Marxist. They passed resolutions against capitalism, called itself socialist, and said that when the war came it would resist and would overthrow capitalism and would not go into the capitalist war. It was educated on certain documents and ideas. It studied, more or less, *Capital*. It read and believed, more or less, in the *Communist Manifesto*. Bernstein had written, Kautsky had written, and various other Social Democrats had written, so that basically the movement subscribed to these or some adaptation of these. There were small groups on the left that were more Marxist and more revolutionary than the big ones. They went their own way. But by and large when they met in conference this was the kind of theory they listened to, that they educated themselves upon. And an advanced worker was advanced because he studied this and knew this.

Then came Lenin and the 3rd International with its tremendous break with them. The 3rd International and certain elements in the 2nd International educated itself upon the old Marxist doctrines and the new doctrines that Lenin had introduced to form the 3rd International. As the 2nd International became more and more reactionary, it paid less and less attention to any political theory, but it kept on, more or less, believing in the *Communist Manifesto*. Although not revolutionary, it thought that Marxism was correct but it didn't go in for revolution, etc. The 3rd International followed the doctrines of Lenin, until Stalin began to rewrite the whole history of the Russian Revolution, whereupon a powerful section of the working-class movement began to follow the ideas and theories of Trotsky. So that in the working class and left-wing movement as a whole, even among the underdeveloped countries, they wavered about between the 2nd International and the 3rd International that Lenin had founded and a few of them also followed Trotsky's theories and basic ideas in which he proved that Stalin was wrong and would restore capitalism in Russia, etc.

So those were the ideas by which the working-class movement and the people in underdeveloped countries educated themselves. All of them were based on a conception of the political party, but when Stalin began to rewrite the history of the Russian Revolution and to prove that Trotsky and all the others were traitors, the Russian ideology fell to pieces. Everybody knew that he was making it up to suit the particular needs that he had. And when Trotsky's predictions failed to come through, the rest of them began to fall apart. Until today Marxism as such is utterly discredited in the world. Not only is Marxism discredited, bourgeois democracy has no doctrines by which it educates or develops people. What have the working-class movements or the underdeveloped countries anywhere, what have they got to teach anybody? Absolutely nothing. The old doctrines before 1917, those have been discredited by Lenin. The Leninist doctrines lasted up to '20–'23 and Stalin corrupted them, twisted them up, so that they have no significance now for anybody. And Trotsky's doctrines themselves have been proved so utterly false and wrong, based upon the certainty that Stalin was going to restore capitalism in Russia, and that the different sections of the 3rd International were all going to join their own bourgeoisie, so that today there is no doctrine anywhere. And all of them, from before 1914 on, all stick to this doctrine of the party.

Now I want to make a clean break and show our organization, what it stands for and how it has arrived at that, and then to draw some conclusions.

In 1958 we published a document which came finally to certain conclusions. It is called *Facing Reality*. It drew some conclusions to which we had been moving all the time, but the thing that really brought us to it was the Hungarian Revolution. And this is what we said:

> The parties, the administrators and the planners have claimed always that without them society would collapse into anarchy and chaos. The Workers Councils recognized the need for an official center and for a head of state. Early in the revolution, because they believed Nagy to have the confidence of the people, they proposed that he assume the national leadership.

Follow this please with extreme care.

> But the councils finished once and for all with the delegation of powers to a center while the population retreats into passive obedience. . . . The Workers Councils made it clear that the power to legalize, incorporate, indeed disestablish an official center, rested with them. They drew no distinction between the work of production and the work of government. They decided who should occupy government posts, who should be dismissed, which ministries should be retained, which should be dissolved.[10]

That is what the Hungarian Revolution and the Workers Councils decided at once. I hope you get the full significance of that. They broke completely with the conception that a party was necessary. We saw that, we had been moving to it.

One of our comrades in France, a very able man and a devoted Marxist, in discussions for the preparation of this book, had said about Leninism, and we agreed, "The Bolshevik Party of Lenin was the greatest political party the modern world had known. In its heroic days it was incontestably the party of the proletariat and there is no greater testimony to this than the fact that before it could enslave the Russian proletariat, Stalinism had to destroy the party almost to a man, discredit, disgrace, and villify its leaders, rewrite the history of the Revolution, and suppress or re-interpret its historical documents."[11] But we go on to say:

> Even this party in the last analysis was a type of parliament with representatives of the workers divided into debating factions, increasingly removed from the actual condtions of social and particularly proletarian life.

Now these are the words:

> Today a party on this model, in an advanced country [and I'm not so sure it's only in an advanced country] can be nothing else but an instrument of oppresssion, tyranny, and failure.[12]

This is the absolutely final statement in terms of political parties today. Political organization of the old party type is certain to fail, oppress, tyrannize over the working class. The party formula has been exhausted, it can't work any longer, something new has to take its place, what exactly we don't know yet. But the moment you have a political party, don't look to it for carrying out the correct policy or for doing this that or the other. It is bound to fail.

Now a woman called Hannah Arendt, who has written very well over the years, published in 1963 a book which she calls *On Revolution*. She studies the Russian Revolution, she studies the French Revolution, and she studies the American Revolution. She studies the history of revolution. She comes to some conclusions, this bourgeois woman. She says that to know what has been happening in the world today "we must turn to the February Revolution of 1917 in Russia and to the Hungarian Revolution of 1956, both of which lasted just long enough to show in bare outlines what a government would look like and how a republic was likely to function if they were founded upon the principle of the council system."[13]

Now on page 275 she makes the final statement, final for us: "parties — as distinguished from factions . . . — have thus far never emerged during a revolution; they either preceded it, as in the twentieth century, or they have developed with the extension of popular suffrage. Hence the party, whether an extension of parliamentary faction or a creation outside partliament, has been an institution to provide parliamentary government with the required support of the people, whereby it was always understood that the people, through voting, did the supporting, while action remained the prerogative of government. If parties become militant and step actively into the domain of political action, they violate their own principle as well as their function in parliamentary government, that is they become subversive, and this regardless of their doctrines and ideologies."

In other words, the modern political party, whatever its policy or program, the moment it takes hold of any government, whatever its democratic intentions, becomes a system and a method and an organization which is opposed to the masses of the people. The only way you can look forward to that being changed is by a formation of independent councils everywhere. We have seen them twice.

I want to make about one reference to what is happening in the underdeveloped countries. The underdeveloped countries are now experiencing to the full, and in the most complete way, the devastation which this kind of political party and parliamentary government, with its government and opposition according to the British model, is carrying out in all the countries that have come into independence. The parties function well until the independence is achieved. But when the independence is achieved they begin to go to pieces.

U Thant[14] has said that the countries in Western Europe, the advanced countries, must accept the idea of the one-party state in the underdeveloped countries. I do not agree with that formulation at all, because a one-party state means the kind of state they have in Russia and the Socialist countries, which is only an extreme form of the political party that we, my group of people, and this woman, and a lot of people today are recognizing is absolutely hopeless for a modern government.

Chisiza, whose book I recommend to you,[15] Chisiza understands what is happening, but Chisiza recommends that at the moment of independence, the government which wins the majority in an election should automatically invite members of the minority to form a national government. This isn't bad, I mean that boy is dead, but he said don't have government and opposition, he says that is ruinous. I think differently, I will go further than Chisiza. I state that in an underdeveloped country, if a political party organizes itself properly and has a real program devoted to the mass of the people and the improvement of their situation, it will win with nearly all the votes, so that in fact it will become a one-party state. But the oppositions can take place, but there is no real room in most underdeveloped countries for any opposition to a party which is a genuinely mass party. That is the problem. U Thant formulates it wrongly. Chisiza has got closer to it.

Now I will give you an example of the way you cannot carry on politics and cannot carry on organization without disaster. For the last 18 years, I think, in Austria, there has been a government consisting of a combination of the Christian Democratic and the Social Democratic Party. I don't know if you know about it. They have been in existence for 18 years. You know what trouble they are in now? They are in trouble because the Hapsurg young man says that he is coming back to Austria to live, and that has thrown them into complete disorder. There is a tremendous battle going on, whether he should come or not. Why? They say because they are afraid that if that Hapsburg, who has been selling motor cars in the United States, comes back to Austria he will be able to gain a mass of support, particularly from the peasantry and other sections of the people. Now I want to ask you, you have been in power for 18 years and still you are afraid of a Hapsburg coming back and having influence with the peasantry? What have you been doing to those peasants all the time, if after 18 years that he has been in disgrace, chased out, he can still come back and still have influence? It means that something was wrong. And that is the situation, that is this cut-throat business that is taking place in underdeveloped countries between two parties because no party puts forward a genuine mass democratic program. So they have the opposition and all this business. There is no need for the opposition party and for the government party. This sort of business is an absolutely hopeless consideration to be carried out today. I hope you get that clear, you can discuss it afterward, but that must be established.

Now I want to go on to our organization. You saw in 1958 we had arrived at that position, that the whole party business whether of the democratic type or the party in the one-party state, and so forth, that was a hopeless failure. It is no longer suited to the 20th century; it is bound to oppress the masses of the people and follow a false line and corrupt them, disorganizing the country. How did we arrive at that? I want to tell you something about our organization. I am not asking you to join it, I am telling you to go and do likewise, or something else. About 1941 three of us came to the conclusion about Trotsky and his theory of the party that, if all he had to say for Russia after all these years was Stalin must be overthrown and the party reorganized, that was all, that was no good, and we decided to work and to establish new principles.

Now I want to go into detail as to what we did. In 1943 we published a document called, "Education, Propaganda and Agitation," it is still there to be read. Nobody bothered with it at the start but after two years when the party started to feel that it was going to pieces, all over the country they were reading it. In 1943 a member of our organization [Raya Dunayevskaya] published a study of the Russian question, the development of the Bolshevik Party, the Russian Revolution and what had taken place in the Russian economy. At the time no such study had been published anywhere. That girl did it, she went and started. She said, I want to see your first Russian documents, at the [Library of Congress] in Washington, beginning from 1900 and she came up the whole line, every one of them, until we reached to 1943. People who read the documents stated that they had not seen or read anything like that before.

A little later, in 1947, we published a document called *The Balance Sheet*. We analyzed parties in the U.S., the political parties that remained, and we traced their origin back to Abraham Lincoln, John L. Lewis, Franklin Roosevelt, and the rest of them. We placed them for the first time — you all will be able to test these matters — we placed the revolutionary organization in the framework of the life and history of the U.S. I have told you what was the education and the theories of the 2nd International, of the 3rd and of the 4th. We were breaking out of that.

In 1947 we published a document called *The Invading Socialist Society* And there for the first time we suggested that Stalinism was not a party which had gone wrong. Poor Trotsky, the moment you leave a basic political line you fall into subjectivism. His analysis of Stalinism was that the Stalinists had "supple spines," they were weak people who could twist all ways. His analysis of the Russian bureaucracy was that they wanted power and beefsteak. In 1947 in *The Invading Socialist Society* we said that Stalinism is a new formation. It was a new type of political leader and trade union leader, and a new type of intellectual who recognized the breakdown of capitalism and was suggesting that they themselves should take charge. They were not prepared to go along with the traditional capitalists. The fascists were another threat of the same type. We did this in 1947, we began. I remember it well and the sensation it caused among certain people when they saw it. But we didn't publish too widely.

In [1951] Hannah Arendt published *The Origins of Totalitarianism.*[16] There she stated that the Stalinists and the fascists and the rest of them were a new formation in society. We had hinted at it in 1947, but we came out with it definitely in a political resolution in 1951, a resolution called "State Capitalism and World Revolution," a resolution that stands substantially today as the best analysis you can find anywhere, political analysis, of the development of the Russian Revolution and the revolutionary movement. 1951. [Hannah Arendt] was just in front of us, but she was writing from general knowledge, we were writing from the working-class movement. We said this was a new social type that is based upon the development of world economy. They are not people with supple spines, they are not people who are bad people or greedy people or hungry people or wicked people; they are people who are filling a certain social need in the development of the economy. We published that resolution in 1951. In 1947 we published *The Invading Socialist Society* in which we stated this first.

In 1948 I published at the conference of the party we had joined [the Socialist Workers Party] a document and a speech on the Negro Question in the United States. It was recognized then by all of them as the best analysis of the Negro Question which had ever been done by the Marxist movement in the United States. It is today still the best. The key to that resolution was that the Negro movement was an independent movement. It would be able to hit the bourgeoisie a tremendous blow and by hitting the bourgeoisie a tremendous blow it would bring the proletariat on the scene and break up the Democratic Party. Don't you know that? That is what is happening, and that resolution has it. That resolution insisted on the independent validity of the Negro Question in the U.S. as a Negro question.

If I may make a reference to the underdeveloped countries, I have already put forward the formula to my friends, that the real peasantry of the advanced countries today are not some peasants in France giving De Gaulle trouble, and some peasants in Britain having extra special prices and so forth; the real peasantry of the advanced countries are the millions of peasants in the underdeveloped countries. Today, the economy of the world is one. And just as in previous centuries and previous decades the advanced elements in the population exploited the peasants, just so at the present time the populations in the advanced countries as a whole are exploiting the peasantry of the underdeveloped countries.

And this is the question to be drawn from it in relation to the analysis of the Negro question. A revolution, a genuine social and economic revolution, in the underdeveloped countries will hit the advanced countries and awaken the proletariat, the proletariat will have to move. Do you follow me? That was the resolution on the Negro question, that the proletariat might hang around, and the intellectuals, but if the Negro Question hit them they would have to change. That is what is happening to them in the U.S. today, this is only the beginning. And the genuine social movement in the underdeveloped countries would hit the advanced countries here and pull the proletariat from under the domination of the bourgeoisie that it is hanging around. That, however, is a point that is to be developed. That is what we did, we did that Negro resolution.

Furthermore, we did something else. We tackled the historical aspects of the U.S., one of our comrades did that [William Gorman]. We have got him back now but he had already done sufficient to show that we were able to put forward ideas and develop historical conceptions in regard to the history of the U.S., that no Marxist or proletarian movement in the U.S. had ever done. That was not all. There were cetain questions in Marxism, such as, for instance, the early Economic-Philosophical Manuscripts, which are being printed today, we published them mimeographed. There were publications by Lenin in the Russian, his Philosophical Notebooks, we [translated and transcribed] them, we, a group of a few dozen people. We did more than that. We did some literary criticism, of a Marxist type. I wrote the book.[17] We did more than that. I wrote, and it is there now, about 80,000 words, and I could not have done it by myself, it was the comrades I had. I wrote an analysis of Dialectical Materialism, the philosophy of Hegel, as carried out by Marx, in relation to the Russian Revolution and the development of the working-class movement. We call it now *The Nevada Document*.[18] 80,000 words. It is there still.

Now I want you to ask yourselves, how does it happen that a few dozen people, in all these fields, this tremendous range, should perform absolutely unknown, and to that time untouched work? My most recent work has been that book on cricket.[19] The reviews that are being published, the letters that people are writing to me, say that is the finest book that has ever been written on cricket in Great Britain. That is the general opinion. Why? It is because of the particular Marxist method. I don't make any fuss about saying that I am a Marxist in the book and that I am using the Marxist method, that it is very clear to everybody, and that I don't believe in capitalist society, and that cricket has declined because capitalist society had declined and that if cricket is to come back again the M.C.C.[20] can pass as many laws as it likes, that will not fix it, society will have to change before cricket changes again. That is plain in the book.

Now that is a fantastic achievement and I want to tell you, and all those who are hearing this, that this particular line of things that we have done remains to this day, I wouldn't say unparalleled, but some of them are untouched and unsurpassed in the whole history of the revolutionary movement. Others have been living on the Second International which has gone to pieces and has had to give up its Marxism. Then they try to live on the Third International which Stalin has corrupted with any number of lies, which now they are saying is no good, and they are abolishing his books and pulling down his statue. And then you have to go by Khrushchev or they went with Trotsky, who said Stalin was going to join the bourgeoisie. There is nothing at all.

That is the list. I have asked the comrades in the U.S. to make a list of these things and to publish them. It is in reality an astonishing achievement. And do you know why? Why is it we were able to do it? When I tell the comrades that so and so has done that and that, some of them get very impatient, some of them may get very angry. But I have already written in some one of my articles what happened. I say that when a group of people or some others find something new, it is as if they have been living on a level with everybody else but by some chance they happen to get up on a great height. When you get to a certain height above the others it is as if you have discovered a new field, a new prairie, a new landscape, and all you have to have is the energy and the drive to go on and you immediately begin to pick up a whole lot of new things which others on the level below don't see, it never crosses their mind. Well we had managed, by reasons which I needn't go into, to make that move up, that leap, whereupon our various people began to move and to find out. Everybody who had any energy or anything was just going to go forward, discovering and developing in fields that had not been touched by Marxists for the previous hundred years.

We also did something else. I am not going to go into detail. But we picked up some people, uneducated, not literary or historical, not in the slightest, and we found that they were able to do work which had never been done before by people who had had twenty times their education and their opportunities. It happened three times in our organization, and it should have happened four times.

Now what to do, what conclusions do I draw from that? The conclusions I draw are three and they apply not only to members of the organization, but to all others. Number one: please go through Lenin's volumes 1–12 of the *Selected Works*, begin from 1 and go through to 12, two or three people can do it, and select every statement in which he says that every new creation in the working-class movement has got to be the creation of the working class itself and not the work of intellectuals and others. Not only the actual change in society and the creation of new political forms, but even methods of struggle. He says that political leaders, for any serious methods of struggle, have to depend on the working class as such. Go through the *Selected Works*, 1–12, and find out all those passages and put them in a list with the dates and get them into your head. Publish them, let everyone be aware of them, you in particular be aware of them, and know what is happening, and know also how wrong you can go if you are not aware of that. And the chief example is Mr. Trotsky with his "supple spines."

Number two: I am suggesting that you educate the organization on its past and what it has achieved and how it has achieved it. You give classes, so they know who they are, where they have come from and where they are going. That is my second conclusion. I regret bitterly that I am in no position to do that myself. They have to know and to appreciate what they have done, it is the only way that they can know what they will be able to do.

Number three: it is closely related to number two. They have to organize themselves and prepare the publication of a journal or a paper. I believe it should be once a week, if necessary, one page, one piece of paper, page one and page two. The first thing I want to tell you is that the paper is not for the public, that is the mistake all these people make. When you just have a small group of people, the paper is for the organizers and for the political organization to be aware of itself and to know what it is doing and where it is going. If it does that properly, it is sure of an audience.

The second thing I want to say about the organization and the publication of the paper is that the paper has to be written and prepared by the membership itself. The old organizations got the special advanced clever people, and that is not only not necessary today but is totally reactionary and the working-class movement today does not want advanced, capable workers who will do what Lenin was saying these advanced, capable workers should be doing, what he was saying in 1900. The world has gone beyond that. The paper should be divided into various sections. Next time that we discuss I am going to go into that, what should be the central direction of the paper, what should be the associate sections. But each and every section should be under the direction and coordination of a section of the organization or such people whom that section of the organization should incorporate into its activities. And there should be no misunderstanding about it.

I want to take, for example, that section of the organization which will deal with the question of the underdeveloped countries in Africa. I am prepared to work with them and help them. I, for example, have got a manuscript which I have prepared especially for publication, I haven't finished it yet because I haven't had the opportunity, on the development of the revolution in Ghana. I have done eight or nine chapters and one or two chapters remain.[21] I am prepared to submit that to the various comrades and friends who will take on themselves the responsibility for dealing with the African question in the underdeveloped countries. There must be one or two friends or associates who will deal with the question of the West Indies, by which I mean all of them, Cuba right down to British Guiana. There are others who will deal with literary subjects, there are others who will deal with the basic economic questions. But every section of the organization is responsible for a particular section of the newspaper and they are *responsible* for it. No rushing around now and then to the leader to ask him to write an article on this or that. That is absolutely outmoded, reactionary and bound to lead to confusion and disaster today.

Furthermore, I would like to add to that that the past of the organization and sections of the work which I detailed today, and which I have asked you beforehand to get together and have asked you to publish as a list — sections of the organization which will be dealing with certain sections of the paper should also be directed towards working at those particular parts of our previous work which are connected with what they have to do.

For example, there is literary work at the present time which the paper will have to take care of. I used to be bitterly opposed to any reviews of books or literature, etc., in the old paper. I knew why I was, I know why I have changed from that. I will give you the best of my experience and advice. But those that are handling that should also be able to take up the book, *Mariners, Renegades and Castaways,* and they should carry out the educational policy of the organization in regard to the past of the organization; a particular section of the organization that is dealing with that in the paper should take up that section of the work and carry it through. They should be responsible for it, and to be able to bring in anybody whom they want.

That particular section which is dealing with the Negro Question should begin with certain books which I shall tell them and also should master that Resolution on the Negro Question in the U.S., which still remains the best Marxist resolution that has ever been done there. They should begin with that and they should be the ones to educate the organization on that question and should be the ones to bring it up to date. So that the past of the organization and all that is important in it, etc., should be brought to the organization by different sections of people who are doing it; they can always do it, you can help them. And that should be whether your organization consists of ten or ten hundred.

Now I think we have done enough for tonight. I will just review what I have done, so that there will be no misunderstandings. First of all, I made it clear that a new type of person was the political leader and the political representative of the progressive classes in 1963, different to the type of person whom Lenin wrote about in 1900. That Lenin and these others were forming and aiming at building a political party, that today the political party is completely outmoded, a different type of organization and government are required. Our organization has arrived at that conclusion, and other people, students on a historical scale, have arrived at the same conclusion and stated it almost as brutally as we have stated it. Chisiza in writing about Africa has come very near to the same thing. This kind of political party and government and opposition is what will ruin all those underdeveloped countries until they finish up with it. But they are not therefore to run into the one-party totalitarian state.

I have shown that we came, having broken away from these old ideas, and were able to develop all sorts of things which were not being done in the Marxist movement at all. It was because we had got up on a height and a whole new world was before us. And you all didn't know that from 1953– 1963, that's what happened to you. You have to know what happened up to 1952, and see it and understand it, and then you will know what happened to you between 1953 and 1963, and what you have to do from 1963 on. Otherwise you just have an instinct and you have some scraps of information, etc., and you are just wandering around.

You don't know what I have just told you, you are not aware of it. You are not aware of your place in the historical development of all these political parties and the bankruptcy of all these political parties. There is nothing to them anywhere, they don't know what to say, they don't know what to do. It wasn't always so. At one time they had something. The 2nd Internatonal had something; the 3rd International had something; and the Trotskyist movement at one time had something. Today none of them has anything, they have nothing to go by. And the underdeveloped countries, what have they to go by? India is developing something, Mao writes something. The chief thing I remember about Mao Tse-tung is a resolution: one day he said, "Let a hundred flowers bloom." Everybody must have talked. Forty-three days after he put everybody who bloomed in jail. What kind of mentality, what kind of thinking is that?

That is how our organization, having got to a height, found out all sorts of things and it explored tremendous areas. When I look back at it, I am somewhat astonished and it has given me the idea of the power that an organization with a few people can find once they have discovered something that corresponds to the necessities of the age.

Now you will go through it and battle with it and work it out.

"McNamara"

Tonight I propose to do the talk in a manner different to some degree to what I originally proposed. This one is for all of us, in Britain and elsewhere. Let me strike the first note clearly. Whoever we are, wherever we are, we have to concentrate on two elementary things. The first is adequate reproduction of material that is typed. That naturally means, of course, typing, but I don't think that typing is too difficult. Adequate reproduction of material that is typed or material that comes from a newspaper, magazine or book. And, secondly, the question of tapes. I am very concerned that any tape that I make here, people in Glasgow or in Dublin or in Sheffield or in Dover should be able to listen to as a normal thing; and any tape that they make, we here should be able to listen to as a normal procedure. That is the age in which we live and if we do not practice and get into the habit of using these conveniences we will still be living in one age when the political development, which is also basically an economic development, has carried us into another age. There are one or two things which I wish to refer to at the end also, but I want to make that clear: those are the things that I want to know that you are paying attention to.

Now, tonight I want to speak to everybody. I have had two talks before. They may be reproduced for you in whatever way that it will be convenient. But there are one or two things which have been absent and which are necessary tonight. That first thing I have said I will show you later how necessary it is.

But now I want to go into something which must be permanently in our minds and which we are apt to forget. I want to begin with a woman who is known but we have not done much with her work. She had a lot to say that was valuable. I mean Rosa Luxemburg. And I have here a pamphlet by Rosa Luxemburg, *Leninism or Marxism*. It was written in 1904 and I want you to watch it particularly.

On [the page] where she is speaking about the small part played by the conscious initiative of the party leadership in the shaping of tactics, she says

[The title of this section, taken from the name of the Secretary of Defense of the United States, is intended to indicate the unified political-economic-military form and movement of the society in which we live. — *editor's note.*]

that this "can be observed in Germany and other countries. In general, the tactical policy of the Social Democracy is not something that may be 'invented.' It is the product of a series of great creative acts of the often spontaneous class struggle seeking its way forward."[22]

I hope that you have that clear. I will go on: "The unconscious comes before the conscious. The logic of the historic process comes before the subjective logic of the human beings who participate in the historic process. The tendency is for the directing organs of the socialist party to play a conservative role. Experience shows that every time the labor movement wins new terrain those organs work it to the utmost. They transfer it at the same time into a kind of bastion, which holds up advance on a wider scale."[23]

I will spend a minute or two explaining that, for that is the historical process in 1964 as much as she explained it in 1904. It is the mass movement which creates the forms and the methods of struggle on a large scale and on a small. Lenin made no mistake about that issue. It is the mass movement that creates, and she says that it having been created, the Social Democratic leadership (for which you can substitute the Stalinist leadership) then proceeds to draw conclusions from it and establish this which becomes a barrier in the way of the further development of the mass movement. And that has been taking place steadily all through. That is exactly what the Stalinists have done, they have taken 1917, the great upheaval of the masses, and tried to establish it as the norm and basis of all procedure and thereby they have stultified and absolutely crushed the imperative development of the mass movement. Trotsky was another; he tried to do it in a revolutionary way, they did it in a bureaucratic way.

Now Lenin knew this very well, there is a passage which I recommend to you and I will read because it is necessary to have these things constantly in mind, otherwise what you are doing becomes routinized and reactionary, not only in regard to the Socialist movement but in regard to yourselves. Lenin says as early as the 1905 revolution: "The point is that it is precisely the revolutionary periods that are distinguished for their greater breadth, greater wealth, greater intelligence, greater and more systematic activity, greater audacity and vividness of historical creativeness, compared with periods of philistine, Cadet, reformist progress." And then he goes on to say, "But Mr. Blank and Co. picture it the other way about. They pass off poverty as historical-creative wealth. They regard the inactivity of the suppressed, downtrodden masses, as the triumph of the 'systematic' activity of the bureaucrats and the bourgeoisie." I may interject here that that is precisely what the Communist Parties and the Labor Parties everywhere are doing. Lenin goes on: "They shout about the disappearance of sense and reason, when the picking to pieces of

Parliamentary bills by all sorts of bureaucrats and liberal 'penny-a-liners,' gives way to a period of direct political activity by the 'common people,' who in their simple way, directly and immediately destroy the organs of repression of the people — in a word, precisely when the sense and reason of millions of downtrodden people is awakening, not only for reading books but for action, for living human action, for historical creativeness."[24]

This is what Lenin was saying in 1905. This is what he never lost sight of, never at any time. In 1904 Rosa Luxemburg knew this. She knew this very well and she pointed out the instinctively, naturally conservative process of Social Democracy and any organized party. But then she went on in the same pamphlet to attack Lenin. She says: "The ultra-conservatism asked by Lenin is full of the sterile spirit of the overseer. It is not a positive and creative spirit. Lenin's concern is not so much to make the activity of the party more fruitful as to control the party — to narrow the movement rather than to develop it, to bind rather than to unify it."[25] In other words, her criticism of Lenin was absolutely wrong. She understood the conservative character of the political leadership. But she attacked Lenin for what Lenin was never guilty of, never.

That was the situation in 1904 and 1905, both of these people thinking and talking in these terms. It was natural to them to do so. If anybody in 1963 still believes that the political party is necessary for the education of the masses, to make them understand, to teach them Marxism and the essentials of socialism, he is crazy. This what they knew and what they thought in 1904, 1905, over 50 years ago. The situation today is such that if you still are of the belief that the mass of the people have to be taught the elements of socialism by a vanguard, then the whole situation is a waste of time. They have not learned it in 50 years. Trotsky, by the way, in some of his last writings, came to that conclusion. He says that if they don't make the revolution in the course of the coming war then we have to look upon the idea of a socialist revolution as utopian and we have to find something else to do. That's where you find yourself. And we have pointed out in *State Capitalism and World Revolution* the particular kind of mistake that he made.

Now, I think it is necessary that in all plans and discussions, etc., this must be the central issue around which thought moves. We come now to the question of Marxism and the small Marxist party. The small Marxist party in the old days was a vanguard party, it sought to educate the workers, the most advanced workers, the best people, so that they could lead and teach the others. Today the small Marxist party, or any section of society that is concerned with getting out of the tremendous burdens that capitalism has placed on us, has to do the exact opposite. An organization today, of whatever kind, has to understand that it hasn't got to teach the masses anything. What it has to do is recognize that leadership has always existed under all forms of society. You have to take up any old book, the Bible or anything, and understand that the creation of a body of leadership for a specific task is a natural human result of human intelligence and human association. That is no problem. What the Marxist organization has to learn is to be able in 1964 to see and understand the socialistic and revolutionary instincts that exist in the mass of the people. We have said this before but never very clearly. It is absolutely clear to me now, the socialism that exists in the population, the resentment, the desire to overturn and get rid of the tremendous burdens by which capitalism is crushing the people. That is what the Marxist movement has to learn, to see it, to understand it, and to be able to develop it. In other words, it is not so much concerned with educating the masses, the masses don't need any education at all, absolutely none. The Marxist organization and the rest of them have to educate themselves.

The process of the organization and the intellectual development is entirely opposite to what the Vanguard Party used to do. And I want to add again, it is to be concerned with learning to understand the socialistic instincts, the socialism inherent in the working class (Engels wrote about that some 80 years ago), and it has to realize the persons whom it needs to educate are the members of its own organization and those people who like every other section of society seek to do something. You have to educate yourself in the business and process of Marxism, whereas the Vanguard Party was concerned to educate its members to the degree that it was possible in order for them to go to educate the mass. Today the absolute opposite is required. You have to educate yourselves and those people who are in your circle in order to be able to understand the socialism inherent in the masses, what we have written and called *The Invading Socialist Society*. Unless you are thinking that way, you would not have much influence on the mass movement but to disturb yourself and get yourself into a complete mess and break up your organization.

We have had during the last few months the most tremendous proof of that possibility, we have had the Negro movement in the U.S. Who have led it? The Communists have preached for years in the U.S. about what the Negro people ought to do. Recently we have had the Black Muslims who were to tell them what to do, the NAACP did a legalistic business and it attacked the Communists and it attacked the others whom they thought would be telling the mass of the Negro people to take steps which were adventuristic and so forth. What does all this mean today in 1963? It means not a thing. Who educated the Negro mass movement? Who? Nobody knows. It is certain that those millions of people who are acting together thousands at a time and have dragged so many white people into the movement with them and have shaken the whole of the U.S. Government, have Congress and Kennedy and all of them in disorder, and have made themselves the center of attention of not only revolutionaries but of progressive peoples everywhere, who taught it to them?

But what I have to say and what I want you to understand is that, as far as I have seen so far, nobody has fully explained or understood that movement. And I want to give you some idea, and I want to give all the comrades some idea, of what it is to be a Marxist. You have many quite intelligent people who are not Marxists, but the Marxists have the method. What is that movement? Is it that the Negro people in the U.S. have at last picked themselves up to make the great struggle for their equality? That is a lot of nonsense. That movement, I deeply regret that I'm not there, is an indication of what the proletariat and the revolutionary elements in society are able and are driven to do in 1963. People talk about the Negro movement having been stimulated by what took place in Africa and the role of the Africans. That to me is without sense. Let me give you an example. I have been taught in school, and many famous historians have written, that the great movement of painting and so forth in the Renaissance, in learning in general, in Italy came from the defeat of the Byzantine regime by the Turks in Constantinople and the rush of the Constantinople Greeks to Italy. That dominated the books for many years. Within recent years, at least recent to me, a new process of analysis of the Renaissance in Italy has developed. They are saying that what took place in Italy may have used the expulsion of the Greeks from Constantinople but that it was inherent in the Italian development and would have taken place under all circumstances whether Greek historians and students of Greek literature and Greek science had been expelled from Constantinople or not. That business, that the Renaissance was due essentially to the Greek influence from Constantinople, that is now dead. They say that that was something inherent in the Italian development itself. And the Negro movement in the U.S. today was inherent in the movement of society in the U.S. They are merely the first section of the revolutionary forces developing in the U.S. and in any modern country.

What you have to note is, first of all, some obvious things. Children, why are the Negro children right in the front of this and taking part as they are? Children did not take part in revolutionary movement before, that is part of 1963. With television and radio the children now are a part of the family, nothing of a social nature takes place without the children being involved, they are affected profoundly with the importance of the state organization and the state penetration into the life of the family. They are not left out, so that both organizationally and as a matter of communication they are part of family existence. Therefore, when anything is to be done, young and stimulated, they take part. It is not something that is specifically Negro. We can be certain that in any tremendous revolutionary movement, any upheaval of the great mass of the population anywhere else, the mass of the children are going to take part also. That is what that means. Furthermore, why has the thing spread with such rapidity, something like the General Strike in Russia in 1905, the first general strike, in the most backward country of Europe, immediately after which they formed the Soviets? It is means of communication, an advanced means of communication, rapidity of contact, number one. And number two, the sharpness and the backwardness of the population in regard to all that they see around them and their needs. That is what has given the movement its tremendous power. It is part of the U.S. society in the second half of the 20th century. It is because the Negroes feel themselves so deprived and so eliminated from what they see all around them and what they are experiencing in the second half of the 20th century in one of the most advanced countries in the world, that that movement has got the extraordinary power that it has. Later I am going to take up our particular role in regard to the Negro struggle in the U.S.

Until that Negro movement is analyzed in terms of the fact that it is a part of the U.S. society, a revolutionary movement, it will not be understood at all. And it is the Marxists who have to do that, nobody else can do it, put before the public what that Negro movement in reality symbolizes. It symbolizes the revolutionary movement of the people of the U.S. because the Negroes are a section of the people of the U.S. and their tremendous actions only have significance and can only be understood when it is realized that they are acting as they are acting because they are a revolutionary part of U.S. society. I can only touch upon this subject here but I want my comrades and all the friends to realize what is their responsibility. That is the kind of thing that depends upon them and them alone. Nobody else can do it, because you have to do a lot of hard work and you really have to absorb Marxism and to understand what Rosa Luxemburg understood and what Lenin understood and has left for us to follow along. Otherwise you go in for a lot of psychology and believe that it has happened to the Negroes because Africa is free and all sorts of nonsense.

I have brought all that in because we have to say certain things, but it is necessary that we never forget that the Negro movement in the U.S. today is one of the most tremendous historical developments of the age, and it is not a question of Negroes, it is a question of the revolutionary development of U.S. society.

Now, that being understood, and that being a part of our outlook which we never forget even if we have to go out and give out 150 leaflets, because if we forget it we lose ourselves, I now want to move on to what I have called "Mc-Namara" but which will not really be McNamara. I want to move on to the function of Leninism and what we have learned from him, what Rosa Luxemburg attacked him for. It is of profound significance to us today. She understood the historical creative function of the mass movement, but she believed Lenin's emphasis on centralism and the role of the party was reactionary. She was entirely wrong, she never went further than Lenin in understanding what the mass movement stood for. But he insisted on the absolute importance, particularly under Czarism, of having some sort of central, functioning and active and precise organization. It was because he understood the inherent power of the mass movement that he thought that it was necessary to have something that would correspond to that, but he never showed that he didn't understand that it was the mass movement that would create everything. And I want tonight to move very rapidly and abruptly to some kind of centralized conception of the organization of comrades wherever they are.

Now I believe that it is necessary for somebody to put forward a system, a centralized procedure. You can object to it, you can say you don't like that, but if a centralized procedure is put before you then you can say you don't like it but a necessity is then imposed upon you to substitute something else instead. And I am going to put this forward very confidently because it means that if you don't like it or you don't like certain aspects of it, you will have to do something about it, substitute something else. No absurd talking here, there and everywhere and "I wish that" and "I like that" and "I don't like that." I want to say at once that I am referring not only to centers, recognized centers, but any group of people anywhere who wish to function.

I believe that there should be a centralized organization, a meeting once a week, every week, as sure as day on let us say a Monday or a Tuesday or whenever you like, which is automatic. There must be no misunderstanding or uncerainty as to whether or not, it just takes place, and the organization gets to know this and other people get to know it also. Now that centralized organization should consist of, it seems to me, for the first hour, business, a rapid dispatch of business, and for the next hour and a half, of the central political attitudes and ideas of the organization. When you come to this meeting, and everybody should come to it, it should be a general meeting in which for the first hour there should be business matters (and I will tell you in a moment what I mean by "business matters" in an hour), and then for an hour and a half the central political business of the organization.

The secret of that is not merely coming on time and paying attention to the business, the secret of that is the proper preparation of the meeting. That is why you need two people, somebody in an office who performs the routine organizational secretarial functions of the organization, somebody who is paid, comes in at nine in the morning and leaves at five, and why you need a political leader. I believe that the political leader and somebody else should be the persons responsible for this meeting, not two, three people. Some kind of organizing secretary should be responsible for the business side of the meeting with the political leader very much aware. And the political leader and somebody else should be responsible for the second half of the meeting in which problems, which we shall call "McNamara" for the time being, will be dealt with.

The secret of the effectiveness of such organization rests in the preparation. When you come to that meeting, all aspects of that meeting must be thoroughly prepared and the people who are in charge of that meeting are able to say what it is they are going to do, what it is they expect, and carry everything rapidly through. The British Cabinet meets every Wednesday morning, I think, for about two hours. Now and then Macmillan calls an extra meeting. It is because, among other reasons, the meeting is properly prepared. I don't think the second half of the meeting should be the responsibility of one person, I think a meeting of this kind should be the responsibility of two people, of two of the most responsible and effective political leaders in the organization. Between them they must handle that meeting and that meeting is the central core of the political life of the organization. It should also be, in time, the meeting at which the basic elements of the newspaper should be adequately discussed and decisions as to points which are in dispute be taken, because I do not see the political life of the organization as being too separate from the journalistic life of the newspaper. Not in the way that I see the functioning of the organization and functioning of the newspaper.

Now let me develop that point to some degree in regard to the organization as we know it. We have got a certain past. I believe that the first stage of the political education of an organization in regard to the problems that have been posed by McNamara, and I have gone into them and I will go into them later, must be what our organization has done in the past in regard to these matters. We have a past, it is a remarkable past and the time has come when we not only have to be able to tell people about it, but we have to know something about it ourselves. The past of the organization on the question of the stage of capitalism which we have reached, upon the function of the working class, what we have done in the past is the inescapable preliminary of the studies and activity, the work that we are going to do at the present time and in the next period. So that right away, from the beginning of the meetings of the organization that I have described, the past of the organization becomes a central thesis and activity. The study of McNamara demands a study of what the organization has done in the past and its views about the analysis of society in general and the society of a particular country.

Now I want to switch that over to the Negro question. I said the other evening that on this question work that we have done is still looked upon, as far as I know, as the best that has been done in the U.S. on this question. And in my opinion it still is. Not only is that so but the recent events have shown it to be so and formed an inescapable preparation for understanding what is happening today and what will happen tomorrow. Do any of you know what is the basis of the analysis of the Negro Question that was put forward by our tendency some 14 or 15 years ago? You don't. And that is the thing that is strangling the organization, that has helped to strangle it, and will prevent it from being able to lift itself forward. The basis of the analysis put forward and accepted by the Socialist Workers Party, although as soon as we split they fell back again, was this: that the Negro Question in the U.S. had a validity of its own, that it was a force that was able to and should be encouraged to act independently, irrespective of the proletarian elements in the population, that it was to act on behalf of its democratic rights and that it would act on behalf of its democratic rights. And then the resolution and analysis went on to say that this action by the Negro people on behalf of their democratic rights would be an action which could and would unloose the proletarian struggle for socialism in accordance with historical experience in the past. That is the analysis of the Negro Question. And also it went into the effect of this independent struggle of the Negroes upon political life in the U.S. and the effect that it was certain to have on the political development of the U.S. as a whole and the consequences for the proletarian struggle for socialism. What do you all know about that? Not a goddamn thing, nothing. It is there. I haven't been able to develop it because I wasn't there, but you don't even know it.

Now I want to go a little further. That is not the particular business, the particular business (note my phrasing please) of what I call McNamara, it is not its particular business. I believe that while the political leaders of the organization plus some secretarial element should hold a meeting once a week or once every ten days, but you should have it regular as the clock, the other members of the organization should be divided up, two or three in a group to do, one, the Negro question (and this work must begin with our past and not only on that subject) then two or three others would do the underdeveloped countries; two or three others would do literature, I hope two or three would do science, according to how the organization can develop itself, and they will meet and function in such a manner as is satisfactory to them, they can meet and discuss and involve anybody whom they can get and go their way. At the center there is the regular meeting of the organization which deals with business and deals with political business that the political leadership looks upon as central to the whole. And these individual sections go their way doing their independent, specific work on some particular sections. If you don't do it that way, you will never be able to do it.

Now the particular sections, two or three at a time, they may find eight or ten people. I went half way with that in *Facing Reality*, but it takes time to get to the full analysis of these profoundly difficult problems and to get rid of what has been hanging upon our heads and our shoulders since the Russian Revolution. That is what Rosa Luxemburg is talking about. When something of this kind takes place, then the political organization settles down, examines it empirically, draws conclusions from it, and that stands in the way of the future creative development of the great mass movement. She knew that in 1904. Lenin knew that too. That is why in 1922 at the Fourth Congress he said, now look here, these resolutions that we have written, there's nothing too much wrong with them but they are unsuitable, they are too Russian, they don't suit the Communist International. That is his last statement to them. He says that I suggest you go home and for one year you study them over and then bring them back and let us see. He understood what was wrong, what was fundamentally wrong, because to organize and put forward resolutions, etc., in that way was something foreign to his whole conception. And he knew that it was all wrong. Trotsky starts with the 4th International and he says he begins with the first Four Congresses of the Communist International. This is a comedy today. At any rate we have to begin the different sections divided up, taking up the past and finding out where we shall leave it behind, what is necessary to us, and going on with our business. I recommend to you that a great part of your work should consist, apart from much working of tapes and so forth, should consist of preparation of material which for the moment I will call articles, something that you can hand round, and which in time can easily become the means of preparing material for the paper.

I hope you see in general what I'm talking about. If you don't understand me ask me about details. But that is a concrete, specific procedure for action. How long it will take for you to function in this way, I don't know, nobody knows. A political organization does the best it can. You may be able to divide yourselves into four or five groupings of three each. You may be able to divide yourselves into two or three. If you can only divide yourselves into two, it means in reality that you cannot function on a very large scale. But it is necessary to divide yourself, to have a center which can keep an eye on everything and which you can consult and which will deal with the organizational and political prospects as a whole, and the rest divided up into sections, systematically carrying on activity in some particular sphere, and in the world in which we live breaking out and not bothering yourself too much about who is a member or who is not, but all people who are ready to function with you, coming in with you and carrying on the activity. Periodically the central organization will take up some of the points that have been raised, circulated by the individual groupings. The center will say, on this particular occasion and for this particular period, or this evening or for the next two or three evenings, we shall deal with this matter as part of our general political activity. I hope that what I am saying is quite clear. I don't know that I have too much to say on that. I have spoken in general, what we are to have in mind always, and then I have spoken about a specific procedure and proposal which you can begin within one week. You may be able to divide into five, maybe you are only able to divide into two. I don't know about that, that you have to settle. But what is important is that you work out clearly what you are going to do, the procedure you are going to follow, the organizational procedures by which you will give expression to your political activity, and then you see what happens.

There are two other points which I wish to refer to. I shall just state them. One of them I referred to before and I was told that, well you are not thinking about that at the present time because you didn't see your way. You are in my opinion absolutely wrong. A certain sum of money is required. I wouldn't tell you what I think the amount is, but it is a sum of money that should be divided into three parts. One section of the organization requires it, another section of the organization requires one-third, and the organization itself requires one-third. I leave you to struggle that out. The amount of money, I wouldn't say what I think the sum should be. All I wish to say is that the organization cannot possibly subscribe it or one-quarter of it. If you attempt to do that you will strangle and ruin yourself. But you must have it in mind. You must let your people, your friends and acquaintances and others, know that you have that in mind. You must work towards it. And whatever work you are doing, it must be clear that you are doing it in this limited way because of your limited finances, but that you have something else in mind and you are trying here, there and everywhere, and letting everybody know that that is your perspective. Don't be afraid to set your sights high at something substantial so that anybody who listens to you will know that you mean business and that you are not fooling around.

Do you know the story of a particular movie star? He got interested in some section of the movement and he let it be known that he was willing to help them out. So they said, could they send somebody to talk to him. He said, yes, and this fellow went to talk to him. The representative said, Mr. "X" I understand that you are willing to help us financially. He said, yes, what can I do? He was told $50. And Mr. X says I'm not giving any money to an organization that asks me for $50. These people are not serious. And he was absolutely right. He said, I'm not having anything to do with that. Particularly in the U.S. which, with all its defects, at any rate is ready to subscribe money, you have to want a substantial amount of money for substantial reasons and you must be able to say so. It may take you a year or two to get it but you must know what you are doing. I have very clearly in mind what I would circulate among the membership to let everybody know what I want and what I intend to do if I get it, and that what I'm doing at the present time is limited and cannot expand because I haven't got the money and you all cannot subscribe the money. If you have in mind that somebody among you is going to do so much work and give so much and so forth, you will not only make a mess of the organization, you will ruin and tire yourself out.

The second thing is, there should be in 1965 a Conference in Belgium.[26] Everybody will be able to cross the water and get there. But we must have in mind that everybody is going to meet in Belgium in 1965. We have that as a perspective, and money for holidays and savings of large expenses, how much you can squeeze out of your father and mother, or out of your uncle or cousin, etc., you have all that in mind. We should all meet for a conference and I think Belgium would be the easiest place where from all parts of Europe we will be able to get together.

So there are three things with which I would end. Number one, have a clear, centralized perspective, precise activity, what Rosa Luxemburg attacked Lenin for. But at the same time have clearly in mind always, never do without it, what Lenin always had in mind as far back as 1905 and without which today any sort of political activity is nonsense — the creativity of the masses. Have in mind also the financial perspective, a serious one and broad one. And have in mind also an international Conference in 1965 at which we shall not have representatives, the days for that are over, everybody will come to it, because everybody will prepare for it.

Now there are comrades in far away Edinburgh, there are people who think they are members of the organization in Edinburgh, there are sympathizers in Sheffield. As long as they are prepared to function there is this that you have to remember: they cannot do everything and try to make themselves into a small replica of the center. Give them, work out with them, some particular activity which they will follow out and by means of tapes and other communication keep them in touch. But specifically, I should say, wherever they are, two or three of them, get down to some specific task which it will be the function of the center to keep integrated with the work in general.

Now that is as much as I want to say.

Notes

1. Robert McNamara was one of the so-called "whiz kids" who, after service in World War II became influential in the Ford Motor Co. McNamara eventually became president of Ford and later became Secretary of Defense in the John F. Kennedy and Lyndon B. Johnson administrations.

2. Engels was the towering Marxist figure during the early years of the Second International. However, he did not "form" the International, which was only loosely Marxist.

3. See note 17, Chapter 2.

4. See note 15, Chapter 1.

5. The reference is to Martin Glaberman.

6. C. L. R. James, Grace C. Lee and Cornelius Castoriadis, *Facing Reality*, Detroit: Bewick Editions, 1974, pp. 86–89; original edition, Detroit: Correspondence, 1958. Pagination is identical in both editions.

7. Lenin, "What Is To Be Done," in *Collected Works*, vol. 5, pp. 349–529, especially pp. 472–73, Moscow: Foreign Languages Publishing House, 1961. The language of the quotations in *Facing Reality* is slightly different than the language in the *Collected Works*.

8. See Lenin, "Five Years of the Russian Revolution and the Prospects of the World Revolution, Report to the Fourth Congress of the Communist International," Nov. 13, 1922, in *Collected Works*, vol. 33, Moscow: Progress Publishers, 1966.

9. See Notes 8 and 9, Chapter 3.

10. *Facing Reality*, p. 9.

11. Ibid., p. 94. The reference is to Cornelius Castoriadis.

12. Ibid.

13. Hannah Arendt, *On Revolution*, New York: Viking, 1963, p. 270.

14. Then Secretary-General of the United Nations.

15. Dunduzu Kaluli Chisiza, from Malawi, published two pamphlets, *Realities of African Independence*, London: Africa Publications, 1961 and *Africa; What Lies Ahead*, New Delhi: Indian Council for Africa, 1961 and N.Y.: Africa-America Institute, 1962. Chisiza was killed in an auto accident.

16. New York: Harcourt Brace.

17. *Mariners, Renegades and Castaways*, New York: C. L. R. James, 1953. Several subsequent editions were published including, Detroit: Bewick Editions, 1978, which omitted the final chapter.

18. Published as *Notes on Dialectics: Hegel, Marx, Lenin*, London: Allison & Busby, 1980.

19. *Beyond a Boundary,* London: Hutchinson, 1963; an American edition was published by Pantheon in New York in 1983 and by Duke University Press in Durham, NC in 1993.

20. The Marylebone Cricket Club, the governing body of cricket.

21. Eventually published as *Nkrumah and the Ghana Revolution,* Westport, Conn.: Lawrence Hill and Co., 1977.

22. *The Russian Revolution and Leninism or Marxism,* Ann Arbor, Mich.: University of Michigan Press, 1961, p. 92.

23. Ibid., p. 93.

24. "A Contribution to the History of the Question of Dicatorship," (Oct. 20, 1920) in *Selected Works,* Vol. VII, N.Y.: International Publishers, undated, p. 261. This same article also appears in the *Collected Works,* vol. 31, pp. 340–61, with the quotation on pp. 360–61. The quotation is from a much longer quotation from a pamphlet Lenin wrote in 1906, *The Victory of the Cadets and the Tasks of the Workers' Party,* and which appears in the *Collected Works,* vol. 10, pp. 199–276, with the extract on pp. 253–54. Apparently, a different translation from the Russian was used in the *Collected Works* than in the *Selected Works* since the wording is not the same although the meaning is consistent.

25. Luxemburg, p. 94.

26. "Belgium" was fictional, designed to avoid or circumvent the reactionary American laws prohibiting international connections with radical groups.

Appendix: Theory and Practice

Introduction

Every revolutionary movement has to face conditions that are unique, unique and unprecedented, because that is precisely what a revolution is, the creation of something new and hitherto unknown to the world. Those who foresee what is coming and devote themselves to advancing the cause are naturally affected by the uniqueness of the situation. Most often they are intellectuals, motivated above all by a sense of historical development; and while this pushes them away from the crimes and catastrophes associated with the breakdown of a social order, they run the extreme danger of being caught in the organizational structure and ideas of a previous age.

To be more concrete, over a hundred years ago Marx and Engels were able to put forward their ideas and programs in conflict with other organizations similar to theirs in size and potentiality. By 1914 Lenin and the revolutionaries had to deal not only with governments, but with the tremendous power of the Second International. By 1939 the revolutionary elements had to deal with the Second International, the Third International, and a powerful state claiming to be the representative of the revolutionary movement. Today the tendency which has been very obvious during the later part of the 19th and during the 20th century has reached its climax. A revolutionary movement is now faced not only with two world political organizations which claim to represent the interests of workers, but also with two states, centered in Moscow and Peking, which are actively organizing all over the world what each claims to be the center of the movements that reflect the urgent necessity felt by most of the world for fundamental change in a decaying order.

From the days of Marx and Engels, most probably before that, the problems of those who saw the necessity of total change was always the relation between the general ideas which understood and expressed the decay and breakup of the existing social order, and the translation of this into terms of programs and policies which the great mass of the population, or that section of it which was prepared to take action, could understand and accept. The difficulty is perhaps best expressed by Oliver Cromwell in his statement that he knew what he was against, although he couldn't say exactly what he was for. The problem of a revolutionary in the middle of our disturbed century might appear at first sight to be, and in some respects is, of a difficulty far beyond that of a revolutionary in any previous age. The Marxist today has got to analyze the actual situation and clarify his ideas not only against the ideas of bourgeois society, but against the doctrines claiming to be Marxist of Moscow and Peking. So that before the task of translating ideas, analysis, and theory into concrete programs and policies, the task of theoretical clarifications and understanding faces obstacles which can be and have repeatedly proved, as we have unfortunately seen, ultimately insuperable. The task is not made any less onerous by the fact that any theory or continuation of a historical development with perspectives for the future can only take place in constant communication with the actual movement of the masses, not necessarily to lead it but at any rate absorbing the constantly new experiences which are the basis for the explosions of the future.

This task I was fortunate enough to see in all its profundities and difficult ramifications many years ago, and on the whole have been able to move with the times, maintain the historical development and yet be a part of a total movement which not only never lost touch but was always guided and im-pelled in particular directions by its contact with the concrete mass move-ment. The documents and experiences of Facing Reality are, I believe, as good an example as can be found of the strenuous effort needed for a Marxist movement in the middle of the 20th century to maintain its relation with fun-damentals and yet to move, as any movement must, or perish. In this critical situation the history and development of our movement over nearly 30 years is the best evidence of the vigorous and quite successful struggles with what might appear to be an insoluble problem.

I am confident that today more than ever we have survived the perils and are well established and moving in the right direction. The proofs that I here submit are two. The first is this document, Theory and Practice, an address by Martin Glaberman, where, as never before, the relation between the basic principles and ideas of Marxism and the concrete activity of a small organi-zation are stated with an easy confidence and precision which express what we have learned through 30 years of study and struggle.

The second proof is that whereas one can easily be overwhelmed by the size and furious activity of the large organizations which compete for the support of the great masses of the population, the substantial fact is that they no longer occupy any position of influence or authority among the great mass of the people trying to find their way out of the social and political morass in which they live. Therefore, as never before, the road to the masses is wide open for the small organization which has known how to preserve itself in theory and practice during the years previous to the present crisis. The only program, policy, perspective is the recognition that those with ideas will not lead the mass. As we have once more seen in France, the mass movement, as it has done for hundreds of years, will register its rejection of the social order in decay. And today more than ever the road is open between the mass movement and those who have ideas corresponding to the needs of the day.

C. L. R. James
November 23, 1968

Theory and Practice[1]

The Conference starts under somewhat unusual circumstances. It was organized in great haste. A lot of what is ordinarily done for a conference will have to be done at the Conference itself. The usual kinds of proposals in mimeographed form that people read and study for a few weeks before a conference just aren't available. It is also unusual in another respect. It is one of the characteristics of Facing Reality to be as objective and candid about ourselves as we can, it is a conference that was called by the organization in opposition to the Chairman. I thought that we had no special reason to run with such haste into a conference. Everybody else thought otherwise and, on the basis of why the Conference was called, I suspect everyone else was right. Without being able to put your finger on any particular thing, things were happening with such rapidity in the world, in the United States in particular and in the world in general, that everybody felt that there was some need for all of us to get together to examine what is happening in the world and to see to what extent Facing Reality could meet the responsibilities of an organization, a revolutionary organization, in these times.

And things didn't stop happening because we called the Conference, and I think the only place to begin in discussing what the world is like today at a political conference is to begin with France. We can't end with France because France is a continuing revolutionary situation. In some respects, what happened was startling and surprising. To most people it was startling and surprising. Even for us to some extent. About a week ago I received a letter from C. L. R. James, who said that he was surprised by the events in France. I understand that within a certain framework. We have lived with the understanding and expectation of events of this kind for almost all of our political lives and the political life of the organization. And what was meant specifically was that, while things would inevitably break out in France, it seemed more likely that they would break out on the death of deGaulle or the retirement of deGaulle. But apparently the French working class and the French students decided not to wait.

What is happening is almost a classic demonstration of what a revolution is in modern times. You have the wave of student demonstrations, posing issues which are originally limited to the university, but even in that limitation already indicate a conception of the society as a whole, its weaknesses and its limitations, and the alienation which people suffer under it. And then the rulers, again inevitably, spur the thing on with what Lenin called "the whip of the counter-revolution"—the excessive brutality in getting the students out of the Sorbonne brought the majority of the students over to the rebels, and very quickly all of French higher education and a good part of French lower education was in the hands of the students with the support of much of the faculty. And then, again in almost classic form, although the concreteness is specifically French—every revolution is specifically the revolution of that country—the thing is transformed into a fundamental social movement by the participation of the working class, the participation of the working class against its own organizations.

It begins—to their surprise—with what leaders of the trade union movement keep calling "the people we last expected"—the women in the aviation plant in Nantes, the young people who never joined the union until after the strikes began, whole plants that were unorganized, unavailable to either the Communist or the Catholic or the Social Democratic unions, sit down and then march over in a body to the union halls and say they want to become members. The fact is that all the organizations of the working class—and in France that means, above all else, the Communist Party and the Communist-controlled C.G.T. (General Confederation of Labor)—are not only to the rear of the students and the workers, but what is much more pertinent to our times and to an understanding of the situation, opposed to the workers.

The opposition is reflected in the fact that it takes them about two days to catch up with where the workers are. But it's a kind of catching up which attempts to impose limitations and restrictions on the movement. First they say the workers are sitting in for a whole series of economic demands: increased wages, increased social security benefits (which were cut by the Gaullist regime), and so forth. Everybody seems satisfied with those demands. And then they win the demands in negotiation and the two top leaders of the C.G.T, the Secretary-General and the President, both of whom are top leaders of the CP (the president of the union is a member of the Political Committee of the Communist Party) are publicly repudiated in person by the workers in Citroen and Renault in Paris, and the whole damn thing falls apart.

The attempt to keep it in the limited framework of economic demands and a political shuffling of the government, replacing [Prime Minister] Pompidou with a Socialist-Communist government of one kind or another, obviously has no relation to what is happening. And what is also obvious is that the working class itself is developing during this period. What seems perfectly reasonable to the workers on one day—a 35% increase in the minimum wage or a 10% increase in wages across the board all across France, for example—becomes very unreasonable the next day when it is finally granted.

And what is crucial in the whole situation; and what was terrifying everybody; and what forced deGaulle into the only position that he, as leader of French capitalism, can hold, is the fact that—unlike strikes in which workers are walking the streets, unlike election campaigns where everything is within the framework of parliamentary democracy—what is happening in France is based on the fact that the workers are in the factories, the students are in the schools, the clerks are in the shops and offices. This includes government offices, this includes, I believe, the naval arsenal near Marseilles. In other words, it is not simply a matter of starving the workers out; the workers are in a position of power unparalleled in the history of France or any other country. And deGaulle, who, if anything, understands the seriousness of the situation, has decided simply not to capitulate, which means that the inevitable confrontation reaches a new stage.

The degree of violence is not determinable, not in advance. But again, I think what has to be realized in this particular situation is that the basic social power in France is today in the hands of the workers, and that the only thing that can cause them to give it up, outside of an absolute and overpowering military defeat, which at the moment doesn't look likely—there's no way of predicting that either—is that the French Communist Party can reassert its influence over the working class in such a way that the movement is limited, restricted, or led to some kind of defeat. There is no way to predict that.

The background for the history of France in the last ten years was presented in *Facing Reality*. A selection from that is reprinted in the November 20 issue of *Speak Out*, on France in the fifties. In a series of battles, the French working class separated itself from the French Communist Party and went over to direct industrial action, and any influence that the French Communist Party had in France was limited to the parliamentary field. Now, while that influence has been extended in the last few days, it is on a very tenuous basis. It is extended only to the extent or the degree that the Communist Party can keep running after what the working class is demanding or what it is thinking. It is perfectly obvious that at every particular point the Communist Party just does not know. They were certain that the workers would accept the favorable economic benefits negotiated between Pompidou and the trade union leaders. They were completely surprised by the fact that they were voted down and booed. And this has been happening at every stage.

Now this kind of development, the fact that this is one of the fundamental tendencies of modern society, has been part of the political basis of Facing Reality almost from its foundation. Those of you who are aware of what the state of socialist politics was in 1956, for example, are aware of the fact that all of the various viewpoints that called themselves Marxist or socialist or revolutionary around the world, based themselves fundamentally on the analysis that the revolution could really not take place. It couldn't take place in the totalitarian East, because what workers need for a revolution is a certain amount of political freedom to form their own organizations, to have a press, to discuss questions, to be able to choose a leadership and on the basis of this move on to the seizure of power. And it couldn't happen in the West, because what workers need to make a revolution is poverty, is a kind of economic exploitation which drives them to resist those who are oppressing them; and in the West, because of the post-war affluence, any hope for a revolutionary development was lost.

The first part of that theory was destroyed in 1956, and it is on that destruction that *Facing Reality*, our book, is based. And the second part, if it hasn't been destroyed up until now, is destroyed in France today. It doesn't matter whether this revolution is successful or not. What matters is that this is what drives the modern industrial working class in all industrial societies, whether they are totalitarian, whether they are welfare-state capitalist, whether they are politically relatively free or politically relatively unfree.

I insist on the fact that we have been able to base our politics on this kind of development to indicate the kind of role that a small Marxist organization has to play in this world that we're in, the United States in particular. There are lots of people around the world, it's in the nature of revolutionary times, that when they see a revolution say, "Great, we are for it, we support it, we will do what we can." And you don't have to be a Marxist to be able to say that, to say you are with the French workers. But that is relatively temporary and limited. And it seems to me what is necessary in these times and, again, particularly in the United States, is the kind of total view, a kind of fundamental analysis which makes these huge events not surprises, except in the very immediate sense of when they break out and how they break out, but an integral part of the political philosophy and a political theory which is then applied day to day and on the basis of which people live and function in whatever manner the society makes possible.

We came to that, not by accident, not because we willed revolution, but because we felt that the only way to live in these times was not by a ritual kind of Marxism in which Marxism is equated with a political line. What is crucial to Marxism is that it is a living doctrine. It is not a political line. It is a method of analysing the society in which we live.

We spent a good many years in developing an analysis of both *Capital* and its application to today, a new stage of capitalist society, that is, state capitalism; and dialectics and its application to an understanding of what's happening in the world today. In 1948, under very different circumstances (because we were an opposition group within the Trotskyist movement, we had no public press, no way of discussing this freely, and this particular document couldn't be discussed because it would have meant immediate expulsion for the ideas which were so radical to the Trotskyists at that time, and today for that matter), we produced a document called *Notes on Dialectics* which was intended to study how a Marxist organization can apply dialectical materialism to the events — serious events — in the world. A progression is presented and it is applied to the development of the working-class movement and certain stages are indicated. The category of the working class, the category of the organization of the working class, is taken from the days of Marx and the First International, the Second International, the revolution of 1917 and the Third International, and the conclusion is reached in abstract form — necessarily because the events weren't there to make it concrete and because it was merely a theoretical projection — the conclusion was reached in 1948 that the next stage was the abandonment or the destruction of the vanguard party, which was the character of all organizations up until then, and the functioning of the total working class as a political body.

The confirmation of that came eight years later in Hungary in 1956, for without a political party of any kind and with the total destruction of the only one that was in existence, the Hungarian Communist Party, the Hungarian working class formed its workers' councils. And the reports of workers' councils have already appeared in the capitalist press, the [London] *Observer* in particular, in relation to the events in France. Communication is extremely difficult. It is difficult because it is difficult physically, but it is even more difficult because it is difficult politically, for the average correspondent has no idea what to look for and can't recognize it when he sees it. So that years later, you find out that all these wonderful things happened. While they're going on, they seem to have a much more limited character than they really have in fact. Because to me it is inconceivable that the workers at Renault with a long union and Communist tradition would vote down a major economic victory and boo down a member of the Political [Committee] of the Communist Party and the Secretary-General of the Trade Union Confederation unless they already had functioning informally or formally on the shop floor their own independent working-class organizations or formations; the embryo or the equivalent or the beginning of the workers' councils. And that has to be true, if not everywhere, at least substantially, all across France.

What is involved fundamentally in our analysis is that capitalism is in a new stage, a stage that we have called state capitalist. There are a number of state capitalist viewpoints in the world today, but mostly they are descriptions of Russia. They say, "Well, Russia is capitalist like the West." They have reached that conclusion, which we came to in 1941. But that a conception like that means a stage in the world; that labor leaders in France, in England, in the United States have to reflect that same situation; that Reuther in the UAW can function only in the same way as a Stalinist trade union functionary functions in France, a Labor Party and trade union functionary functions in England, and a Communist Party functionary functions in Russia — that is beyond most groups and organizations in the socialist movement. It requires a kind of totality of conception of the nature of the stage in which we live, which, it seems to me, only an intense concern with the events but in relation to a living continuing theory can provide.

Before the events in France broke out we were working on a book which is called tentatively, *The Gathering Forces*, which is to be an analysis of the world 50 years after the Russian Revolution.[2] Everybody was celebrating the Russian Revolution last year, the 50th anniversary of the Russian Revolution, celebrating or mourning, as the case may be. Our interest was not in either celebrating or mourning, but in taking the Russian Revolution as one of the tremendous turning points in world history, examining the world and how the Russian Revolution has shaped that world in the 50 years. And here, again, the French Revolution, or the beginning of one, continues concretely what we have begun to develop theoretically.

One of the main characteristics of the most recent period, particularly the period after World War II, is the revolution in the Third World, the winning of independence by the major nations of Asia and Africa and the Cuban Revolution. And while there have been certain things said about agricultural societies, peasant societies, by Marxists, these were rather scattered and many of them were not applicable to the times in which we live. Yet it was relevant to the development of a total theory or a total conception of the world in which we live, because one of the things that happened after World War II was the apparent domination of the industrial world by Russia and the United States and the apparent immobility of the working class. The revolutionary activity in Africa and in Asia combined to give most people [a limited] idea of a revolution in the industrialized world, above all in the United States and Russia. And those theories abound; they abound to this day, in the Negro movement, for example, in the New Left, the idea that, well, perhaps American capitalism can be overthrown, but not by the American working class. It will have to be overthrown by its colonials—the equivalent of a Cuba or a Vietnam in Africa or South America will destroy American capitalism.

What is the relation of the revolution in the Third World to what we have to do in the United States in particular and the industrialized world in general? Here again, some totality of conception is necessary. It is not enough to say "We are for," or, "We are against." And it is not enough to treat the question as it is traditionally treated, as all questions are traditionally treated, as a matter of political line. You take a society; you say you are for or you are against; you like it or you don't like it; it is good or it is bad; it is revolutionary or it is counter-revolutionary; it is socialist or it is capitalist or state capitalist or something of that sort. What gets lost in the process of this kind of analysis is the fact that any analysis has to be a moving, living thing; and it loses sight of the fact that the period in which we live is a revolutionary period, which means it is not a static period consisting of so many societies of one kind and so many societies of another kind. It is a period in which societies are constantly changing, being overthrown, being modified, and unless categories with which you think are being modified to suit the real world in which we live, your thought does not reflect, cannot reflect, that world.

To take one case in particular, Cuba. It is possible to apply the principles of 1917 and the disputes between Trotsky and Stalin and say, "Workers' state or capitalist state?" Socialism in one country is impossible, and if it was impossible in a country as huge and with as many resources as the Soviet Union, it surely is impossible on as small an island as Cuba. But socialism even in 1917 was not a formal determination of which side the state was on in any narrow sense. Lenin called the Soviet Union state capitalist; he said it was under workers' control. And what is involved fundamentally in our understanding of these new emerging nations, in particular those that are attempting to achieve some kind of socialist future for themselves, is not whether ultimately that future is possible without a socialist world which includes the industrialized nations, but for now, whether the conditions under which they live are conditions under which the masses of the people in those countries are participating in the transformation of those countries or in the maintenance of some kind of direction or movement. In other words, do you have, as I believe you have in Cuba, for example, essentially a broad participation from below?

With all sorts of defects, with all sorts of limitations — if that wasn't true, Cuba wouldn't be a backward country, Cuba wouldn't have had to, a few years ago, fight the battle against illiteracy, Cuba wouldn't have the problem of any kind of industrialization — but because it is that kind of country, the kind of participation that is available to the people of that country is therefore not the kind available to the workers of Paris or the workers of Budapest. But it seems to me nevertheless to be a genuine participation. A genuine exchange exists between those who are leading Cuban society and those who make up the basis for Cuban society, and within that framework it is not a matter of saying Cuba is a socialist society or Cuba is not a socialist society. It is possible to say that Cuba is developing in a direction, to the extent that it can, of building a socialist society, but that the building of that society is possible only in the framework of the transformation of the industrialized world. That is, ultimately, if revolutions do not take place in North America and in Europe, then it is impossible, no matter what the participation, to prevent the development of bureaucracy, of planning from above, of trying to lift the nation up in spite of its citizens, so to speak, which was the old characteristic of Stalinism and to some extent is the characteristic of Mao in China.

But that is ultimately. In the same way that you can't set conditions on the Hungarians, you can't say, "Well, you should have known you were going to be invaded by the Russians and lose," you can't say to the Cubans, "You should have known you can't build socialism in one country; you've got to sit back and wait until the Americans make a revolution or the Europeans make a revolution." And, by the way, the theoretical equivalent of that is to say to the Negroes, "You should know that you can't transform American society unless the working class makes a revolution, so you should sit back and wait." Unless you are prepared to say that to the people in the underdeveloped countries, you can't set the kind of rigid formal test that used to be traditional in the Marxist movement and which I think is terribly out of place and inapplicable today.

Hopefully, *The Gathering Forces,* when it appears, will put the revolution in the Third World and the attempt to create some kind of socialism or tentative socialism in the Third World in a Marxist framework. Not everywhere. In a lot of places there isn't even any attempt. In other places there is the apparent attempt which is not in fact an attempt to create socialism. But where it is, I think we have to accept it and incorporate it as part of our thinking about a stage in society which is revolutionary, in which all kinds of transformations are taking place, in which people are experimenting with new forms and new possibilities.

The kind of relation that exists between some of the problems of the Third World and some of the problems of the industrialized world is reflected here in the United States. One reason the Negro question in the United States and the struggle for black liberation in the United States has the attraction all over the world that it does is that it tends to combine within itself some of the problems of the Third World and some of the problems of the industrialized world. It is clearly a national question and not simply a class question. And yet, clearly, questions of class are involved. Now, again, what is true of the French revolution is true of the struggle for black liberation. You don't have to be a Marxist to know which side you are on. You don't have to be a Marxist to understand how to function in the day to day struggle. However, one of the things that happens after a period of struggle is that the struggle itself, while important, is not everything. People want some kind of conception into which to fit what they are doing, so that they can understand the struggle that they are participating in in relation to other things. And it is here that some kind of total theoretical and political conception can contribute.

And it can contribute more directly. We were talking in the car coming up, pointing out the scenery of Detroit, which is essentially a scenery of plants, ghettos, riot areas and former ghettos that have been urban renewed and now have high-rise, high-cost housing. One of the characteristics of the explosion in the United States and the explosion in Detroit last summer, which was not just typical, but reached a kind of peak, was the total surprise by which it took the Negro nationalists, all the black militants. They weren't even in town; they were off in Newark holding some kind of convention discussing how to liberate the cities. I don't say this, by the way, in the sense of criticism because this thing happens all the time, you are really taken by surprise. But their first reaction was very ambiguous: "Well, we were thinking of revolution, but is this really a revolution, people rioting and looting and so forth?" I know some SNCC [Student Non-violent Coordinating Committee] kids; it took them about two days to realize that this had better be the revolution and they had better be in it or they would be really out of it.

The reason it surprised everybody is that in Detroit, above all other cities, the Negro ghetto reflects the society and the misconceptions that people have about that society. There are substantial numbers of Negroes in Detroit in auto. That is, they are not what people thought you have on 12th Street and you do have to some extent in Harlem and Watts, the most miserably oppressed, unemployed, transient, marginal people in the society. These are people who are making the best industrial wages in the country. Right now, with the new contracts, it's over $3.25 an hour. There are people with 10 or 20 years seniority and they have been making that kind of money for long enough to have bought houses and cars and sent some of their kids to college. It is a community in which there is a substantial middle class. And one of the consequences of the other Civil Rights movement, the political Civil Rights movement, was that a lot of Negroes were in the last three or four years introduced into other occupations from which they had been excluded, sales people downtown, bank clerks and things of that sort, and up into the lower executive echelons. Plus you have the so-called sophisticated liberal Democrat Cavanaugh as mayor of Detroit. You have the most massive outpouring into the anti-poverty program anywhere in the country—and this town blows and it blows because there was a misconception to begin with on what causes revolution.

It is not oppression, poverty and despair that causes revolutions; it is the possibility of a new society, a possibility of ending alienation; nobody could be bought off from that by the fact that he has his own house, in the city or in the suburb, it really doesn't matter. Marx wrote about it a long time ago, but people don't really believe that that's what Marx said. People believe that Marx said that everybody gets paid too little. If anybody is interested, in the summary, I can read you quote after quote from *Capital* where Marx said the exact opposite. He says this society will die—the term he uses is under penalty of death—unless it transforms work and the detailed labor which makes of everybody a fragment of a man to the fully developed individual, fit for a variety of labors, and where his social functions—not merely industrial functions, all the social functions—become merely different ways of expressing his natural and acquired characteristics. Not a word there about low wages; not a word there about unemployment; although obviously those are factors. That kind of conception applies to the black liberation struggle as it applies to the French revolution, as it applies to Hungary.

But there are certain specific problems that relate to the relation of a small Marxist organization to various movements of this kind and to the socialist revolution itself. I said that we, in our analysis a number of years ago, reached the conclusion that the age of the vanguard party was over (not that the vanguard party was over, the vanguard party was confronted by the French workers in France today). It has to be pushed out of the way, destroyed to make any progress at all. That means, specifically, that because we have all these very fine ideas, etc., it does not thereby become our function to lead all these masses, that without this leadership they are lost, they don't even understand what they are doing. That's a lot of nonsense and anybody who thinks that there's any truth in that is in real difficulty. And the basic reason that the Old Left in the United States is in such constant difficulty is that they have no other conception of how to function.

I want to give you a specific example of what is involved, a very peculiar dialectical relation between what a Marxist organization can contribute and what concrete organizations of struggle are about. We have the experience in our own organization. We attend some of the meetings, black liberation meetings, and we are confronted by a demonstration of hostility to whites. And you think to yourself, because you know the Negro struggle is independently valid, that it is making all kinds of changes in the society, but for this society to be really overthrown it has to be overthrown by a total revolution which means fundamentally the American working class. And where we differ from a lot of other people — I don't want to go into that unless somebody wants to raise it — is that we have a conception of the American working class which considers it, not non-racist, not that it is going to be won over to the black liberation struggle, but that it is inherently revolutionary on its own because it has to struggle against capitalists and capitalism in any way that it can; and ultimately it will have to explode the way the French have exploded and the way the Hungarians have exploded.

It is very easy, therefore, to think to yourself, "Don't these people realize that? If they don't, we've got to tell them that." Not quite. Not quite. Because in the fact of the liberation struggle the militants are trying to establish their independence, trying to shake off their backs the years of liberal white, radical white — and let's not play around with the words; the radicals were as bad as or worse than the liberals — domination of the various organs of black liberation, the NAACP, the Urban League, CORE for a number of years, and a lot of others, the marches on Washington, the Southern Christian Leadership Conference and so forth. There is always, through money or direct political intervention, the influence of whites. It you are attempting to form a viable organ of struggle against this society in the ghetto, you can't possibly end every speech with, "We're going to do this; we're going to arm; we're going to fight the cops; we're going to do the other things; and, when all is said and done, you've got to know that the white workers are going to overthrow American capitalism." Because that last sentence completely vitiates everything you have said before. Well, okay, we can sit back and wait. It is a practical political matter; it is impossible for that to be part of the functioning background of the black liberation movement. Not that they are wrong and we are right; they have a different function from a Marxist organizaton.

But that doctrine has to be available to the black liberation movement for people to see and understand — there are a lot of people in the movement particularly in Detroit who know that, because they know the Negro industrial workers and they know the white industrial workers and they know their revolutionary capacity. But it can't be part of the black liberation struggle directly, it has to be part of what a Marxist organization contributes to that struggle in terms of its press which is available, in terms of the people in that struggle who become members of the Marxist organization, not to capture the liberation struggle, not at all. They are willing to participate where they can in the struggle for socialism in the United States where it is. And unless you understand there can be that contradiction between the needs of an independent mass struggle and the needs and purposes and functions of a Marxist organization — not opposition because the two supplement each other, but at the very least a contradiction between the two — you begin to think of the Marxist party as the party that has to organize everybody and win everybody over, because unless you know what we know, you're wrong, which is nonsense. Or, on the other hand, you say "What do you need a Marxist organization for?" Then you begin to lose the grasp of the totality, of the conception of the total society as it really is.

One of the reasons France can explode in one day, and Hungary can explode in one day, and it took just about a week or two for the Revolution to cross Russia, is not just modern technology but because the ideas which in 1917 were limited to a handful of people, Lenin and the Bolsheviks and so forth, are today part of the world. You don't have to be a Marxist to know that the state has to decide all sorts of things which can't be left to private business anymore. That wasn't understood in 1917; everybody understands that today. So you get this peculiar and specific kind of relationship for our period between a Marxist organization and a liberation struggle.

And that contradiction applies in other ways. There was a report or a series of articles — they appeared in the *New Republic* a couple of years ago before the battles had reached the ghettos. There were some people in the South who participated in the liberation movement there and were already reaching the mature ages of their late twenties and were looking back on their radical youth and determining what made them function the way they did. One of the kids said, one of the black kids from Mississippi, that his father, whom he had always respected, who he had known had taken part in black liberation struggles years before, when he came to him in the later fifties to discuss what could be done, everything he had to propose his father had gone through. And his father gave him the wisdom of his years. The wisdom of his years was, and it was the literal truth and his father would have been less than honest if he had said otherwise: "It wouldn't work. You want to picket? We picketed; we got our heads beat in. You want to do this? You want to do that? You want to do the other thing? We have a tremendous experience that shows that you can't do it."

And that has been essentially the role of the Old Left, not just the old militants in the black liberation struggle. And one of the basic reasons why in this world today, not in 1917, when there was a lot of reason for a vanguard party, but today, there again has to be that separation, that supplementation one of the other, is that only by being in a specific organ of struggle not burdened by years of doctrine and theory, a lot of which is right and some of which is wrong, are you free to experiment, to make all kinds of mistakes and to find out that things which were impossible 5, 10, 15, 20 years ago are now possible. To find out that racist sheriffs who were all-powerful in 1940 are not quite as powerful in 1960. To find out that the Democratic Party in the South which was a solid racist organization can be broken up.

That's in the struggle for black liberation. It applies to SDS and the student movement. It applies to the anti-war movement. Every Marxist can give you a thousand reasons why an anti-war movement as such is doomed to failure. Why? Because war is inevitable under capitalism and unless you overthrow the capitalist system, you can't prevent war. True, absolutely true. But also absolutely useless to anybody who is participating in an anti-war movement. That Marxist theory and doctrine has to be present, has to be available to illuminate, to clarify, to combine in a totality, to be able to relate the anti-war movement, the black liberation movement, the working-class movement and the movement of the Third World and the movement abroad. But you can't replace the concrete struggles which can only live by experimentation, by making mistakes, by what Hegel calls risking your life, without which you cannot be free. The Marxists tend to have too much doctrine at stake to risk their lives, and I say this as a Marxist, as someone who believes in the absolute necessity for a Marxist organization in our world.

Unless we live by that understanding of the kind of dialectical relationship between the specific function of a Marxist organization to develop and apply theory as a living thing to continually understand the world in which we live, to make it available to the broadest possible number of people, people who are functioning in all sorts of ways in the concrete struggle for liberation, we don't have the conception of the purpose and nature of a Marxist organization. Nor do we see the nature and fantastic strength of all these organizations that have been set up, some permanent, some temporary, some not as good as others, but still all of them set up to carry on specific struggles in all sorts of fields — the field of black liberation, anti-war, the student movement, women, almost anything you can name; because there isn't a section in this society in which there isn't disaffection, alienation, and an attempt to achieve some kind of change.

But it is never a matter of theory versus practice, because if it is, the theory will in the shortest possible time, come to an end as rigid doctrine and dogma. It will be fit for libraries and nothing else. Unless the theory is integrally related to practice, it is no theory at all. It has to be a theory that is applied constantly to what is going on in the world today. And that means that the Marxist organization, although it is not a vanguard party of the past, although it does not try to encompass the whole of what is going on in the world or all the people that are functioning in the world, it has to have within itself, and base itself on, representative sections of the society and participants in all the concrete struggles. Not, as in the old days, front organizations. You had fractions—the Communist fraction of this union and the Trotskyist fraction in this Negro organization. Your ultimate objective was to take over the organization and impose your line. So, if you have left that behind, then it becomes absolutely necessary that, for your organization to live as a Marxist organization, and to make its contribution to the totality of the struggle, you have to have as members and participants in the constant revision of your theory and your ideas, people who are taking part in the concrete struggles as participants, contributing what they have. If they have qualities of leadership, they become leaders. If they have qualities of mimeograph machine operators, they become mimeograph machine operators. If they have qualities of carriers of picket signs or walkers of picket lines, fine!

The point is there is no imposition; there is a free exchange of personnel and experience and then the organization is able to learn from the movement. And unless it learns from the movement, it cannot develop its own theory and thereby contribute in turn to the movement. And it can't learn from a movement in terms of reporters for a press. I don't know how many times this has happened with the best will in the world—if you are a reporter and you come up to somebody who just got out of jail, or just got off a picket line, they'll tell you and they'll try to tell you as honestly as they can and you'll try to write it down as honestly as you can, but between the experience and the telling and the writing there will be two sets of transformations, and it won't be the same. It will be a formality. It will be an abstraction. It will be an approximate reflection, which is already wrong, of what has really happened in that particular struggle or that prison or whatever. And unless the organization lives in the struggle itself and doesn't merely sit by—I'm not against sending out reporters; if you're not somewhere and something happens, you send to the factory gate and say to the workers, "What happened? Why are you on strike?" And so forth—but hopefully a Marxist organization can build itself up to the strength, the capacity, not only to carry out its own specific functions, but so that it can be a participant in all the significant movements and organizations that are existing in the society in which we live.

We have lived for many years on the conception of the revolutionary capacity of the working class, the American working class above all, because we are an American organization, not because the American working class is the greatest working class in the world, the industrialized working class. But even there, the working class has certain limitations. I don't know if anybody has participated in a wildcat strike. Working-class democracy, working-class-action, is a very unique and distinctive thing. It takes several forms. One of the forms which is very frequent, and the kind that short wildcats usually take, is that you're working on a machine or on a line and you see some people coming down the aisle heading toward the time clock. And you look up, and it isn't lunch time and it isn't quitting time and there are too many people to be going to the tool crib. So you know they're leaving the plant. So what you do, literally, is shut your machine. If you've got tools, you put them in your tool box; you lock your box and you wipe your hands and you walk out; you punch out. You have no idea what's happening, none whatsoever. All you know is that the plant's being struck; and the sight, visually, is fantastic. You see a factory melting away, until the last man is out the door. Then you go outside and say, "What the hell's going on?" "Oh, such and such happened." And then you might say, "Well, great; it's about time. We've been taking this shit for too long." Or you might say, "What kind of nonsense is that? You mean you walked out for that?"

The point I'm getting at is when you get outside you might find that you support the strike or you oppose the strike, but the basic characteristic of the working class is that first you strike. Unless everybody strikes there's no meaningful action. You can get ten college professors and you have four for the war and four against the war and two who don't know where they stand. And so the four who are against the war will organize an anti-war movement; the four who are for the war will organize a pro-war group and the other two get argued at by these first eight. But the working class can't function that way. Everybody strikes. You don't wait until you get 51% of the vote. Unless you have an awareness, by the way, that 90% really support you, you don't even bother. Five guys just don't walk out to strike. Well, once in a while, some kind of issue will happen and somebody will get up a picket line all by himself in front of the plant. That is very rare. That isn't the natural way that the working class functions.

But there's a peculiar element in that. To shut your machine down in full confidence that everybody else is, is not an instinct that you're born with.

When you get out of the womb, you don't know how to run a wildcat strike. It comes from a long experience in a particular plant, a knowledge of the particular form of production, of your particular workmates on the whole and what you can expect of them and what they can expect of you. Not just in general but in particular. Who is a good speaker? Who is a good negotiator? Who is an intransigent bargainer? Who is a hard-nosed goon who will beat up scabs? You've got to know all of these things. And it takes a long time to develop, because it's not developed in terms of formal discussion; it's developed in terms of living experience.

And so what is characteristic of the working class in its struggles is three things basically. One, it is not public because it is not vocal; workers don't read or speak, and workers don't write. So you don't read about it in the press or hear about it at mass meetings. It just happens in the factories, and unless you're there, you don't know what's going on. Two, it takes time; it's not a moral question which suddenly excites everybody. It's a slow developing kind of thing, and as capitalist production changes, which it does constantly, it requires the workers to change. The period of the fifties, for example, in Detroit was a period of wholesale automation; plants shut down, new plants built, workers transferred. Which means that all sorts of new relations have to be determined and built up and new experiences made. But it also means that when the explosion finally takes place, it takes place with immense power—France, ten million people across the country in one day. You don't have to slowly build up an anti-war committee; it's a different kind of thing, but it's also a slowly maturing thing with a sudden explosion at the end. And it's because of that that there are years where even in a Marxist organization, people who are not in the factories (and it becomes true of the organization as a whole if it does not have immediate contact with people who are in factories) begin to develop a ritualistic but more and more meaningless attachment to the idea that the working class is revolutionary.

That was true, by the way, over a long period of years, of Trotskyists and the Communists; they're the ones who insist all the time on the proletarian revolution—they will lead it, but the proletariat will make it. It has become a ritualistic thing with no conception of the proletariat. The fact that you're not as ritualistic to start with—this is the real world in which we live and it's not a world of abstractions—you can't maintain that fidelity to theory and to fundamental ideas unless it is in living relation to the reality, unless you have people who are workers in your organization to constantly check you, to say, "Hell, no, you're wrong," or, "Don't write us off," or something of that kind.

What I'm trying to say in other words is that we begin with a certain conception of the world, a revolutionary conception. Our primary concern is not that all facts are equal or all events are equal. Our primary concern is an attachment to those events, those facts, those people who are revolutionary in this world. It's that that we base our politics on. Then we have beyond that, a specific relation to particular revolutionary movements and developments, and then beyond that, those revolutionary developments and those particular classes and sections of society involved in it have to be part of our organization, not because we have to run it all, but precisely because unless we do have these people in our organization, we might be tempted to run it all; we might be tempted to neglect or forget our theories, and say the working class really seems to be backward so we've got to try to achieve leadership over it or educate it or bring it into our organization or do all sorts of things which aren't very strange because organizations are doing it all the time. That's why Marxism has such a bad reputation in the world, because Marxist organizations are always trying to do that kind of thing. That's why even the term Marxism is such an ambiguous term these days; we say we're Marxist; so does the CP; so does the SP; there must be a dozen organizations in France alone that say they're Marxist. What I'm saying is this: that to be a living doctrine, that is applicable to the world, that makes the world intelligible, it has to be also a living organization; it has to be an organization which lives in this world and has people who participate in the revolutionary struggles in this world.

The purpose of this conference, the following points on the agenda, is first to find out what is really happening in terms of the concrete reports of people who are participants in particular struggles, and then, to the extent that it is possible in this kind of political framework, make our decisions on what we have to do, what we have to publish, the kinds of organizational steps we have to take, all sorts of decisions, some of which are routine for any organization, some of which are very specific to us, in terms of a press. The kind of political orientation that I described implies above all else the fact of as intimate a connection in terms of a press with the society as is possible, where you are reporting what is taking place in the building of socialism in the United States and everywhere in the world, through which you are participating in those struggles to the extent that you are participating in those struggles, and in which you are making your specific contribution; where you can say what Johnny Watson,[3] for example, can't say: that the American working class is revolutionary. Provided you don't say, therefore wait and depend on it. Where you can say, this is what the anti-war movement has accomplished and these are the conclusions we can draw for social movements in general, for this society in general, for the world in general, for theory, Marxist or any other kind. And it is to work out the concrete conclusions from that kind of an attitude that the rest of the agenda is set up. That concludes the introductory report, and the floor is open for discussion.

Martin Glaberman
May 31, 1968

Notes

1. Opening speech to a conference of the Facing Reality Publishing Committee, May 30, 1968.
2. The book was never published because differences about China and some other matters could not be resolved. A draft in mimeographed form was circulated among members and friends.
3. John Watson was one of the leaders of the League of Revolutionary Black Workers. He was for two years the editor of *The South End*, the Wayne State University student newspaper, which was used as an organ of revolutionary black militants.

Index

Communist(s), 149; American, xi, 6, 7, 18, 37, 169
Communist parties, 4, 11, 12, 15, 18, 25, 27, 28, 32, 59, 97, 99, 104, 116, 132, 153, 167, 184, 185, 188, 196, 198, 199
Communist states, 50
Communist unions (C. G. T., General Confederation of Labor), 184, 188
Congress of Industrial Organizations (CIO), 5, 10, 22, 23, 30, 37
Constantine, Learie, xi
CORE (Congress of Racial Equality), 193
Correspondence, xviii, xix, xx, xxi, xxiii
Croce, Benedetto, 63
Cromwell, Oliver, 182
Cuba, 128, 164, 188, 189, 190
Czech Spring (1968), xvii

D'Addario, Filomena, 68
Debs, Eugene V., 23
DeGaulle, Charles, 61, 105, 184, 185
DeLeon, Daniel, 30
Democratic Party, 160, 195
Detroit, xiii, xiv, xv, 81–82, 83, 84
Deutscher, Isaac, 52, 89, 94, 112
Dewey, Thomas, 5
Diaghilev, Sergei P., 54
Dialectical materialism (historical materialism), xiv, xvii, xxvi, 3, 17, 20, 23, 25, 29–31, 32–33, 44, 45, 47, 54, 82, 83, 140, 150, 161, 187
Dobbs, Farrell, 111
Dostoevsky, Feodor M., 54, 56, 57
Douglass, Frederick, 38
Dühring, Emil E., 34
Dunayevskaya, Raya (Rae Spiegel, F. Forest), xii, xiii, xv, xx, xxii, 67–68, 75–77, 80, 83, 84, 86, 112, 126, 143, 159
Durkheim, Emile, 63
Dutch Party (socialist), 11

Eastman, Max, 25, 32, 33
Eliot, T. S., 65
Ellis, Douglas, 33

Emmett, W. H., 33
Emory University, xxii
Engels, Friedrich, xiii–xiv, xxvi, 20, 24, 27, 29, 31, 33, 34, 38, 47, 60, 96, 99, 131, 169, 181
English Revolution (English Civil War), 65
Europe, 92
European Common Market, 75

Facing Reality, xx, 69, 70, 77, 92–93, 99, 125, 147, 149, 156, 175, 185, 186
Facing Reality (the organization), xx, xxii, xxiii, xxiv, 182, 183, 186
Fascism, 13
Fascists, 160
Fichte, Johann G., 53
First International, 187
Fokine, Michel, 54
Ford Rouge plant, xiv
Fourth International, 12, 69, 132, 153, 159
France, 4, 12, 19, 28, 59, 75, 95, 96, 97, 99, 105, 183, 184, 185, 186, 187, 188, 192, 199
French Revolt (1968), xvii, xxii, 183, 191, 194, 198
French Revolution, 53, 157, 188, 192, 193
French Turn, 12, 40 n 12
Freud, Sigmund, 63

Gaitskell, Hugh, 105
Gambino, Ferruccio, xxii
Garvey Movement, 38
Gates, Albert, 14, 27
Germany, 4, 19, 62, 97, 100, 103, 105,167
Gettysburg Address, 88
Ghana, xxiv, 90, 131, 135, 164
Glaberman, Jessie, xv, xxiv, 68
Glaberman, Martin, xi, xii, xiii, xiv, xv, xvi, xix, xx, xxi, xxiii, xxv, 87, 116, 120, 182
Goethe, Johann Wolfgang von, 54
Gogol, Bessie, 68, 90

Gogol, Louis, 68
Gogol, Nikolai V., 54
Gorman, William (Morris Goelman), 68, 84, 87–88, 128, 161
Great Britain, 4, 19, 43, 58, 64, 75, 84, 90, 92, 99, 103, 108–09, 121, 131, 149, 161, 188
Greece, 170

Hacker, Louis, 30
Hansen, 31
Hapsburg, 158
Harris, Abram, 30
Healy, Dennis, 57, 141, 143
Hegel, Georg W. F., xiv, 33, 44, 45, 53, 60, 82, 86, 103, 126, 161
Henry, Paget, xxv
Herzen, Alexander I., 17
Hill, Christopher, 64
Home, 61
Hook, Sidney, 16, 32, 33, 34, 35
Howe, Irving (Fahan), 33, 34
Hume, David, 45
Hungarian Revolution (1956), xvii, xx, xxvi, 51, 89, 156, 157, 187, 190, 192, 193, 194
Huxley, Julian, 63

Independent Labour Party, 11, 79, 124, 144
India, 58, 101, 134, 165
Industrial Workers of the World (IWW), 37
Inevitability of socialism, 44
Interim period, xvi
International African Opinion, xii
International African Service Bureau, xii, 134, 135
Isaacs, Harold, 112
Italy, xxii, 28, 95, 96, 97, 99, 170

James, C. L. R. (J. R. Johnson), xi, xii, xiii, xiv, xv, xvi, xvii, xviii, xix, xx, xxi, xxii, xxiii, xxiv, xxv, xxvi, 69, 78–81, 83–85, 124–27, 137, 161–62, 183
James, Selma, xix, xxiii, 86

Jefferson, Thomas, 23
Johnson-Forest Tendency (Johnsonites), xii, xiii, xv, 26, 90

Kamenev, L. B., 91, 139, 144
Kandinsky, Vasili, 54
Kant, Immanuel, 45, 60
Kautsky, Karl, 14, 60, 154
Kennedy, John F., 48, 61–63, 105, 170
Kenyatta, Jomo, xii, 125, 134, 144
Khrushchev, Nikita, 101, 106, 114, 133, 154, 162
Knights of Labor, 23
Kravitz, Nettie, 76
Kusterer, Ken, xxiv

Labor Action, xii, xv, 4, 7–11, 13, 14, 15, 16, 19, 22, 24, 25, 26, 27, 30, 31, 32, 38, 39
Labor movement, 19, 21, 22, 23, 34, 37
Labor party, 8, 30, 38, 167
Labour Party (England), 59, 70, 105, 117, 125, 133, 134, 144, 149, 188
Latin America, 100, 189
Layers in organization, xviii
League of Revolutionary Black Workers, xxiv
Lenin, Nikolai, xi, xiii, xiv, xvii, xxvi, 11, 14, 16, 17, 19, 20, 21, 27, 28, 29, 30, 31, 33, 34, 35, 36, 38, 39, 43, 44, 46, 47, 48, 50–53, 55, 56, 57, 58, 59, 60, 61, 62, 63, 64, 65, 69, 89, 91, 95, 96, 99, 102, 103, 104, 106, 112, 127, 132, 133, 138, 140, 141, 144, 145, 147, 148, 149, 151, 152, 153, 154, 155, 156, 161, 163, 165, 167, 168, 171, 172, 175, 177, 181, 184, 189
Leninism, xv, 4, 18, 37, 52, 69, 70, 76, 82, 83, 85, 98, 126, 128, 172
Leonard, Joe, 34
Leveller Party, 64
Lewis, John L., 23, 39, 159
Lilburne, John, 64
Lincoln, Abraham, 52, 53, 159
Logical Positivists, 63
London, Jack, 10
Lund, Ernest, 7, 14, 21

Luxemburg, Rosa, 31, 34, 56, 166–68, 171, 172, 175, 177
Lyotard, Jean-François, xxii

Macdonald, Dwight, 25
Macmillan, Harold, 105, 134, 173
Makonnen, T. Ras, 134
Malinowski, Bronislaw K., 63
Mao Tse-Tung, 70, 97, 98, 165, 190
Marx, Karl, xiii, xiv, xvi, xvii, xxv, xxvi, 14, 20, 24, 29, 30, 31, 33, 34, 35, 38, 43, 44, 45–50, 54, 57, 60, 61, 62, 65, 82, 86, 95, 96, 99, 126, 131, 161, 181, 187, 192
Marxism, xi, xii, xiv, xv, xvi, xvii, xxi, xxii, xxiii, xxiv, xxv, xxvi, 7, 10, 11, 13, 15, 16, 17, 18, 20, 23, 27, 28, 30, 33, 34, 35, 36, 38, 43, 44, 45–50, 51, 52, 53, 54, 55, 57, 58, 60, 61, 63, 64, 65, 67, 68, 69, 71, 72, 73, 74, 76, 79, 82, 83, 85, 96, 99, 102, 107, 112, 113, 114, 121, 122, 123, 126, 127, 140, 154, 155, 161, 162, 168, 169, 171, 182, 187, 199
Marxist-Leninist, 98
Marxist organization or movement, xii, xv, xvi, xviii, xix, xx, xxiii, 8, 9, 10, 13, 29, 43, 59, 64, 65, 70, 73, 74, 75, 77, 80, 93, 98, 111, 113, 117, 121, 123, 125, 126, 165, 168, 169, 170, 182, 186, 187, 190, 191, 192, 193, 194, 195, 196, 198, 199
Marxist paper, xviii, xx, 8, 9, 72, 74, 79, 117, 122, 163–64, 173, 175, 199
Marylebone Cricket Club (M. C. C.), 162
Mass, masses, 6, 7, 9, 13, 14, 15, 23, 31, 35, 111, 131, 168, 183
Mass parties, 12, 18, 19, 36
Mass party, 3, 6
Maupassant, Guy de, 54
McCarthyism, xviii
McKinney, Ernest R. (David Coolidge), 40 n 5
McNamara, 130, 166, 172, 174, 178 n 1
Medici, Lorenzo, xxi
Melville, Herman, xix

Michelangelo, xx
Michelet, Jules, 57
Milan, xxii
Missouri, strike of agricultural laborers, 6, 21
Morrow, Felix, 13
Moscow, 181, 182
Moscow Trials, 13
Moussorgsky, Modest Petrovich, 54

NAACP (National Association for the Advancement of Colored People), 9, 169, 193
Narodniki, 17, 34
Napoleon, 141–42, 143
National question, 27
Nazism, 104–05
Nearing, Scott, 14
Negro movement, 189
Negro Question, xi, xvi, 25, 38, 64, 84, 128, 160, 161, 164, 170, 171, 174, 190, 191
New Deal, 23, 31
New International, 5, 14, 18, 24–38
New Left, xxi, 189
News and Letters, xx
Nkrumah, Kwame, xii, 134–35, 139, 144
Novack, George, 25

Oberlin, xxi
Old Left, 192, 195
Owen, Si (Matthew Ward, Charles Denby), xix

Pablo, 116
Padmore, George, 125, 134, 135, 144
Padua, xxii
Paine, Freddy, xx, 68
Paine, Lyman, xx, 81, 84
Paine, Thomas, 23
Pannekoek, 60
Pareto, Vilfredo, 34, 63
Paris workers, 190
Parti Ouvrier Internationaliste (POI), 12
Party building, 3, 6, 9, 11, 14, 32, 36, 75, 76, 113–24, 125, 126, 127

Peasantry, 160–61
Peking (Beijing), 181, 182
Perlman, Fredy and Lorraine, xxiii
Permanent Revolution, theory of, 58
Phillips, Wendell, 38
Picasso, Pablo, xxi
Pioneer Publishers, 18
Plekhanov, Georg V., 14, 38
Political Action Committee (PAC), 9, 22
Pompidou, Georges, 185, 186
Popular Front, 13
Populist movement, 23
POUM, 4, 40 n 3
Proletariat (working class), xii, xiv, xv, xvi, xvii, xviii, xix, xx, xxii, xxiv, xxv, xxvi, 3, 4, 5, 8, 9, 10, 11, 15, 21, 22, 35, 36, 62, 64, 70, 82, 99, 100, 103, 111, 113, 115, 163, 169, 173, 174, 186, 188, 189, 193, 197, 198, 199
Proudhon, Pierre Joseph, 34
Puritans, 64
Pushkin, Aleksander S., 53, 54
Pyatakov, G. L., 139, 140

Quock, Tom, 68

Rawick, George P., xxiv
Recruiting, 3
Renault, xxii
Reuther, Walter, 188
Robeson, Paul, 136
Rochester, Anna, 14
Roosevelt, Franklin D., 28, 39, 105, 116, 159
Rosenberg, William G., 129 n 24
Russia, 18, 19, 28, 32, 53–57, 63, 64, 69, 75, 80, 95, 98, 103, 104, 116, 131, 133, 136, 147, 153, 154, 158, 159, 171, 175, 188, 189
Russian Factory Committees (shop steward movement), 89, 93, 117, 128
Russian movement, 16
Russian people, 17, 131, 136
Russian Question, 12, 13, 24, 80, 82, 159

Russian Revolution, xxvi, 43, 45, 47, 51, 52, 53–57, 58, 59, 63, 93, 95, 97, 99, 110, 131, 132, 150, 151, 155, 156, 157, 160, 175, 188
Russian Social Democratic Party, 17

Schelling, Friedrich W. J. von, 53
Schmitt, Peter, 11
Schumpeter, J., 34
Second International, 8, 56, 99, 103, 131–32, 135, 150, 153, 154, 155, 159, 162, 165, 181, 187
Shachtman, Max, xii, xiii, xv, 14, 39, 74, 90, 103, 112, 142
Shakespeare, 64, 127, 145
Simons, A. M., 14
Sinclair, Upton, 10
Slavophils, 56, 57
Social Democracy, 4, 10, 11, 12, 15, 28, 29, 116, 154, 167, 168
Social democratic unions, 184
Socialism, 12
Socialism in a single country, 13, 40 n 15, 95, 189
Socialisme ou Barbarie, xx, xxi, xxii
Socialist-Communist Government, 185
Socialist Labor Party, 10, 11
Socialist Party of America, 10, 11, 12, 23, 32, 37, 199
Socialist Workers Party (SWP), xii, xiv, xv, xvi, xviii, 12, 80, 111, 116, 121, 124, 125, 160, 174
Socialistische Arbeiter Partei (SAP), 11
Sojourner Truth, xxii, xxiii, xxiv
Solidarity Group (London), xxii, 43
Solidarity (Poland), xvii
Sorge, F. A., 38
Southern Christian Leadership Conference, 193
Souvarine, Boris, xi, 52
Soviet Union, xii, xiii, xvi, xxvi, 4, 15, 75, 79, 80, 132, 133, 152, 189
Soviets, 56, 171
Spain, 4, 13, 19
Spanish Revolution, 111
Speak Out, xxi
Speaking Out, xxiv